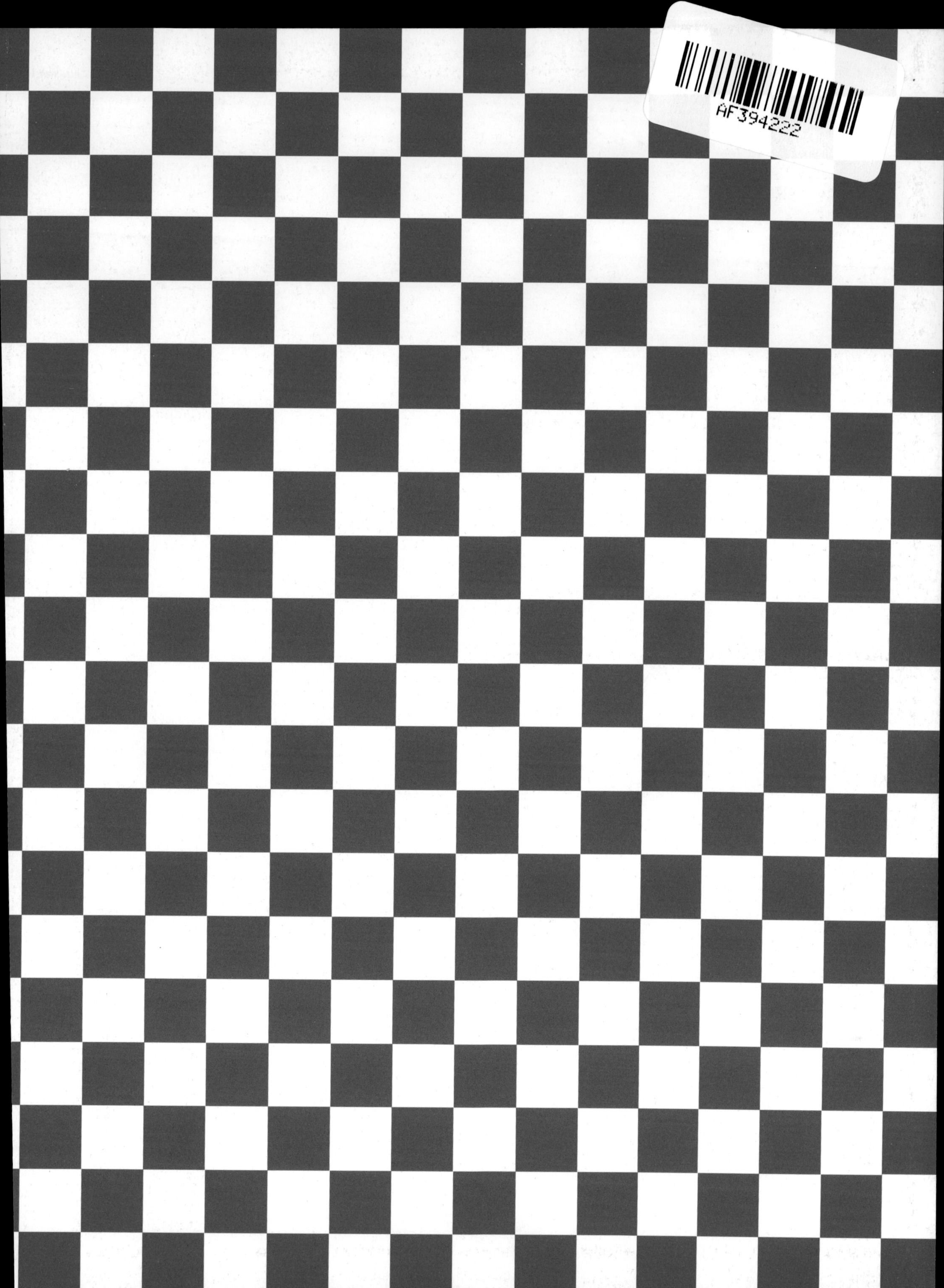
AF394222

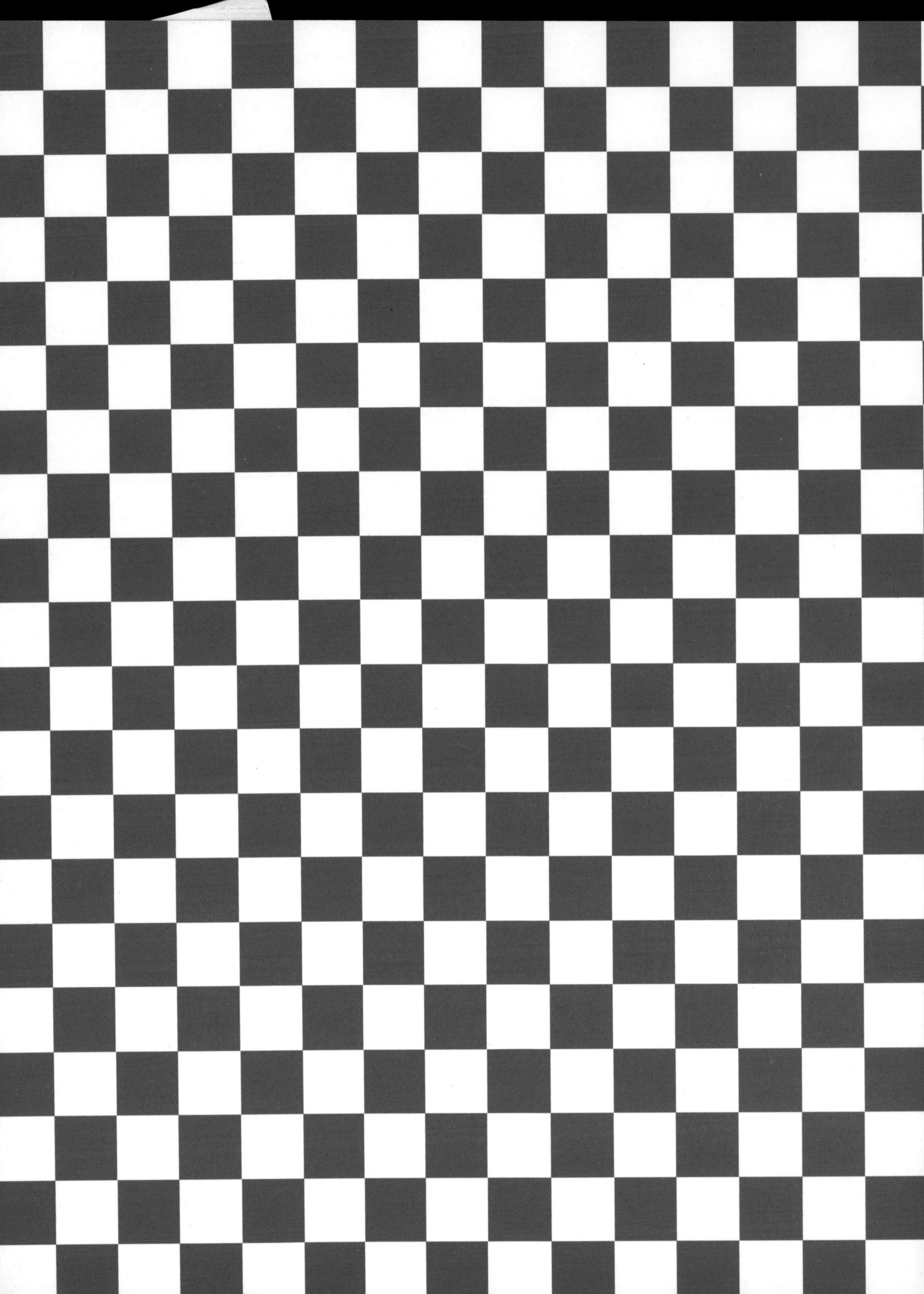

Pizza Love

100+ RECIPES PERFECTED FOR THE HOME COOK

Featuring Old-World Italian Traditions and Beloved American Styles

MAESTRO LEO SPIZZIRRI

weldonowen

CONTENTS

FOREWORD

Leo Spizzirri was born to be a teacher. I say this based on one important observation: He genuinely loves the craft of teaching as much as he loves the craft of pizza making. (And if you know Leo, you know how much he loves his pizza.) This book is the work of a master teacher; every word is infused with the joy he feels when transmitting the knowledge of his life experience to the thousands of people whose lives he has touched during his classes, presentations, and videos.

I first met Leo at the 2014 International Pizza Expo where I was scheduled to moderate "Tinkering with Your Dough," a panel discussion with pizza masters John Arena and Brian Spangler. One of my website sponsors asked if, since I was there, would I also serve as emcee at the company's booth for a chef I hadn't yet met named Leo Spizzirri. After my panel session ended, I sprinted my way through the enormous cavern-like convention hall to their booth. There I saw Leo for the first time as he was about to make some kind of focaccia-like product with an obscure name. I liked him immediately because, like me, he was short and stout, but he had far more charisma. There were, maybe, five or six people present when he began. And then, within minutes, the magic happened, and as people walked by on their way to somewhere else, they changed their minds and decided to stick around to watch this electric bundle of doughboy energy wearing a red neckerchief and a white pizzaiolo cabbie cap. He was putting on his show, explaining in colorful detail everything he was about to do and how he was going to do it, and then, he went ahead and did it.

By the end of the demo, well over 125 people were surrounding the oven, vying for a sample bite of Leo's fanciful focaccia bread. Once Leo had served the last bite and was just catching his breath, I introduced myself and asked how he wanted to stage our tandem performance, scheduled for later in the day. He said, "Can I get back to you in a couple of hours? I'm late for my next demo at another booth, and I have to rush over there right now." And off he ran.

As I soon discovered, he was booked to perform demos throughout the day for several product clients—cheese and tomato producers, cooking schools, flour and yeast companies—and he had to keep hopping around the expo to stay on schedule. As I walked around the hall, I'd occasionally hear his voice a few aisles over describing the details of yet another arcane but traditional Italian specialty he was about to make, and I saw, again, how the crowds kept growing around him. When we finally reconnected back at the booth, I experienced firsthand how the audience grew from a few initial stragglers to huge crowds because of how compelling Leo was.

Our friendship has grown over the years as we have worked and taught together. So I was thrilled to learn he is now, at long last, going to share all his knowledge in a book.

At the beginning of this foreword, I called Leo a born teacher. Yes, he's a certified and highly decorated *pizza maestro* (one of fewer than one hundred certified master instructors from the oldest pizza school in the world) and a tireless, charismatic showman and performer. But I think his enduring legacy will be as an educator, which I believe is an even higher calling. It means he stands as a link in the transmission of knowledge and wisdom from one generation to the next, intuitively utilizing what I call the "rabbinical method of teaching." That is, he tells stories as he teaches, and he illustrates the countless and detailed technical aspects of his craft with colorful images, examples, tales, and, of course, by answering questions with his own questions. But it takes an additional talent to translate performance skill into the written medium, and so I was delighted to see Leo's same joyful enthusiam on display here, illustrating ideas and knowledge through the use of colorful anecdotes and examples. His stories are like parables, and as history has shown, that's how great ideas penetrate our muscle memory and psyche.

In my writings, I often refer to the personal quest for the perfect pizza as a metaphor for my own self-discovery process, ultimately realizing that there is not just one perfect pizza but, instead, many perfect pizzas. Likewise, there are now a growing number of excellent pizza books, each one adding new knowledge to what came before, so I wondered if we might have run out of anything new to add to the category. But I hadn't factored in the combination of attributes that add up to a Leo Spizzirri, who is unique among teachers and pizza-book authors. Not only are his pizza skills and craft exemplary, having been forged in the crucible of training under many demanding teachers and mentors (who you will learn about in these pages), and not only does he possess natural performance and entertainment talents, but what sets him apart most of all is his God-given love for teaching and for transmitting knowledge and wisdom to those who are hungry for it. Joy like this cannot be taught. It must be honed and preserved and is consummated only when it is shared. When that happens, as you will discover as you read on (and as you may already know if you've seen Leo in action), a connection—call it a kind of communion—is forged between teacher and student, between maestro and audience, that results in a deep collective sigh of satisfaction and mutual joy and, perhaps, the feeling that our work here, at least for the present moment, has revealed to us new meaning and purpose.

Peter Reinhart
Charlotte, North Carolina, 2025

INTRODUCTION
La Mia Famiglia

So many memories race through my mind every time I think about how I got to this place in my life—a life obsessed with cooking and with the love of making pizza. It has been a wild ride, to say the least, and my path has been greatly influenced by my Italian heritage.

For a chubby little kid wearing husky corduroys from Sears growing up on the North Side of Chicago, life was pretty friggin' good. I always looked forward to Fridays because my grandparents would come over to our house for dinner, then we'd watch *Dallas* on TV. Afterward, a Bialetti Moka pot from Italy would be put on the stove, filling the house with the incredible smell of Italian coffee. Of course, a coffee cake or chocolate donuts from Entenmann's would be on the kitchen table waiting for everyone to sit down.

At the end of the night, I'd usually fight with my younger brother and sister about who would get to spend the night at our grandparents' house. That's because we all knew that when you woke up on Saturday morning you got to watch Bugs Bunny cartoons while eating corn flakes and reading the back of the cereal box. My grandmother called every cereal corn flakes unless they were actually corn flakes, then she called them Cheerios. Saturdays at my nana's house were the best. It was like having a staycation every weekend: three squares a day and some snacks in between along with visits to the neighborhood market where my grandparents would grab fresh bread and definitely some mortadella, plus whatever else was needed for the next few meals. Being there meant I got to get away from everyday life without a thought in the world except spending time with them—that is, until Sunday came around. I always hated Sundays because the reality of both going back to school all week and knowing that I'd never done my homework would set in. So when I finally did get dropped off at home, the party was over.

Once in the door, my mom and dad would first make me sit at the table to do my schoolwork until at least two p.m. If you're Italian and reading this, you know that Sunday at two is the international dinnertime for Italians. My mom would have been up since around seven a.m. so she could start a pot of sauce and get everything ready for dinner while everyone else was still in bed. I can vividly remember lying in bed asleep as the stovetop aromas of garlic and basil filled the entire house.

In Italy, my nana worked in a bakery and my grandfather, whom we called Nanutz, was a cobbler. They got married and my mom, Josephine (who was born on Saint Joseph's Day, March 19), was born a while later. Around the time my mom was about a year old, there was an opportunity to leave Italy with my nana's sister and her husband and head to England. As I look back, I feel that this side of my family played a major role in influencing everything that happened to me in the future.

Both of my parents were born in the province of Cosenza in the region of Calabria, Italy, the part of the boot between the heel and the toe in which southern Italian traditions were steeped in farming and making the most of whatever could be produced from the land. My maternal grandparents (Francesco and Gilda), with my infant mother under arm, left Calabria for England with what little they had. Once there, they bartered their labor on a local farm in exchange for housing. About a year later, they had a son, my uncle Tony. After many years of backbreaking work, my grandparents scraped together enough money to apply for visas to the United States. On December 2, 1967, they left England for Chicago, where other family members had settled before them and where there was a large Italian community ready and waiting to embrace them. I still wonder what it was like for Nanutz to pack up everything they had and head to America. If you have ever been to Chicago in December, you know that it is cold—probably colder than anywhere they had ever experienced in their lives.

My paternal grandparents (Leopoldo, after whom I was named, and Matilda) were also from Calabria. When World War II broke out, they had two very young daughters. At the time it was mandatory for Italian males who had reached the age of eighteen to fight in the war, so my grandfather left Calabria to fight in Libya with the Esercito Italiano (Italian Army). At the time, Libya was an Italian colony, and the Italian land forces were dispatched there to help protect it. His battalion was overpowered during a battle, and he and his fellow soldiers became prisoners of war who were used as laborers. He spent seven long years being moved around Algeria, often under harsh conditions, and eventually ended up back in Tripoli. At the end of the war, some Italian prisoners of war were released from Libyan camps and told to find their own way home, my grandfather among them. He made his way back to Calabria to his wife and children, and soon after my father was born.

My dad grew up on a farm and learned invaluable skills from a very young age, such as how to grow nearly everything imaginable, how to butcher a pig to make soppressata and capocollo, and how to press grapes for making wine. At the age of eighteen, he, too, was forced to serve in the army, and once his obligation was completed, he rejoined the family in Calabria. Around this time, my grandfather became serious about the entire family immigrating to the United States. The cost for the journey was too great to move everyone across the Atlantic at once, so it was decided that he and my father would head out alone and leave the rest of the family in Calabria. They found factory work in Chicago and were able to rent a small apartment on the North Side. After a short time, my grandfather sent enough money back to Calabria for the rest of the family to join them.

One day, there was a big family get-together and, coincidentally, both sides of my family had been invited. There is an old saying that all Italians either know one another or are related, an adage that was especially true in the early 1970s on Chicago's North Side, which was so heavily Italian that the neighborhood seemed like it was home to one giant family. That day was when my parents first met, and the rest, as they say, is history.

I grew up a stone's throw from the nearby genteel suburbs of Oak Park and River Forest, which were also home to some of Chicago's most notorious gangsters. It was common to hear stories of crazy things going on around us, like robberies, fires, and even the occasional Cadillac with a body in the trunk. My dad was always telling us to watch where we went and who we hung out with, because while that lifestyle might have seemed glamorous to a kid, we could have whatever we wanted if we just worked hard and earned it.

On the whole, the rhythm of my life was carefree and good. Growing up in an Italian American home meant everything in daily life revolved around family, with food and cooking at its very core. At a young age, I learned how to cook from watching my mom and my nana. I can remember the first time I made lasagna with them. My mother had me help her roll tiny meatballs, which were then fried in a skillet and scattered throughout the layers. The problem, however, was that every time she'd pull them out of the pan, I would eat them almost faster than she could layer them in the lasagna!

I also learned how to make pasta dough and use a pasta machine. My family would make large batches of fresh pasta at least once a month. My grandmother would lay the pasta on bedsheets to absorb the excess moisture. But she would make so much pasta that there were bedsheets on every surface of the house, including the top of the bed, which was always her preferred place to dry it.

But perhaps my favorite dish was the rustic pan pizza we made regularly. The dough was hand mixed and made with warm water, some yeast, a bit of salt, olive oil, and whatever flour was in the pantry at the time. I can remember them putting a bit of oil in the bottom of a large bowl, adding the big dough ball, and then giving the ball a turn so it had a slight sheen. Next, out came a paring knife for scoring a cross into the top of the dough, and finally the bowl was covered with a towel and the dough was left to rise. When asked why they scored the dough with a cross, their response was simply, *Cosi Gesù lo aiuterà crescere* (Like this, Jesus will help it rise).

After the dough had blown up like a balloon, they would uncover the whole thing, punch it down, and allow it rise in the same manner a few more times. They tested the dough by pulling on a corner of it, and if it stretched without much resistance, it was time to move on to the next step. Out came the famous wooden-handle paring knife again, which this time was used to divide the dough into four pieces. When the dough was officially ready, a thin, rectangular pan was pulled out. They would spread a bit of oil in the bottom of the pan and then a portion of the dough was added. I can remember the dough getting pulled and dimpled, but at this stage, it never extended to the edges of the pan no matter how much they stretched it. A little more olive oil was drizzled on top, and then the pan was placed inside the oven, the oven light was switched on, and the dough was left to rise. This process was repeated with three more pans until there was no dough left. After about an hour, the pans were pulled out of the oven, and like magic, the dough had stretched almost all the way to the corners of each pan. Once the dough filled the pans, the four pans went back into the oven for an hour to proof the dough one last time.

While the dough was rising, my nana would take out her stockpot, drizzle in some olive oil, and drop in a few whole cloves of garlic. The garlic was allowed to

cook until it just started to brown and then a couple of mason jars of homemade tomato sauce or *passata* (uncooked tomato puree) would be added and left to simmer. She would then pull out a box grater and shred different types of soft white cheese, such as mozzarella and scamorza (a southern Italian cow's milk cheese), into a big bowl. Once the pizzas had each risen to the top of their pan, they were removed from the oven, sauced, and a generous amount of cheese was scattered on top. Since we always had plentiful amounts of sausage and fresh vegetables on hand, some array of them would be added too, along with a light dusting of pecorino or parmigiano and a dash of dried oregano. We called this Nana's pizza before I had ever learned about the grandma-style pan pizzas that were becoming popular on the East Coast. With their appealingly crispy bottoms and soft, bread-like interiors, it's no wonder people love them.

Although Nana is no longer around to make pizza, I still occasionally find time to make this pan pizza for special occasions. It always reminds me of her and those incredible times we had in the kitchen together. And you'll find a version of it on page 166 (Vecchia Scuola), an homage to my Italian roots.

Pizza's Journey to America

Pizza as we know it in America today was practically nonexistent in the States before World War II. Think about that for a minute. Pizza had very little identity in the United States before the 1950s. That's a deep and profound point that I often think about as I begin to prepare for a class or lecture on this topic, especially when you consider how popular pizza is now. In one widely recognized ranking of the most popular foods in the world, pizza comes second to rice, which is number one. I think whoever is in charge of this food list needs to rethink how it's done. Pizza *is* the most popular food in the world!

For the record, Italians were immigrating to the United States in large numbers by the late 1800s. Many of these newcomers settled throughout the East Coast in places like New York and New Haven, Connecticut, where some of them opened pizzerias. But there was very little mention of these new establishments unless you lived in one of those Italian neighborhoods.

It has taken years for pizza historians (yes, they are a thing) to sort through public records and newspaper clippings to unfold the story of pizza in America and to try to figure out who truly opened the first pizzeria in America. Wiener, who is arguably the most famous pizza historian in the United States and is also the owner of Scott's Pizza Tours in New York (he is one of my students and an old friend as well), has supporting information on this topic.

According to Scott, the earliest known evidence of a pizzeria in America is an 1894 listing. Found by pizza historian Peter Regas, this evidence is from a business directory that lists "Forno e Pizzeria" at 59 ½ Mulberry Street in Manhattan. Previously, Lombardi's on Spring Street was thought to have been the first pizzeria in America, but several business listings prior to Lombardi's opening disprove this. Lombardi's does have an exceptional history going back to its founding in 1898 by Filippo Milone. Lombardi's didn't get involved until several years later, which is why it wasn't technically called Lombardi's until 1940. Originally named Pizzeria Napoletana, the existing pizzeria was purchased in 1908 by Gennaro Lombardi, who quickly sold it only to buy it back a decade later from then-owner Francesco D'Errico.

It wasn't until American GIs who were in Italy during World War II discovered pizza for the first time that mentions of it started popping up in the States following their return home.

My grandparents and parents were leaving Italy around this time and heading to America. I always felt like one of the lucky kids growing up because eating pizza at home was a common thing. The only phone number I needed for placing a pizza order was my nana's number, or I could just yell down the hall to my mom, who was, by the way, usually in the kitchen.

What we recognize as pizza today pretty much started in Napoli—at least, Neapolitans were the first ones to take a small round disk of dough and eventually top it with tomato sauce. However, the first pizzas didn't have tomato sauce on them at all. But before we get to that, we need to travel further back in time.

If we go back about two thousand years to Pompeii and Herculaneum, we find early evidence of communal ovens made of stone. These two ancient cities were covered with volcanic material and ash after the eruption of Mount Vesuvius in 79 CE. As workers slowly excavated Pompeii, they uncovered the many treasures buried beneath the rubble, including the well-preserved communal stone ovens. Today, we can see how these ovens were constructed, which provides clues as to how they were both heated and maintained temperature. This helps us begin to understand the integral role shared ovens played in the creation of bread and other foods in Roman times.

In the eighteenth and nineteenth centuries, Napoli was a very different city from what we know today. Many of the people were poor and struggling to survive. The streets were overcrowded and noisy, with vendors of all kinds selling their wares. Imagine each vendor shouting to advertise their goods to those passing by, all trying to outdo the guy next to them.

And by the end of the nineteenth century, the streets were riddled with sickness, making for dark times in this densely populated port city.

As you walk the streets of Napoli today, you can feel the story of the city under your feet. Pizzerias dating back over three hundred years are still standing, reminders of an earlier time. While the pizzas were baked in wood-fired ovens inside the pizzeria, pizza in Napoli was originally a street food. On the sidewalk outside a pizzeria, baked pizzas were displayed, ready to be purchased. The pizza was placed on a square of paper, then folded in half, and then folded in half again. Imagine a wedge with four layers encasing a small amount of tomato sauce, some fresh garlic, a pinch of dried oregano, and a splash of olive oil. Today, this walkaway meal is still called *pizza a portafoglio* (wallet pizza) or *pizza a libretto* (booklet).

L'Oro di Napoli (The Gold of Napoli), a famous 1954 Italian anthology film featuring the beautiful Sophia Loren, captures a very different Neapolitan pizza, *pizza fritta* (fried pizza). Sophia plays a pizzaiola (pizza maker; *o* at the end is masculine and *a* at the end is feminine) making *pizza fritta* on the sidewalk outside of her family's pizzeria. The film does an excellent job of showing what an authentic Neapolitan pizzeria looked like during the hard times of the 1950s. In one of the major scenes, Sophia is shown stretching dough

in the Neapolitan method called *schiaffo* (slap). If you ever misbehaved as a kid growing up in an Italian household, you probably knew the word *schiaffo* before you ever knew what pizza dough was.

As passersby called out their orders, they would often ask to pay *pizza a otto* (eight-day pizza). Remember, this was a time when people were so poor they could barely afford to eat, so it was a common practice for the pizzeria to give a pizza to the customer and allow payment over eight days. Another typical practice was something called *pizza sospesa* (suspended pizza). This was when a customer would order one pizza and pay for two, putting one on credit for someone who can't afford one, a custom similar to the pay-it-forward concept sometimes seen today.

Now, returning to street food: There was one other way to market pizzas outside of your pizzeria. In the early days of pizza in Napoli, a *stufa* (stove), a round copper vessel with a chamber on the bottom for holding hot coals from the wood-fired oven, was sometimes put to use. *Pizze a portafoglio* were stacked inside above the coals, and a large copper lid sealed the whole thing shut. Think of the *stufa* as a mobile warming unit that could be carried around the city, allowing the pizzaiolo to sell pizzas away from the pizzeria.

There are many stories about the roots of pizza, most passed down from generation to generation without much supporting evidence on their origin. What we do know is that, hands down, the most famous Neapolitan pizza to this day is the pizza Margherita. Its origin dates back to the end of the nineteenth century when Queen Margherita of Savoy went to Napoli with her husband, King Umberto I. Due to the hardships of the common people, there was fear within the hierarchy of a revolution. To restore faith among the people, the queen wanted to show them that she considered herself one of them, rather than above them. *Pizza popolare* (popular pizza) was something eaten by peasants, and the queen thought that if royals were to be seen eating the same thing as commoners, their popularity among the people would grow.

A pizzaiolo named Raffaele Esposito came to the Palace of Capodimonte where the royal couple was staying and created three special pizzas for the queen, one of which highlighted the colors of the Italian flag, with green basil, white mozzarella, and red tomato sauce. It proved her favorite, and Esposito named it in her honor. The story goes that she loved this pizza so much that, during her stay, she continued to request it from Esposito, who was the pizzaiolo at a nearby pizzeria, which was named Pizzeria Brandi at a much later date. If you travel to Napoli today, you can still sit at a table and eat a pizza Margherita at the original location. And not surprisingly, as word of the queen's new favorite Neapolitan food spread, so did the idea of pizza throughout Italy.

It is important to remember that a lot happened between the time Queen Margherita ate pizza at the palace, when Gennaro Lombardi arrived in America, and the point that we are at now. Pizza was created in what seems like primitive times in Napoli, when people lacked the technology and other conveniences we take for granted today. Electricity did not make it to Milan until 1883, when a flip of the switch illuminated the lights of the Teatro alla Scala for the first time. Neapolitan pizzaioli were using ovens heated with wood fires, had no refrigeration, and were making dough with flour stone-milled from wheat grown in nearby fields. And despite those limitations—possibly because of them—one of the most perfect foods we know was created.

The pizza of Gennaro Lombardi was taught to him by other Italian immigrants who had made it to New York many years before him and had set up small pizzerias around the city. While they didn't have the same flour or ovens they had used in Italy, they found ways to get very close to their old-world pizza. Flour was sourced domestically, and ovens that could achieve the high temperatures of a Neapolitan dome pizza oven burned coal instead of wood. The result of this inspired adaptation was the birth of the coal-fired Neapolitan pizza in New York and New Haven,

Connecticut. As this hybrid of the Neapolitan pie became more widely recognized and popular, the demand to learn how to make it increased. New technology was gradually introduced to meet this demand, like the natural gas deck oven and the electric planetary-style dough mixer.

In time, New York pizza began gaining its own designation as a style. The ovens baked at a lower temperature than a wood-fired oven, so the pizza spent more time in the oven but also ended up being crispier. Since the pizza took longer to bake than the original Neapolitan pizza, which was done in under ninety seconds at a temperature of around 900°F (485°C), the dough formula had to evolve too.

Neapolitan pizza dough is traditionally made with four ingredients: flour, salt, water, and yeast. This combination along with a long rest at room temperature and no refrigeration allowed the dough to rise naturally for up to twenty-four hours. When this dough was baked in an extremely hot wood-fired oven, the result was a light and airy crust with notes of fresh-baked bread. Since the new pizzas being made in New York were now using electric mixers and lower-temperature gas ovens, these two factors gave the crust certain distinct characteristics. The crust needed to bake longer, and to keep the interior structure tender and not too dry, solid fat or oil was added. Slowly the New York pizza became a completely separate category, and new pizza chains in America began adapting their idea of what the public was looking for around these New York characteristics. As these adaptations took hold, the American pizza slowly moved away from its Neapolitan origin and traditions.

In New Haven, for example, pizza makers created their own style of coal-fired Neapolitan pizza called *apizza* (pronounced ah-*beetz*), which has a thin, crispy and blistered crust. But New Haven was not alone. Suddenly, regional varieties were popping up all around the country. In my classes, I say that every style of pizza in America can be connected to one of the four styles in Italy: Neapolitan, *pizza classica*, *pizza alla romana* (which has three subcategories, *pizza in teglia* [pan], *pizza alla pala* [made on a peel, then baked on the hearth of the oven], and *pizza a mattarello* [rolling pin]), and Sicilian *pizza in teglia* (pan). The New York pizza of Gennaro Lombardi and those who came before him all started as a type of Neapolitan pizza. As pizza traveled outside of Napoli and spread throughout Italy, ingredients, equipment, and techniques changed as well. The round pizza eaten in Italy that's not from Napoli is called *pizza classica*. The pizza eaten in New York today is a cousin of *pizza classica*, and in this book, I teach you how to make it using my Italian Artisan dough (page 58). I'm also going to teach you how to make the Classic New York dough (page 68) that's used for making New York whole pies and slices.

When we talk about pizzas from Chicago, everyone goes straight to what comedian Jon Stewart referred to as "a (bleep)ing casserole." In Chicago we have the deep dish as well as the thin and crispy tavern pizza. For the record, Chicagoans usually only eat deep-dish pizza when we have visitors from out of town or when we have the occasional taste for one. Our go-to for pizza is the thin-crust tavern style. The roots of the deep-dish pizza lie in Sicily. Some might argue that Sicilian *sfincione* (fluffy, thick pan pizza) is its cousin. The same is true of New York Sicilian pan and Detroit pan pizza. The tavern pizza from Chicago is closely related to a Roman pizza that uses a small wooden rolling pin called a *mattarello*.

There are eight master doughs in this book, two of which will include variations with a preferment. Each one will give you a specific result when done in a certain way. I've perfected them for enthusiasts to make at home to achieve results similar to what you will find in pizzerias around the world. I hope you make each of them and perfect them on your own. I'm always around through my many @askchefleo social media platforms and YouTube. I'd love to see and hear about your results as you begin your *Pizza Love* journey just as I did so many years ago.

Pizza is a product of the skilled hands of the Neapolitan pizza maker, and in 2017, the United Nations Educational, Scientific and Cultural Organization (UNESCO) added Art of the Neapolitan "Pizzaiuolo" to its list of Intangible Cultural Heritage of Humanity. This was a huge moment for all of us who have dedicated our lives to preserving the traditions and techniques of the Neapolitan pizza. I will always remember the moment it was officially named on television. Although I was in Italy, I was up north in Padua, near Venice, watching the festivities from afar. I had been receiving calls all night about the celebration that was about to take place in Napoli, as friends from around the world all made their way there. I'll never forget seeing the late Sergio Miccù, who was then president of the Associazione Pizzaiuoli Napoletani (Association of Neapolitan Pizza Makers; APN), interviewed for news programs around the world after the announcement was made. He said, "Pizza was here before all of us, and we have an important responsibility to ensure that it continues to be respected after we are gone." These same words were said to me in 2018 by Antonio Pace, president of the Associazione Verace Pizza Napoletana (AVPN), when I was officially named Ambassador to the United States of America by the organization.

I have a deep love and respect for Napoli, for its people and culture. While my entire family is from the region of Calabria, which lies just below Campania and its capital of Napoli, people from Napoli have often said to me, "*Potresti essere cento per cento Calabrese, ma il tuo cuore e' cento per cento Napoletano*" (You may be one hundred percent Calabrian but your heart is one hundred percent Neapolitan.) Man, even writing that chokes me up. To understand the journey that I've been on for my whole life with this pizza thing and the amount of study and practice I have done to try to perfect every style of pizza is to know that all this kid from Chicago ever wanted was to be recognized as an Italian pizzaiolo instead of an American pizza maker.

THE SCIENCE OF PIZZA MAKING

No matter if you're a seasoned pizza maker, a professional chef, or simply a pizza-making enthusiast who wants to learn how to make an incredible pizza, you'll soon discover that there's a lot of science and plenty of calculations that go into making consistently good pizza. To be clear, I'm a pizzaiolo and not a scientist, but after years of studying my craft, I've learned a lot of things—science, math, physics, and more—along the way that allowed my successes and failures to improve my pizza making every day.

Start by grabbing a notebook, something that you can use to take notes in so you can journal everything you do. I have boxes of notepads and composition books filled with years of information that I still refer back to from time to time. The reality of forgetting something important is going to happen, so I like to use composition books to keep a snapshot of what I'm doing as I dive deeper into a dough formula or a specific pizza I'm developing. The worst thing that you'll ever encounter is creating a pizza that your friends, family, or clients are raving about only to discover that you can't remember a measurement or a piece of the process that got you there. So take good notes when making pizza.

As you begin to study individual pizza styles and understand what part of the world they came from, you'll notice similarities that begin to occur. A Neapolitan pizza will have certain parameters when it comes to making the dough, but what happens to that dough between mixing and baking is more important. Every pizza style that you encounter will fall under these same principles. The goal here is not to intimidate you but to give you some basic tools that will take your pizza making from good to great. Learn and apply these simple steps to your experimentation, and I promise the results you're looking to achieve will soon become a reality.

There are seven simple steps that every dough needs to go through to make a great pizza. Let's break them down.

1. **Scaling:** Gather all your ingredients before you start. Chefs practice mise en place, a French term that means having all your ingredients prepared and ready before cooking. Start by reading through your recipe to make sure you have all the ingredients on hand. Then scale, or weigh out, each ingredient so everything is within reach when you begin and you're not scrambling around the kitchen looking for something. Also, use this time to determine if you're making enough dough. The recipes in this book may only make enough dough for a couple of pizzas. This is the point where you need to decide if want to double or even triple a batch to make enough dough balls for the number of people you will be feeding.

2. **Mixing:** Properly mixing a dough involves more than adding all the ingredients to a bowl and swirling them around until they come together. The most critical aspects of mixing are time and temperature. The world of pizza making revolves around these two variables, and once you understand how they relate to your dough, you'll be able to have dough ready as quickly or as slowly as needed—and, most importantly, on your schedule. Calculating water temperature to achieve a certain final dough temperature is a life skill of every good baker, and I'm going to teach you my method later in this section. Once flour and water meet, the formation of gluten begins. The art of mixing is to understand and recognize the stages through which your dough passes before it is overworked and ultimately becomes heavy and/or difficult to work with.

3. **Bench Rest:** This term describes the time period after mixing when the dough is allowed to sit and slowly absorb the water that was just pushed into the flour. An artisan bread baker often refers to this step as bulk fermentation and uses the term "bench rest" for a pre-shaped loaf that needs time to relax before receiving its final shaping. A bench rest of 15 to 20 minutes after your pizza dough is removed

from the mixer will allow Mother Nature to finish the mixing process for you. I like to remove the dough from the mixer before it reaches the final stages of development and allow it to bench rest to ensure it will not be overmixed, which can cause problems working with the dough later in the process.

4. **Dividing:** A straight-edge dough cutter, or bench scraper, a scale, and your hands are all you need to divide dough to the desired weight. Accurately weighing your dough is critical to ensuring you have the correct amount for the size pizza you want to create and for the crust thickness you want to serve. Once your dough is stretched and goes into the oven, the texture of the dough will change based on the oven temperature and baking time. A precisely weighed dough ball will guarantee that your pizza will bake properly for the temperature you have selected.

5. **Shaping:** I think of creating dough balls as a life skill. There is art behind the way a piece of dough is folded and turned to create a solid round mass that has a tight enough exterior to keep the gases created by the yeast trapped inside. At the end of the day, the dough ball is the precursor to the pizza. You can't make a round pizza without a round dough ball, and the process of shaping the ball should be treated as such. Remember, you're not rolling meatballs, you're making pizza. Once the dough ball is formed, it needs to be kept covered all the time so the exterior cannot form a skin and dry out, making it look like the top of your grandma's hand.

6. **Final Fermentation:** Fermentation in dough is the process in which yeast consumes sugars, converting them to carbon dioxide and ethyl alcohol. This process can happen slowly, if the dough is refrigerated for a long period of time, or rapidly, if it has been held at room temperature. Fermentation is how our doughs get their bready flavors and complexity. Once you have shaped your dough ball, you'll have a decision to make about its maturation and the process for getting there. Do not confuse maturation with fermentation. Maturation is about time, measured from when the dough comes out of the mixer to when it finally hits the oven. In other words, maturation refers to the age of the dough while fermentation refers to yeast eating sugar to create gas.

7. **Baking:** Once your pizza enters the oven, many things happen. But most of us are only watching for the bubbling of mozzarella or the doneness of toppings. The purpose of baking is to transform the raw dough into a baked crust. But more importantly, baking removes moisture from the dough, leaving a light and airy crust that's held up by the spiderweb-like gluten structure. The trend in pizza today is to add as much water as possible to achieve a "better" dough. However, it is important to remember that the more water you add to the dough, the longer it needs to bake to remove the excess moisture. Failure to do so will leave your pizza crust gummy and dense in the middle. Here is a high-level description of what's really happening in the oven as the dough temperature increases.

- 75°F (24°C) to 120°F (49°C): Yeast fermentation and enzymatic activity rapidly increase. Crust formation begins. Gases released by the yeast cause "oven spring."

- 120°F (49°C) to 140°F (60°C): Bacteria, enzymes, and yeast die (yeast dies at about 140°F).

- 140°F (60°C) to 160°F (71°C): Starches begin to gelatinize and crust expansion slows.

- 160°F (71°C) to 180°F (82°C): Final gluten and dough structure is formed.

- 180°F (82°C) to 212°F (100°C): Water turns to steam and gives the crust a final sudden push. Crust growing begins.

- 212°F (100°C) to 350°F (180°C): Maillard reaction (browning created by the heating of proteins and sugars unconsumed by yeast) causes the crust to develop color.

- 300°F (150°C) to 400°F (200°C): Crust continues to brown and flavors develop through caramelization of sugars.

UNDERSTANDING BAKER'S PERCENTAGES

Baker's percentages, sometimes referred to as baker's math, are considered by some a sort of secret language of bakers—especially if you're not familiar with them. I can remember at a very young age being asked by a fellow baker what the hydration percentage of my dough was. I had no clue what he was talking about, so I quickly started asking my baking mentors for an explanation. Baker's percentages are simply the weights of every ingredient as a percentage of the total flour weight. No matter what your flour weighs, it's always represented as 100 percent. I was told that the reason flour was listed as 100 percent back in the day was because it came in 100-pound sacks. Made sense back then, but now, it seems more like a bit of folklore.

Let's use my Neapolitan dough formula (page 55) and convert it into percentages, then calculate a conversion so you can scale the formula up or down based on how much dough you want to make.

Converting a formula to percentages:

Flour	350 grams
Water	210 grams
Salt	10 grams
Yeast	1 gram
Honey	3 grams

As mentioned above, flour is always listed as 100 percent, and each ingredient becomes a percentage of the total flour weight.

To determine the percentages of the other ingredients, simply divide the ingredient weight by the flour weight, then multiply the result by 100.

Here's the breakdown:

Flour	350 grams	100%

Water 210 grams 60%
(210 g ÷ 350g = 0.60 × 100 = 60%)

Salt 10 grams 2.85%
(10 g ÷ 350g = 0.0285 × 100 = 2.85%)

Yeast 1 gram 0.285%
(1 g ÷ 350g = 0.00285 × 100 = 0.285%)

Honey 3 grams 0.85%
(3 g ÷ 350 g = 0.0085 × 100 = 0.85%)

Now that we know the baker's percentages for the Neapolitan dough formula, we can easily scale the formula up or down based on our needs for dough balls. For this example, let's assume that we want to increase our flour weight to 800 grams. The rest is a simple math equation. Start by dividing the percentage by 100 to give you a decimal, then multiply the result by the weight of the flour to give you the new ingredient weight.

Flour 100% 800 g

Water 60%
(60 ÷ 100 = 0.60 × 800 g = 480 g)

Salt 2.85%
(2.85 ÷ 100 = 0.0285 × 800 g = 22.8 g)

Yeast 0.285%
(0.285 ÷ 100 = 0.00285 × 800 g = 2.28 g)

Honey 0.85 %
(0.85 ÷ 100 = 0.0085 × 800 g = 6.8 g)

So how many dough balls will this formula make?

To determine how many dough balls a formula will make, we need to calculate the total amount of dough in the batch, then divide it by you desired dough ball weight. For this example, let's assume that we are making the newly increased batch of Neapolitan pizza dough using the 800 grams starting flour weight.

Let's add up all our ingredients to come up with our total batch size:

Flour   800 grams

Water   480 grams

Salt   22.8 grams

Yeast   2.28 grams

Honey   6.8 grams

(800 g + 480 g + 22.8 g + 2.28 g + 6.8 g = 1,311.88 g)

Now we need to decide how large we want our dough balls to be. Let's use 260 grams as our dough ball weight. To determine how many dough balls this batch of dough will make, divide the total dough weight of 1,311.88 grams by the desired dough ball weight of 260 grams.

1,311.88 g ÷ 260 g = 5.04

Based on our calculation, this batch size will make five dough balls of 260 grams each.

DESIRED DOUGH TEMPERATURE

A critical calculation that we use in pizza making every day is water temperature and how it translates to achieve a final dough temperature within our normal working parameters. The reason I say it's critical is because it allows us to consistently control fermentation and to work within a set schedule when making and using our doughs. The optimal temperature zone for pizza dough is between 68°F and 77°F (20°C and 25°C). In the professional baking world, we use Celsius.

So how do we know if the dough temperature should be 20°C, 25°C, or somewhere in between?

Remember when I said that everything we do as pizzaioli revolves around time and temperature? Think of dough temperature as a pendulum: the lower the temperature, the longer the time and vice versa; the higher the temperature, the shorter the time.

With this relationship between time and temperature understood, we can now start talking about the maturation of pizza dough (dough age measured between mixing and baking). If we need a dough to be ready sooner, our target final dough temperature should be at the far right of the optimal temperature zone range, or 25°C. If we plan to cold ferment in the refrigerator for 48 to 72 hours, then we are looking to the cooler side of the zone, or 20°C. Everything between these two points is fine-tuning. For example, if I am making a dough I want ready in 48 hours, the target temperature is 23°C. Simply put, the desired dough temperature is determined by the dough you create and the time you need it to be at its peak for baking.

To achieve your desired dough temperature, you'll need a digital thermometer to collect the temperature of your flour and the ambient temperature of your mixing area. You'll also need one additional temperature known as the friction factor.

What is the friction factor?

As dough spins in the bowl of your mixer, friction is produced by the movement of the dough hook, generating heat and causing the temperature of the dough to rise. This increase in the temperature due to the friction factor must be considered in the calculation of the desired dough temperature. The friction factor is not an exact number because of certain variables, including the type of mixer being used (spiral, planetary, or stand), the amount of mixing time, the mixer speeds used, and the size of the dough batch. Here are the friction factors for the three most common types of mixer:

Spiral mixer = 9°C

Planetary mixer (Hobart) = 14°C

Stand mixer (KitchenAid) = 16°C

If you used one of these factors in your calculation of your desired dough temperature and the temperature you were targeting wasn't achieved, you'll need to make adjustments until you figure out the friction factor of your specific piece of equipment. Take notes and keep adjusting the friction factor until you nail it. My advice is to add or subtract the amount you went over or under the temperature you were targeting from the friction factor you used, and you'll eventually figure out the friction factor number for your mixer.

Here is an example: Assume that we weighed our flour and it had a temperature of 19°C. Next, we held our thermometer in the air near the area where we are mixing, and it recorded a temperature of 20°C. We are then going to mix the dough in a spiral mixer that has a friction factor of 9°C.

Now we need to decide what the desired dough temperature should be. Let's target 20°C.

Here is how we calculate what the water temperature should be to achieve a desired dough temperature of 20°C. Since there are three factors we are calculating (flour, ambient temperature, and friction factor), we need to multiply our desired dough temperature by three. Then we subtract our three temperatures to arrive at what our water temperature should be.

20°C (desired dough temperature) ×
3 = 60°C

- 19°C (flour temperature)

- 20°C (ambient temperature)

- 9°C (friction factor)

= 12°C (water temperature)

Based on this calculation, to achieve a final dough temperature of 20°C, our water temperature needs to 12°C.

A CHAT ABOUT GLUTEN

The whole point of mixing flour and water together is to form gluten, the spiderweb-like structure that develops during mixing and ultimately holds the gases produced by yeast that make a pizza crust rise.

From the moment flour and water meet, two proteins found in flour become entangled to form what is called the gluten net or mesh. These proteins, glutenin and gliadin, are what give doughs their elasticity and extensibility. During mixing, the proteins are stretched and aligned, which gives dough its strength. The strength of the gluten net is determined by the wheat that was sourced to make the flour. As a dough is mixed, it must be checked constantly to note what stage it's at to avoid overmixing it, which can tangle the gluten strands into a knot. It is difficult to produce a light and airy pizza crust from an overmixed dough because once those gluten strands are locked up, it's nearly impossible to unwind them. This is why occasionally you'll eat a pizza and then want to go lie on the couch because you feel like you just ate a brick. Overworked dough is difficult to digest, hence that feeling in your gut.

It is important to source a flour with enough protein for the job at hand. Not every dough needs high-gluten flour, however. In fact, the shorter our maturation time, the lower the protein percentage of the flour needs to be. When using high-gluten flours, it's typical to see maturation times jump to 48 to 72 hours. That's how much time Mother Nature needs to break down the heavy parts of the flour, making it lighter and more digestible. There are, of course, exceptions to this rule, the biggest of which is the more water you use in your formula, the more extensible the dough will be and the sooner it can be used. The dough will still have a chewiness, however, and you'll feel your jaw doing extra work as you eat your freshly baked pizza.

HYDRATION

Let me start by saying that I am sick of the word *hydration*. It has become the "demure" of the pizza world. Everyone who has ever googled pizza dough has suddenly become a master pizzaiolo, and they have taken this simple term and made it pretentious.

So when talking about dough, what exactly is hydration?

Hydration is simply the amount of water used in a dough. As we saw in the calculations for baker's percentages (see page 20), to determine the hydration percentage, simply divide the amount of water in the formula by the amount of flour and multiply by 100.

Now, the critical part to understand when dealing with hydration is to recognize that not every dough needs to be a high-hydration dough. A balance exists between the strength of the flour and how much water it can absorb. Typically, lower protein flours have a lower absorption rate, and while you may be able to get a lot of water into a dough as you mix it, it doesn't mean the flour wants all that water. Think of this example to put this notion to rest: If we took a bucket, held it under a faucet, and then turned the water on, the water will fill the bucket until it reaches the top. If we keep the water on, the water will technically continue to go into the bucket, but everything extra will flow over the sides. Think of your flour as the bucket. When it comes to hydration, every flour has a recommended minimum or maximum absorption rate. The only way to know how much water can be absorbed by a specific flour is to research the flour mill's technical specifications for that particular flour. The technical specs will give you a road map of everything you need to know about what the flour can handle and how you need to treat it.

WINDOWPANE TEST

Part of the art of making pizza is understanding when doughs are ready. In this book, I give you parameters for mixing your dough. In time, and with practice, you'll begin to spot signs of where your dough is in its development. If you watch veteran bakers, you'll notice they're very handsy throughout the mixing process, constantly touching the dough. That's because our hands and our senses are much better at knowing when a dough is done than setting a timer and waiting for it to go off.

One of the common ways to test gluten development is the windowpane test. To perform the test, take a piece of dough from the mixer about the size of a golf ball and, holding it in the air, slowly start to stretch it outward with both hands. The goal is to stretch the center of the dough to a thin membrane, which I like to think of it as the head of a drum. As you stretch the dough, it should become thin enough for you to see through it. And if you look closely, you should be able to see the exposed gluten strands. If you begin to stretch the dough and it quickly tears, it's a sign that your dough is undermixed and needs more time in the mixer. That said, as noted earlier, I'd rather undermix a dough than take it to the point of full development because the dough will finish "mixing" during the bench rest step.

Overmixing will increase your final dough temperature and cause other issues down the line. By using the windowpane text, you can nearly eliminate the risk of overmixing. Here's where thinking of the head of a drum comes in: You'll know if the windowpane test was successful by stretching the dough and then tapping the thinly stretched dough with your finger from the underside. If you can tap it like a drum without it ripping, the dough is ready and you should stop mixing.

AUTOLYSE

Autolyse is a technique that comes from the world of artisan bread bakers and was developed in the 1970s by Raymond Calvel, a Paris-based professor of baking and expert on French bread. It is a resting period at the beginning of mixing using only the flour and water of the dough formula. Typically, the flour and water are mixed just long enough for the flour to get wet (2 to 3 minutes), then the mixture is covered and allowed to sit in the bowl and rest for 30 to 60 minutes, depending on the type and strength of the flour.

During the resting period, the flour fully hydrates and the gluten strands magically develop without mixing. The result is a dough that requires less total mixing time and has better cell structure and more oven spring.

BULK FERMENTATION

Another technique often found in the artisan bread world, bulk fermentation is a great way to develop flavors and gluten during the first stages of a dough's life after mixing. It calls for leaving the dough to rest as a single mass for a period, during which it creates gases from fermentation. The gases cause the dough to rise, increasing its structure and volume. It also gains more of that bready flavor that we love due to the ethyl alcohol given off by the yeast during the process. It is common for a dough that is being bulk fermented to go through a series of folds, which strengthen the gluten net and catch the fermentation gases inside its structure, giving the dough more volume. Bulk fermentation can happen either at warmer (ambient) temperatures while resting between folds or at colder (refrigerated) temperatures for a longer period. When bulk fermentation happens at colder temperatures, the yeast activity slows and the process becomes gentler.

Depending on your desired total maturation of the dough, similar outcomes are possible if you take care to respect the times and the final dough temperature. I always prefer a dough that is cold bulk fermented, especially when my total maturation lasts 48 hours or longer. It's typical to see my doughs bulk ferment for 24 hours in the refrigerator, then get divided and rounded into dough balls before returning them to the refrigerator for another 24 to 48 hours. This yields a crust that is very light and airy with a beautiful flavor. Remember that these are pro techniques and will require an investment of inactive time. If you need your dough right away, you can bulk ferment the dough for even just an hour at room temperature with a fold after 30 minutes, then divide and create dough balls and finish your regular process.

TYPES OF DOUGH MIXERS AND HOW THEY AFFECT YOUR DOUGH

When I first started making pizzas in a restaurant at a young age, I had my introduction to a giant beast of a machine called a Hobart, which is a planetary-style mixer. It looked similar to the mixer my mom had at home in her kitchen, only much larger. At home we had a KitchenAid stand mixer. In 1919, the Hobart Manufacturing Company started a division called KitchenAid that began producing stand-type mixers with a number of convenient accessories for the home baker. The division was sold in the mid-1980s, and now Hobart only manufactures commercial mixers.

So what is a planetary-style mixer?

If you ever watched one of these machines do its thing, you'll notice that the dough hook moves in a manner reminiscent of how the planets orbit the sun. As the hook moves around the bowl, it works from the sides and comes back to the center, ensuring the ingredients are mixed homogeneously. The hook does its work in a tighter mixing pattern in a planetary mixer than in other mixers, so the mixing happens much quicker. Also, it's important to remember that the bowl of a planetary mixer doesn't move when the mixer is on, so more friction is created during mixing. Keep in mind, too, it is easier to overmix a dough and increase the dough temperature quickly if you aren't careful. When bakers start the machine, they often begin on speed 1 and then increase to speed 2 for a short burst of time to finish developing the dough. Typically, it takes 8 to 10 minutes total to mix a dough in a planetary-style mixer.

As you start to search for a mixer, you'll notice other types of mixers are now available for commercial use and, on a smaller scale, for home use. When you're ready to invest some money into upping your mixer game, you'll find that the spiral mixer is the way to go.

What's a spiral mixer, you ask?

Different from the planetary mixer, the spiral mixer has a bowl that rotates in unison with a spiral-shaped dough hook. With the bowl and hook working together, the ingredients in the bowl are fed into the hook and released out the other side as the bowl turns. This process is much gentler than the action of a planetary mixer, and the gluten develops without the threat of overworking the dough. Since the bowl moves independently, there is also much less friction created, ensuring that the final dough temperature does not increase dramatically.

Spiral mixers typically have two speeds, with speed 1 running at approximately 110 revolutions per minute and speed 2 running around 220 revolutions per minute. Each manufacturer creates its own specs for how its machines operate as well as a different-size motor based on the size of the mixer model. The revolutions per minute can fluctuate from manufacturer to manufacturer, and it's important to know this information once you make a purchase. The more revolutions per minute, the faster the machine is working, which ultimately will increase temperatures and change your mix times.

In my opinion, the spiral mixer is the best machine because it does a great job at mixing every possible type of dough. However, you'll have to get yourself a food processor if you're planning to shred mozzarella or chop vegetables, as, unlike the planetary mixer, no accessories are available.

The *forcella*, or "fork" mixer, is another type of mixer, though it is usually seen only in pizzerias specializing in Neapolitan pizza. It has a much different look than the planetary or spiral mixer. First, the bowl has a cone-shaped center, which creates a trough where the ingredients lie. Then, the hook- or spiral-shaped agitator is replaced with a mechanism that spins almost horizontally and looks like a fork with only its two outer tines. While the bowl is spinning, the fork slowly rotates, scraping the ingredients from the bottom of the trough. As it works, it pulls the dough up the sides of the bowl and folds it on top of itself. It looks like the crest of a wave. As the dough develops, it takes on a rope shape. The fork mixer works very slowly and typically only speed 1 is used. A Neapolitan dough mixed in a *forcella* can take upward of 20 to 25 minutes to complete. The slow process creates less stress and friction, which is perfect for doughs that are made of just flour, water, salt, and yeast.

There's one additional type of mixer, the *braccio tuffante*, or "diving arm," mixer, which you may occasionally see in commercial use but is less common for home use. I have started to see smaller versions available, so its popularity may grow. Two arms *bracci tuffanti*—literally plunge into the bowl repeatedly, mimicking the work of hand mixing a dough. As the bowl spins, the arms extend down to the bottom of the bowl, lifting the ingredients before bringing them back down in a diving motion. These mixers are typically used for bakery products like panettone and other higher hydration doughs. Like the fork mixer, it is a lower-stress machine, making it best for mixing soft, delicate doughs.

LET'S NOT FORGET HAND MIXING!

Hand mixing dough is a life skill and everyone who plans on making pizzas needs to know how to do it. First, you can literally make dough anywhere. In the past when I was still competing professionally, I can remember times when I needed to start mixing my dough in my hotel room the night before a competition. The bathroom sink, an empty garbage can, or even a TV stand are all places you can use to make dough if you're desperate enough. Gross? Yes, but

ask around and you'll soon find out that it's not that crazy if that's all you've got. All you need are your ingredients and a vessel for holding them. Everything else that's necessary—your hands, your fingers—is attached to your arms!

Once you learn how to mix dough by hand, it is easy to move on to a mixer. Hand mixing gives you a basic understanding of the stages of development your dough goes through, making it less likely you'll overmix any dough once you start using a machine. Mixing dough by hand is a slow process, and people often think they'll be in for a workout and they'll overmix their dough. Let me be the first to tell you that if you decide to hand mix your dough, you'll be overworked before your dough ever is.

When I teach students how to hand mix doughs, I start by getting the water into the bowl, then the salt, and then half of the flour. Once I begin to pull all that together, the dough starts to look like pancake batter. This is the point I add the yeast. Next, I take half of the remaining flour and continue to slowly add it into the bowl, constantly mixing with my fingers and making sure I pick up every bit on the bottom of the bowl. Once no evidence of loose flour remains in the bowl, I add all the remaining flour and continue to mix with my fingers. At this point, you'll probably see the dough starting to get stiff. That's the sign to move it to a work surface and begin a short bit of kneading. The goal is to get all the flour—yes, every bit!—into the dough. The dough will appear sticky and not at all smooth. Once that's done, I take the bowl that I used to start the mixing, flip it over on top of the dough to cover it, and let the dough rest for 15 to 20 minutes. When I come back, the dough can be pulled like taffy. This is Mother Nature doing the heavy work for you. I give the dough a quick knead—just a minute or two—and then cover it again with the bowl for another 15 to 20 minutes. When I return, the dough will be ready to divide and form into balls.

Hand mixing dough is so simple that literally anyone can do it. It is also a great way to get the kids in your life involved in helping in the kitchen.

GETTING STARTED
How to Use This Book

After spending a lifetime in pizzerias with my hands in flour and countless hours in front of every pizza oven imaginable, I would have never imagined that one of my strengths would be teaching a classroom full of students. I think a lot about a comment that I regularly hear from students about my teaching style: How is it that I have the ability to discuss details at a granular level and at the same time make the information so easy to comprehend for everyone from a weekend pizza enthusiast to a seasoned chef? I think I grew up with undiagnosed ADD, which would make a lot of sense given that the chaos of the kitchen appealed to me at such a young age (as did the chance to play with fire and knives without anyone questioning me). As for my teaching style, I impart information in the same way that I need to learn something for the first time. I have to get down to the nth degree for things to make sense to me, and the same goes for the materials I'm presenting. I want you not only to understand a technique or procedure but also to connect the dots as to why you're doing it.

For this reason, I want to keep the recipes simple and give you some space so you can ask yourself the basic questions as you go and make notes on the answers you received. If you're just starting out in pizza making, your notes may be about accurate measurements or what variety of tomato to use. A seasoned pro might be looking for details and making notes about a technique for a certain style of pizza they've never made before. I've put this book together with this understanding. My recipes are more streamlined than what you might see in other cookbooks, but there's gold in the upcoming pages when it comes to the how and why.

In this book, there are eight pizza styles, each with its own dough formula, and five sauces that are used throughout the pizza recipe chapters. I didn't select the recipes I share here because I think they're the "best" or are "trending." I selected rock-solid recipes that are reliable and produce consistent results. Take each recipe as a lesson and learn something from it. My first goal is to have you making delicious pizzas, though not necessarily beautiful ones. The best part about pizza making is that no matter how bad you may screw up your bake, your mistakes are usually edible, and there are always plenty of people willing to eat your mistakes. I want you to enjoy the process and be successful enough in your journey that you'll want to continue practicing and experimenting. At the end of the day, my hope is that you'll get to the point where you tell people that the best pizza joint in your neighborhood is in your kitchen or backyard.

In choosing the recipes and techniques you are about to encounter, I've taken into consideration what I hear most often from students, which includes things like ingredient availability, timing, oven capacity, and the general skill level of the people using this book, to name just a few.

My dough recipes tend to yield fewer pizzas than many recipes. This is on purpose, as it has been my experience that most enthusiasts only want to make a couple of pizzas at a time and thus have no need for five or six dough balls. The recipes are easy enough to double or even triple if you want to make more, however. I'm also using fairly standard container sizes when it's time to run to the grocery store and grab such ingredients as canned tomatoes. Sometimes I'll give you my preferred brand for an ingredient but also provide a general idea of what to look for in case you can't find that particular brand. Lastly, the ingredients for my dough formulas are all weighed using the metric system (grams and kilograms), but my recipes for the pizza builds use pounds and ounces for weight and cups and spoons for volume measures. It's so much easier and more accurate to weigh the ingredients for your doughs in grams using a digital scale, and I want to encourage you to try to make it part of your regular baking routine.

My last bit of advice is to have fun! Nobody wants to do anything they don't like. I mean, you must like pizza enough to have bought this book. Take what's in these pages and make it your own. The more you practice, the more developed your skills will be. Believe me when I say, there's a very fine line between a good pizza and a great pizza. Enjoy the journey!

Spizzirri

The Essential Equipment

Before I get started, you need to know that I'm a bit of a gadget junkie. No matter if it's my insane guitar collection or my equipment in the pizza garage, if there's something new to try, I've gotta have it. I tell all my students to do their research before investing in kitchenware and always to buy the best they can afford. It's like the old saying, "Buy once, cry once."

That said, there is a clear list of must-haves and nice-to-haves. As you go down the rabbit hole of making great pizza at home, you're going to start with the basics and soon realize that you can't get from good to great without upping the ante with better equipment.

Here's my long list of must-haves (many of which of you probably already own).

SCALES

Digital scale: The most accurate way to measure an ingredient is by weight. All my dough formulas are scaled in grams. While measuring cups can be used, they result in a lot of inconsistency. Find a scale that registers to 1 gram and up to at least 2 kilograms. Digital scales also weigh in pounds and ounces with the push of a button.

Pocket scale: I joke that this is like a small drug dealer scale because it is used for less than 1 gram and accurately weighs to 0.01 gram. Also known as a palm scale, you'll use this scale primarily for measuring yeast.

THERMOMETERS

Instant-read thermometer: A probe-type digital thermometer is always within arm's reach in my kitchen. From water to flour, pizzaioli are constantly taking temperatures. The speed at which your dough will rise is dependent on specific parameters, and you'll need a thermometer to understand if you're going to go fast or slow. Make sure you get a thermometer that's made for testing a range of hot and cold temperatures and not the doneness of a steak.

Infrared thermometer: This is one of those cool laser thermometers made for taking surface temperatures. Look for one with an upper temperature range of at least 900°F (482°C). I use mine all the time to take the temperature of the floor of my wood-fired oven and pizza stones.

Oven thermometer: I like having one of these in my oven because it's a good way to test for any hot and cold spots. It's also a great way to ensure that the temperature you're aiming for is being achieved, rather than just relying on the knob with numbers printed on it. You'll be surprised how much oven temperatures vary, and if you've never had your home oven calibrated, this will be when the reality sets in that it needs to be done. I like the kind of oven thermometer that hangs from the rack and can be pushed out of the way when not in use.

Baking steel: Made from food-grade steel, a baking steel does the same job as a baking stone. But it conducts heat better than a baking stone, and it transfers heat to the pizza crust more quickly, which means faster cooking times. It also recovers its heat more rapidly, which is a plus if you are cooking more than one pizza. Baking on a steel will give the bottom of your pizza the appearance of being baked on a griddle, with uniform browning and a crispy finish.

Baking stone: Also known as a pizza stone, a baking stone is a slab of stone or ceramic that rests on your oven rack and holds your pizza as it bakes. It absorbs and retains heat evenly, mimicking the floor of a brick pizza oven, and because it is porous, it ensures evaporating steam dissipates, yielding a crispier crust.

Bench scraper: Typically made of metal, this straight-edged, commonly rectangular tool is used to scrape work surfaces clean and to divide dough into portions. It is also handy for scraping down cutting boards and pizza stones when you're done with them.

Bowl scraper: Made of plastic, silicone, or nylon, this flexible hand tool with one rounded edge is used for scraping the bottom and sides of a bowl clean. I use mine when hand mixing dough or for such tasks as getting out the last little bit from the bottom of a large can.

Box grater: Since a box grater has four sides, you'll be able to shred mozzarella, grate hard cheeses like Parmesan, slice vegetables, and zest citrus fruits. Don't buy the cheapest one you can find. It will be flimsy. My favorite is from OXO and has a rubberized bottom for stability and a plastic insert to catch whatever it is you've just cut.

Cast-iron skillet: This heavy iron pan is extremely versatile—good for searing, frying, and even baking. It can withstand high heat and retains heat extremely well. Plus, with proper care, cast-iron skillets will literally last a lifetime. When properly seasoned, they become naturally nonstick.

Cooling rack: A raised wire rack that allows air to circulate around your freshly baked foods helps them cool evenly. I love to use a cooling rack to hold my pizza when it comes out of the oven before I'm ready to cut it. It prevents the pizza from getting soggy from the steam and condensation that forms under the crust if it is sitting on a solid surface.

Cutting boards: I keep two cutting boards in my kitchen, a large wooden butcher block and a large polyethylene plastic board. I do most of my prep on the wooden board, but wooden boards need constant maintenance, including regular applications of oil to keep them sealed. My plastic board can be used for everything, and when I'm done with it, I can throw it into the dishwasher.

Dough boxes: Now that you're ready to start making dough, you're going to need a place to put those dough balls. The problem for home bakers is that most dough boxes are made for commercial use and are too large for a home refrigerator. There are two solutions: Use round, stackable Rubbermaid resealable storage containers or the artisan line of dough trays from DoughMate that come with a tight lid and will fit in a home refrigerator.

Kitchen timer: Measuring time is critical to dough processes and baking. I prefer a digital timer to one of the analog types with the big knob on the front that my grandmother used. Find a timer that will count up to at least 24 hours as well as count down. I like really loud timers too, because I'm that guy who's always side-tracked in the kitchen, and if the timer goes off, I want everyone around me to know that something is ready and needs attention.

Kitchen tongs: An essential tool, tongs can be used for grabbing, lifting, and flipping food easily and safely.

Kitchen towels: You can never have too many towels. I use cotton, linen, or terry cloth with sewn reinforced edges. Don't use microfiber towels. The fabric is made of synthetic materials that can melt when the towels come into contact with high temperatures.

Knives: I have three main knives I use all the time and a drawer full of every other type imaginable. The ones you really need are a paring knife, a serrated knife, and a chef's knife. Keep them sharp. Dull knives are dangerous.

Ladle and spoodle: Ideal for portioning and spreading pizza sauces, these tools come in various sizes. For home use, a 2-ounce ($\frac{1}{4}$-cup) to 4-ounce ($\frac{1}{2}$-cup) ladle is all you'll need. A spoodle combines a spoon and a ladle and is sometimes preferred by pizza makers because it has a flat bottom instead of the traditional round bottom of a ladle.

Measuring cups: Used to measure ingredients by volume, measuring cups come in two main types: for liquid ingredients and dry ingredients. For liquid measuring cups, I prefer transparent Cambro brand cups, which are highly durable and can be easily read from the outside. The company makes liquid measuring cups in sizes ranging from 1 cup up to 4 quarts.

Measuring spoons: Great for measuring wet or dry ingredients, measuring spoons typically come in a set with four sizes: $\frac{1}{4}$, $\frac{1}{2}$, and 1 teaspoon and 1 tablespoon. I like a stainless-steel set linked together with a ring at the handle end so the spoons don't get separated.

Mixing bowls: You're going to need an assortment of sizes, from small to large. I prefer stainless steel and plastic rather than glass. The key is to find bowls that are nonreactive, are not porous, and obviously won't shatter if you accidentally nick the edge. You'll use these for everything from making sauces and dough to storage.

Offset spatula or solid turner: I have a lot of these around the kitchen, and I use them for everything from flipping a burger and scraping food from a sheet pan to removing a pan pizza from its pan. I love the turner from Dexter-Russell that is 8 by 3 inches (20 by 7.5 cm) and has a wooden handle.

Oven brush: This tool is often forgotten by home cooks, and you'll need it for cleaning up your pizza stones and steels of any burnt-on residue. It's bristles are also great for sweeping up ash and coal debris from a wood-fired oven and for getting rid of extra flour left behind after you launch your pizzas.

Pan gripper: This tool is like a set of pliers specially designed to grab onto the edge of a pizza pan so you can remove the pizza without burning your hands. With the gripper in your nondominant hand steadying the hot pan, use an offset spatula in your dominant hand to get under the pizza and pop it out.

Pastry brush: Commonly found with natural bristles or nylon fiber, a pastry brush is great for applying oil or butter in a thin, uniform layer to a crust or pizza pan. Newer versions are made of silicone and can withstand higher heat and hold together longer after repeated washings.

Pizza cutter: Over the years, I've collected a ton of cutters. But if I had to pick only one, I like a 4-inch (10 cm) stainless-steel wheel attached to a polypropylene handle because the wheel can be sharpened like a knife and the handle material means the cutter can go into the dishwasher. I like Dexter-Russell brand, which offers its stainless-steel cutter in a variety of colors. A rocking pizza cutter, which has a long, large curved blade and a handle on each end or a single handle along the straight top, is especially handy for cutting some pan pizzas, though a long, sharp knife can be used in its place.

Pizza pans: Over the years, I've accumulated quite a collection of pizza pans. My most revered one is over forty years old, with a thick, black patina built up around the edges. Today, I use a lot of pans from a company called LloydPans. It makes great hard-anodized aluminum pans that are virtually nonstick and come in every imaginable size. The thing I love the most about them is that when you are done baking in them, they cool down fast and can be wiped clean with a paper towel.

Pizza peels: I have a lot of different peels in my kitchen. Some are wood and some are metal; some are solid and others are perforated, and handle lengths range from 10 inches to 72 inches (25 to 183 cm). Every kitchen should have a peel made of wood with a head size of at least 12 inches (30 cm) and a handle long enough to allow you to reach the back of the oven without sticking your entire arm inside. If you plan on baking pizzas that are larger than 12 inches (30 cm), get yourself a peel that will hold the largest pizza you'll be making with the intention of using it for smaller pizzas as well. Keep in mind, however, that the largest pizza you'll be able to make depends on the size of your pizza stone or steel.

Pizza scissors: Yes, scissors are used to cut pizzas. Typically, Roman pan pizzas are cut with scissors because they require less force than a wheel-type cutter, which helps prevent you from crushing the interior structure (crumb) of your pizza. Select a pair with handles offset from stainless-steel blades. This will allow you to keep the cutting part of the scissors perfectly flat while your hand remains elevated, ensuring it can move freely up and down to continue cutting. I also like the type that come apart in two pieces for easy washing.

Plastic wrap: This common kitchen item is used mostly to cover dough to prevent air from drying out the exterior and creating a skin. For dough balls on sheet pans headed to cold storage, I typically first coat them with a bit of nonstick cooking spray, then cover them with a tight layer of plastic wrap.

Rasp grater: This handheld grater has hundreds of tiny, razor-sharp teeth that do an amazing job of very finely grating ingredients. I use a Microplane-brand rasp grater for finishing my pizzas with a dusting of Parmigiano-Reggiano or lemon zest or even for mincing garlic into a fine paste.

Rolling pin: Yes, even I use a rolling pin at times to stretch pizza dough. A stiff dough that must be rolled out very thin is the perfect example of when I use a rolling pin. I have two primary rolling pins: one is very heavy, 18 inches (45 cm) long, and made of maple, and the second one is much lighter, 12 inches (30 cm) long, and coated in silicone.

Rubber or silicone spatula: Used for scraping down the sides of a bowl or folding ingredients, this spatula comes in various sizes. I like mine to have a head with good flexibility for getting into corners better and a long handle for swiping along the bottom of things like big tomato cans.

Sauté pan with lid: A stainless-steel sauté pan can be used for lots of different types of cooking. It is my go-to pan for baking Neapolitan pizza in the home oven, and because stainless steel is nonreactive, it's a safe choice for tomato sauces. It's essential if you plan to sear a piece of meat too. I have a great set of All-Clad pans that I've had forever and a newer HexClad set that I've been using like crazy lately.

Sheet pans: I keep several sheet pans—both aluminum and steel—in my kitchen. I like the kind with rolled raised edges about 1 inch (2.5 cm) high. You'll mostly use half sheet pans, which measure 18 by 13 inches. You can roast as well as bake in them.

Whisk: Many recipes call for whipping or beating an ingredient. I like to use a metal balloon whisk with a nice long handle for a good grip and better control.

Now, here is my list of nice-to-haves.

Dough mixer: You can totally make your doughs by hand, but eventually you'll start working with high-hydration doughs that require mixing at high speed for a long time to complete them.

1. Stand mixer (KitchenAid or similar): Stand mixers work great for almost every type of dough. They can plug into almost any outlet in your kitchen and come in a variety of sizes and colors. Be

aware, however, that because the bowl is fixed during mixing, your dough can easily become overworked or overheated if you're not careful and mix too long.

2. Spiral mixer: There are a few spiral mixers out there now that are made with the home pizza enthusiast in mind. These mixers have a bowl that spins independent from the hook. Sunmix markets a spiral mixer that plugs into any single-phase 110v electrical outlet and comes in different sizes and colors. I've had a Sunmix 6-kilogram spiral mixer in my kitchen for over five years now, and it's a beast. I can literally do every type of dough perfectly in that small mixer without raising the dough temperature too much. Once you use a spiral mixer, you'll never want to mix dough any other way.

Food processor: When you really get into making pizzas and find that now you're turning out dozens a week, letting a food processor and all its accessories help with shredding mozzarella and cutting vegetables will make your prep work a breeze. You can easily do everything with a box grater and some sharp knives, but a food processor will do so much more and faster.

Food mill: This old-school kitchen tool has a hand crank, a rotating blade, and a perforated bowl-like bottom and is used to mash and strain food into a smooth purée or chunky sauce. I use a food mill to create my pizza sauce. I also use it for making other sauces and for mashed potatoes. Food mills can be stainless steel or plastic and have a stationary disk or interchangeable disks with holes of varying sizes. I like a stainless-steel food mill with at least three different disks.

Immersion blender: Yes, it looks a bit like a boat motor, but it's a handheld blender and is so much faster than using a whisk; I use mine to make sauces and emulsify dressings.

High-temperature pizza oven: I say all the time that people getting started in pizza making today have it so much better than I did when I started out. With advancements in equipment and tools, manufactur-

ers have made pizza making much more accessible and affordable, especially for home cooks. As you get into pizzas like Neapolitan style, you'll take your baking to another level as soon as you can get your oven temperature over 750°F (400°C). It's now common to walk through a big-box hardware or department store and find the following ovens for sale in the same aisle as outdoor grills. To help navigate the choices, here's my short list.

FOR INDOOR USE

I really like the electric models, and there are three clear-top options available today, all featuring independent top and bottom heat controls.

The **Breville Pizzaiolo** oven can bake almost every style of pizza using presets for everything from deep dish to Neapolitan pizza.

The **Ooni Volt** series comes in different size models and can also bake a variety of styles of pizza while giving you a boost function to allow for quicker recovery of the stone after multiple bakes.

The **Blackstone E-Series** is my most recommended for beginners due to the fact that the stone rotates inside the oven, which ensures a uniform bake without the need to manually turn the pizza on your own.

FOR OUTDOOR USE

The **Ooni** series of outdoor pizza ovens come in a variety of models that feature open-flame propane burners with some models even capable of burning wood.

The **Gozney Dome** style ovens recreate a professional stone pizza oven using a propane burner. With the added thermal mass that the stone dome provides, it can bake a variety of styles of pizza and recover its temperature quickly.

The **Blackstone** series pizza oven has a rotating stone floor, and some models offer multiple burner configurations to heat the top of the dome and below the stone independently. This is my top pick, and a majority of the pizzas you see in this book were baked in them.

Flour 101

The topic of flour is incredibly complex, but understanding flour and the role it plays in making pizza will pay you great dividends and help you bring your baking skills to the next level. When selecting flour for a specific type of dough, I consider many factors before making my decision, which I will discuss in the pages that follow. For now, just remember that it is important to take into consideration the amount of maturation time the dough will need prior to baking as it relates to the protein level of the flour as well as to the hydration level of your dough, the temperature of your baking environment, and the final dough temperature.

THE ORIGINS OF FLOUR

When talking about flour, I like to start with its fascinating origins. Wheat as a foodstuff has been around for millennia. There is archaeological evidence that it was being cultivated over 10,000 years ago in the Fertile Crescent, a crescent-shaped region that stretches from the eastern shores of the Mediterranean to the Persian Gulf and spans modern-day Syria, Iraq, Turkey, Lebanon, Israel, and Palestine. While North America is known today for having millions of acres of wheat planted across the continent, it was not indigenous and was likely brought over by farm immigrants from Europe.

Wheat is generally classified globally according to season, hardness, and color. The main classes of wheat grown in the United States are hard red winter, hard red spring, soft red winter, spring white, winter white, and durum, with hundreds of varieties within the classes.

WINTER VERSUS SPRING WHEAT VARIETIES

Spring wheat varieties yield high-gluten flours that typically range from 13 to 15 percent protein, while winter wheat varieties are lower in protein, averaging 11 to 12 percent.

In North America, winter wheat varieties are grown in areas with mild winters, such as northern Texas, eastern Colorado, Nebraska, and Kansas. The grain is planted in September and October, grows four to five inches (10 to 13 cm) before winter arrives, and then goes dormant under a heavy blanket of snow. In the spring, the wheat resumes its growth, and harvesting begins in May and lasts through mid-July. Kansas is the top winter wheat producer in North America.

Spring wheat is grown much differently from winter wheat and yields higher levels of protein. It is sown in areas of North America with extreme winters, such as the Dakotas, Montana, Minnesota, Alberta, Saskatchewan, and Manitoba. The seed is planted in the spring, goes through its full growth during the spring and summer months, and is finally harvested in mid to late summer. The strongest wheat variety in the world comes from Manitoba, Canada, is called Manitoba, and its protein percentage tops out at 15 percent. Manitoba flour is the flour of choice for the production of panettone and other baked goods where a strong cell structure is required to maintain the height of the loaf. This loaf is created through a long fermentation period, which helps ensure it holds its shape without collapsing after baking.

When I speak to my students about the differences between winter wheat and spring wheat, I use an analogy that usually gives them an "aha" moment of clarity. I like to say that if two people of the same age and body type started hitting the gym together and each had the same ending date after six months, what would happen if one of those people decided to quit for three months and then returned to finish their training? The person who worked out for six months straight would be stronger than the person who took a break in the middle and then got back into it. Winter wheat, which goes dormant in the coldest months, is like the person who stopped training for three months. Spring wheat, which is planted and allowed to mature fully, is like the person who trained without a break. Just memorize this example and you'll always remember that spring wheat is stronger than winter wheat.

THE ANATOMY OF WHEAT AND HOW IT IS MILLED

Now that you understand a bit about where wheat comes from, what happens to it next? Wheat grains

come in various shapes, typically elongated. The grain itself has three specific parts. The first is the outer covering, or bran, which is rich in cellulose, an insoluble fiber, and mineral salts that are naturally occurring based on where the wheat was grown. The second part, the endosperm, is the largest of the three parts and is located directly below the bran. The endosperm makes up 90 percent of the total weight of the grain and is rich in proteins, vitamins, and enzymes. Its core consists of cells rich in complex carbohydrates (starch). White flour is a result of grinding the endosperm. The third part of the grain, the germ, is a tiny nugget located at the bottom of the endosperm and is rich in vitamin E, oil, and other vitamins.

All flour starts as whole grain, or whole wheat. This was the most common flour type in the past. If you have ever watched an old movie in which grain was being ground into flour, you may have seen a large millstone attached to a wooden frame to which a donkey was harnessed. As the donkey walked in a circle, the mill-

stone would grind the wheat grains. This method was commonly used to mill flour if there was no waterway nearby. Ideally, flour mills were set up alongside a swift river so the current could turn a massive waterwheel that sat just outside the mill. The wheel had a shaft that extended through the mill wall and was attached to a series of sprockets and gears that transferred the rotational motion of the wheel to a giant millstone that ground the wheat grains. The result was whole grain, or whole wheat, flour.

As flour mills evolved, dispensing with both the donkey and the waterwheel, so did the types of flour that could be produced. Modernization introduced a system of sieves and filters to remove the bran and germ from the endosperm, making the milling of white flour possible.

Today, flours produced in the United States are categorized by their protein level. Those with a low protein content, such as pastry flour and cake flour, are best for making delicate baked goods. Higher-protein flours, such as bread flour and whole wheat flour, are ideal for making heartier baked goods. In contrast, European flours are classified according to ash content, or the amount of bran, germ, and outer endosperm present in the flour. To arrive at the content, a small amount of flour is burned, and the ash that remains, which is made up only of minerals, is measured and expressed as a percentage of the original flour amount. The lower the ash content, the more highly refined the flour.

ITALIAN FLOURS

In recent years, the most common wheat flour imported to the United States from Europe is highly refined Italian flour, known as 00 or doppio zero, with an ash content of 0.55 percent or less. Beyond that, there is type 0 at 0.55 to 0.65 percent, type 1 at 0.65 to 0.80 percent, type 2 at 0.80 to 0.95 percent, and integrale, or whole wheat flour, with an ash content of 1.3 to 1.7 percent. Type 00 appears pure white and is silky smooth to the touch, though fine specks of bran are perceptible if you look closely. Type 0 reveals small traces of bran and germ and is slightly off-white, while types 1 and 2 display a lot of bran and germ relative to the others and feel noticeably gritty. Although 00 flour is the most sought-after flour for Italian pizza making, it also has the least amount of nutritional value because all the vital nutrients have been stripped away during milling. It is important to remember that this grading system only refers to the coarseness to which flour is ground and has nothing to do with its protein level, that is, its strength.

Italian flour classifications are protected by law, so only flour milled in Italy can be labeled 00. Note that I say milled in Italy and not grown in Italy. Since there is not enough land in Italy to grow wheat to meet the world demand for Italian flour, the Italians source grain from all over the world to very precise specifications based on the types of flour they are creating. Once these grains arrive at a mill, they are milled into flour to meet the desired classification, from 00 to integrale.

MORE ON HYDRATION

A flour with a lower protein content will almost always absorb less water than flours with higher protein contents. This is another good point to remember when deciding how much water your dough will be able to absorb. Pizzaioli and other bakers love to use a lot of water in their doughs because when the dough bakes and heats to 212°F (100°C), the water turns to steam and leaves only pockets of air that are held in place by the now-solidified gluten structure of the dough. This in turn not only yields a very light and airy pizza but a crispy one as well. But flour can only absorb so much water before it finally can't take any more. This is why bakers often blend a stronger flour with a lighter flour. The addition of a higher-protein flour will give dough a bit of a boost in its overall strength without making it too heavy or dense. For example, replacing 20 percent of your overall flour weight with a slightly higher-protein flour will allow you to add more water than you normally would, which gives your dough extra strength in the early stages of baking. This will result in good oven spring, that final full expansion that causes the dough to hold an air pocket higher without collapsing on itself. We can create a flour mix for a specific maturation process and higher hydration by adding flours specifically for their absorption properties. Check out my New York Pan dough (page 69). It uses a combination of King Arthur bread flour and semola rimacinata (fine semolina), which is a hard durum wheat that is ground twice to give it a silky texture similar to 00 flour. In this case, since King Arthur bread flour is made up of hard red wheat, I am blending it with semolina (durum), which allows me to get more water into the dough without it feeling too loose and sloppy in the end when I'm ready to stretch it. For more information on hydration levels of doughs and what they mean, see pages 22 and 23.

THE ROLE OF GLUTEN

When we talk about the amount of protein a type of flour has, we are specifically interested in the strength of the gluten it will create. As noted on page 22, gluten is made up of two proteins, gliadin and glutenin, that, when combined with water, create a gluten net. While gliadin gives dough the ability to stretch, glutenin gives it the ability to return to normal. The type of dough you make will depend upon the ratio of gliadin to glutenin in the flour. Flour with more gliadin will result in a dough in which the gluten net is more flexible, thus allowing the dough to rise higher. Flour with more glutenin will create a gluten net that is more rigid, so the dough will not rise as high and will usually appear denser. In the chart that follows, you will find not only the protein level of the individual flours but also a description of their gluten strength and the effect of the glutenin on the dough's elasticity.

Remember this rule of thumb: The higher the protein content of your flour, the longer you will need to leaven your dough. A dough with a higher protein content will create a stronger gluten net. If a dough is made with the correct flour for the process, it will be easy to stretch and won't snap back at you unless you manhandle it. If you make a dough with, let's say, bread flour and try to stretch it after refrigerating it for 24 hours, it will feel stiff and be difficult to stretch. If you keep the same dough in the refrigerator for an extra day, or 48 hours, it will feel like it opens much easier without the need to overwork it to shape it. You can usually tell if a dough needed more time to mature once it is in the oven. During baking, you will typically see irregular bubbles form toward the middle or outer edge of the pizza. This is because as water turns into steam, the crust begins to rise, and because the gluten net is still rigid, the steam will find the path of least resistance in its attempt to escape. With a dough that has been properly matured, the gluten net is more flexible and thus a more uniform oven spring can occur.

HOW I DECIDE WHICH FLOURS TO USE

As you bake your way through this book, you will soon notice that there are a few types of flour I use fairly consistently, depending on the style of pizza I'm creating. The factors I use to decide which flour will go into a specific dough are all based on the protein level of the flour and the gluten it will produce. The flours I use the most should be relatively easy to find as you source your ingredients. For my Italian doughs, you will regularly see doppio zero (00) flour from Mulino Caputo. That's because this highly refined flour will yield the all-around lighter, crispier texture that is the hallmark of Italian artisan pizzas. But when it comes to traditional American-style pizzas, you'll notice all-purpose and bread flour from King Arthur are my primary choices. These flours are milled slightly coarser than 00 flour, so they allow me to add more water; they also contain malt to help with

browning at lower temps, such as in my New York Pan and Detroit Pan doughs. Because these pizzas are baked for a longer amount of time, they really benefit from the extra water and malt. The list that follows covers a wide array of flours beyond the ones I use in the book. I feel this additional information can be helpful, especially if you plan to experiment with alternative flours.

Farro (Emmer) Flour: 16 to 17 percent protein with moderate gluten strength and low elasticity

Spelt Flour: 15 to 16 percent protein with moderate gluten strength and moderate elasticity

Durum Flour: 14 to 16 percent protein with strong gluten strength and low elasticity

Stone-Ground Whole Wheat Flour: 12 to 14 percent protein with strong gluten strength and moderate elasticity

Semolina Flour: 12 to 13 percent protein with moderate gluten strength and low elasticity

00 Pizza Flour: 11.5 to 14 percent protein with strong gluten strength and moderate elasticity

Hard Red Spring Flour: 11.5 to 16 percent protein with strong gluten strength and high elasticity

Bread Flour: 11.5 to 14 percent protein with strong gluten strength and high elasticity

Hard Red Winter Flour: 11 to 13 percent protein with strong gluten strength and moderate elasticity

US Unbleached All-Purpose Flour: 11 to 12 percent protein with strong gluten strength and moderate elasticity

US Bleached All-Purpose Flour: 10 to 12 percent protein with moderate gluten strength and moderate elasticity

Hard White Flour: 10 to 16 percent protein with moderate-to-strong gluten strength and moderate elasticity

Soft Red Winter Flour: 8 to 11 percent protein with weak gluten strength and moderate elasticity

Soft White Flour: 8 to 10 percent protein with weak gluten strength and low elasticity

00 Pasta Flour: 8 to 10 percent protein with moderate gluten strength and moderate elasticity

Pastry Flour: 8 to 9 percent protein with weak gluten strength and low elasticity

Cake Flour: 6 to 8 percent protein with weak gluten strength and low elasticity

As you can see from the different types of flour listed, the characteristics of the flour itself gives us an idea of how it will perform in a given dough. I selected the flours for each dough formula in the book based on the amount of maturation time necessary to ferment the dough properly. Most of the doughs will be ready for you to use within 24 hours, and those formulas will call for either 00 flour or all-purpose flour. Since these flours have a lower protein content, they can be ready to perform in less time. Remember that 00 flour refers strictly to the way the wheat is ground. Depending on the type of wheat, a wide range of protein percentages exists in the 00 category, so be sure to check the label before purchasing 00 flour. When I call for 00 flour in this book, I am using Caputo 00 Pizzeria Flour with a protein content of 12.5 percent.

As you begin experimenting with different doughs and flours of different strengths, it's easy to remember that weaker flours require less time to get to their peak than stronger flours. The complexity literally lies within the complex carbohydrates in the flour. Complex carbohydrates are complex sugars that are broken down by enzymes that occur naturally in flour. As the enzymes, primarily alpha amylase, break down the complex carbohydrates, they become simple sugars that yeast then uses to create fermentation. The more complex carbohydrates a flour has, the longer it will take for the enzymes to break them down. If this process is rushed, your dough will feel and eat heavy. This is why same-day doughs or doughs that will be used within 24 hours generally do well with lighter flours, that is, a flour with less than 12 percent protein. But as you start to increase your maturation time, the strength of the flour needs to increase. For instance, in my Neapolitan dough recipe, you will notice the maturation time of the dough is 18 to 24 hours, so my choice of flour is Caputo Pizzeria Flour, which has a protein level of 12.5 percent. But the ideal maturation time for my Classic New York dough is longer, 48 hours, so I use King Arthur Bread Flour, which has a protein level of 12.7 percent, and a very small amount of semola rimacinata (fine semolina), with a protein level of 12 percent. If your dough is made with a flour that is too weak for its process, the dough ball will usually look flat, and when you stretch the dough, it will spread to the point that very thin spots or irregularities will appear in the dough skin. This is why you will find that all-purpose flour or a blend of all-purpose flour with the addition of up to 20 percent bread flour makes a decent substitution when 00 flour is not available.

A NOTE ABOUT KING ARTHUR FLOURS AND MALT

Both King Arthur all-purpose and King Arthur bread flour contain malt. Malted flour is generally great for home bakers. The most common problem I have come across with my students and followers is that their home ovens cannot reach the temperatures of professional ovens. The addition of malt to a flour provides an extra sugar reserve that will caramelize during baking and create more even browning of the pizza crust and a better finished appearance. Keep in mind, however, if you intend to use these formulations in a portable or at-home wood-fired oven (see page 33), these malted flours may cause your crust to burn before the pizza finishes baking properly. If this happens, switch to an unmalted brand of the same kind of flour.

Yeasts

Welcome to the magical world of yeast, a place where this single-celled microorganism is neither an animal nor a plant but a member of the Fungi kingdom. To survive, it must have suitable conditions to thrive, primarily moisture, oxygen, food, and appropriate temperatures. When all these factors come together, the circle of life of the yeast begins.

So, what happens?

As yeast is activated, two major things happen: reproduction and alcoholic fermentation. During fermentation, yeast consumes sugars and converts them into alcohol and carbon dioxide, the latter being what pizza makers and other bakers alike are most interested in.

While there are dozens of types of yeast with hundreds of species and thousands of subspecies, the most common strain used for commercial yeast production today is *Saccharomyces cerevisiae*. Commercial yeast for pizza makers can be found in three main types: compressed yeast (also called cake or fresh yeast), active dry yeast, and instant dry yeast.

For most of the doughs I personally make, I use fresh yeast. However, depending on where you live, fresh yeast can be impossible to find in the average grocery store. This is why I recommend dry yeast for home bakers and even some pizzerias. A lot has to do with the shelf life of fresh yeast. From the time a block of fresh yeast is born (created commercially), it has a roughly thirty-day shelf life. Then you have to take into consideration the supply chain the yeast goes through before it ever hits the refrigerated case of the grocery store. In most cases, the fresh yeast you buy has less than a two-week shelf life. Plus, depending on the way the yeast was handled, things like weather, ambient temperature, and exposure to air can cause it to deteriorate, bringing the shelf life down even further.

Dry yeasts, in contrast, have a shelf life of two years from the time they were born, are readily available in the baking aisle of grocery stores, and are less perishable. For these reasons, I suggest you use dry yeast unless you are completely comfortable that the source of your fresh yeast can guarantee its quality.

No matter which type of yeast you use, buy only as much as you need in the short term. Don't "stock up" because you found a deal somewhere. Also, a lot of "experts" suggest that freezing yeast will extend the shelf life. Again, if you need to freeze your yeast, it means you bought too much. Yeast is fairly cheap, but it can cost you a lot of money and time down the road if it

turns out to be dead or has one foot in the grave. Store your yeast in an airtight container in the refrigerator and you should be good to go.

Think of the two types of dry yeast this way: active dry yeast needs to be activated and instant dry yeast works in an instant, which means it can go in with the flour without blooming it first. I've been preaching this distinction for years, and it's partially my mom's and grandma's fault. As a kid, I watched people put active dry yeast into warm water and then stir in a spoonful of sugar. After ten minutes, the mixture was foamy and ready to go into the mixer. It turns out that because of advancements by major yeast manufacturers, if your dough formula has a high enough hydration percentage, active dry yeast can be added directly to the mixer during the initial stages just like instant yeast and it will work just fine. I typically only bloom active dry yeast in warm water for doughs under 55 percent hydration. Also, the temperature of the water is important when blooming yeast. You don't want to kill it. I like to keep my water temperature for blooming around 90°F (32°C).

Fresh yeast is made up of about 70 percent moisture. During the production of active and instant yeast, moisture is removed to about 5 to 7 percent. Since fresh yeast is so high in moisture, it takes more of it to do the job. If your formula calls for fresh yeast and all you can source is dry yeast, it is important to remember dry yeast is concentrated, so you need less to achieve the same result. Here are my tried-and-true conversions for swapping out one type of yeast for another.

To trade out fresh yeast for active dry yeast, multiply the amount of fresh yeast by 0.40. Let's say your formula calls for 5 grams fresh yeast: 5 × 0.40 = 2 grams active dry yeast.

To trade out fresh yeast for instant dry yeast, multiply the amount of fresh yeast by 0.33. Using the same example of 5 grams fresh yeast: 5 × 0.33 = 1.65 grams instant dry yeast.

Lastly, to trade out active dry yeast for instant dry yeast, multiply the amount of active dry yeast by 0.75. Let's say your formula calls for 2 grams active dry yeast: 2 × 0.75 = 1.5 grams instant dry yeast.

TECHNIQUES
Making a Pizza Dough Ball

As a pizzaiolo, rolling dough balls is one of the life skills that is as critical as having a great dough formula. It's hard to make a round pizza without a round dough ball. Also, for pizzas that will be cooked in a rectangular pan, these need to be oval balls and not round. The process I'm about to give you is one that I have instructed thousands of students over the years to start with.

- After you have completed the mixing and resting stage of the dough you have created, divide the dough into individual portions according to the recommended dough ball weight for the recipe.

- As you divide your dough, try to cut the size into one chunk. I find that if I use a plastic bench scraper, I can place the piece of dough on the scale then cut and remove any excess. If the dough is scant, cut small pieces of dough from the main batch and place them onto the center of the piece already on the scale. Repeat this process until you have the desired weight of your dough ball.

- Once you have your weight, remove the dough and place it onto a clean work surface. I try to keep the dough as it was on the scale with the largest piece on the bottom and any small scraps on top of it.

- With the largest piece at the bottom, try to square the bottom piece off and create four corners to the piece. Remember, the small scraps need to be on top and in the center.

- Grab two of the corners at opposite ends, then individually, bring the points into the center of the dough piece, overlapping them onto any of the small scraps in the center, covering them.

- Repeat this process with the other two ends, bringing them into the center, overlapping the previous two pieces you already brought to the center.

- Now that all four corners are brought to the center, you should see that now you have four new corners and that your dough has formed a small square package. With one hand press your thumb into the center of the dough. Then with the opposite hand, grab the dough in a manner in which you can cup the top, pinching the points between your thumb and index finger and bring the four points together until they touch your thumb that's pressing the center. You can now remove your thumb and pinch everything closed.

- Make sure that as you pinch the dough, your thumb and index finger wrap around the points, creating a seal. There should be the fewest seams and openings as possible to ensure that air cannot escape as the dough ferments.

- Flip the dough over and you should now have a smooth outer skin that is the top of your dough ball. For most pizzas, you'll want this ball to be nice and round. If you are making a pan pizza, form the dough into something more oval rather than round. This will make it easier to press the dough into a pan.

- Place the dough ball into a lightly greased resealable container with the pinched portion of the dough ball at the bottom and the smooth outer piece on top.

- Place a lid on the container and ensure that it is sealed tightly so no air can enter the container.

- Store the dough ball according to the dough recipe you have just made, either in the refrigerator or on the counter, until ready to use.

HAND STRETCHING A PIZZA DOUGH BALL

1. Put about 2 cups (200 to 230 g) of flour into a medium bowl. Use the same flour as in the dough. Remove the dough ball from its storage container gently so as not to disturb the interior gases that have developed.

2. Dredge the dough ball in the flour. This will keep it from sticking to your hands and make it easier to work with.

3. Place the dough ball on a well-floured work surface. Start by pressing the center of the dough ball, then lift your fingers and, moving outward, continue to dimple the dough until you are about a finger's width from the edge of the dough.

4. Flip the dough over and repeat the dimpling process from the center to the edge. You should now have an evenly pronounced ring all the way around the edge of the dough.

5. Hold the dough firmly on one side without flattening the newly formed edge and, with your other hand, grasp the opposite side, again while not flattening the edge, and pull the dough away from you. Rotate the dough a quarter turn and repeat the pulling motion. Repeat this step two more times. The dough should be uniformly thin and even and the diameter called for in the recipe.

6. You can instead stretch the dough on your knuckles. Clench your fists and slide your hands, close together and palms down, under the dimpled dough, then lift the dough on your knuckles and pull your hands slowly apart to the outer edge. The dough is strong, so stretch it to the size called for in the recipe, then rotate the dough a quarter turn and repeat.

LAUNCHING A PIZZA

1. Prepare a pizza peel with a small amount of dusting flour. I prefer semola rimacinata for dusting, but you can use the same flour used in the dough. This helps the pizza slide into the oven.

2. Lay the stretched dough on the prepared pizza peel. (See above for hand stretching.)

3. Top the dough as desired. Just before you are ready to launch the pizza into the oven, give the peel a shake to ensure the pizza is not stuck. If it is, carefully lift an edge and slide a little dusting flour under it. It's important to keep the sauce on the pizza. If any drops onto the peel, the pizza can stick as you're moving it into the oven.

4. Place the pizza peel on top of the pizza stone or steel, holding the peel at a slight angle, and slowly begin to shake the peel forward to slide the pizza onto the stone. Don't shake too aggressively, or the toppings could shift forward onto the stone.

5. As the pizza begins to slide off the peel and onto the stone, slowly pull the peel backward while continuing to shake it until the pizza comes to a full rest on the stone.

6. Once the pizza is on the stone, set the peel aside and quickly close the oven door.

NEAPOLITAN PIZZA BROILER METHOD

1. One hour before baking the pizza, position a rack in the top position of the oven (about 4 inches [10 cm] from the heat source), place a pizza stone or steel on the rack, and preheat the oven to 500°F (260°C) or the highest setting.

2. Preheat a sauté pan over high heat on the stovetop. Gently lay a stretched Neapolitan dough ball in the preheated pan.

3. Cover the pan with a lid and cook the dough on the stovetop over high heat. If your stovetop is electric, rotate the pan every 30 seconds to make sure it cooks evenly. Check the dough after 3 minutes to make sure it's not being scorched. This should take about 5 minutes, depending on your range.

4. Remove the pan from the heat, uncover, and add the sauce and toppings to the dough.

5. Turn the oven setting to broil. If your broiler has temperature settings, set it on high.

6. Place the pan with the pizza onto the preheated stone or steel.

7. Bake the pizza for up to 5 minutes, or until the desired color is achieved.

Panning

PANNING CHICAGO STUFFED PIZZA

1. Grease a 12-inch (30 cm) round pan with a coating of solid vegetable shortening or margarine. A properly greased pan has a uniform layer of fat distributed over the bottom and all the way around the sides.

2. Using a rolling pin, flatten the first dough ball into a thick disk and then roll it out from side to side in an even layer, avoiding any thick or thin spots. It should be about 3 to 4 inches (8 to 10 cm) larger in diameter than the pan.

3. Lay the dough onto the bottom of the pan by first placing half of it down and then adjusting the rest of the dough to cover the pan.

4. Using your fingers, gently press the dough into the edges of the pan, leaving about 1 inch (2.5 cm) of the dough overhanging the rim of the pan. Do this all the way around the pan to prevent any air bubbles from forming under the dough.

5. Once the bottom layer of dough is in the pan, arrange the pizza filling in the pan. The filling should reach at least halfway up the sides of the pan.

6. Once the filling is complete, roll out the second dough ball the same way to create the top layer. Then add the top layer to the pan the same way you added the bottom layer, laying half of the dough over the filling and then following with the remaining dough, again adjusting as you go and allowing the excess to overhang the sides.

7. If the edge of the bottom layer feels dry, the top layer won't adhere and seal properly. Wet your fingertips with a little water and trace along the entire edge, gently dampening it before sealing the top layer to the bottom layer.

8. Use your fingers to press the top layer against the bottom layer along the side walls of the pan, creating a uniform seal. Do this all the way around the pan to make sure the dough layers are tightly sealed.

9. Once the top dough is sealed to the bottom dough, use your fingers in a pinching action to make 5 small, evenly spaced holes (1 in the middle and 4 around the edges) in the top dough to allow steam to escape during baking.

10. Apply the desired amount of sauce, then spread evenly with the back of a spoon or ladle. If there are any spots that lack sauce, add a dab of sauce to each one to prevent burning.

11. Carefully use a sharp knife to trim the excess dough from the sides of the pan. Hold the knife at an angle and slice in a single motion along the rim while turning the pan and lifting the scrap.

12. Remove the excess dough scrap and discard.

13. Finish the pizza with a dusting of grated Parmigiano-Reggiano or other toppings before baking.

PANNING DEEP-DISH PIZZA

1. Grease the bottom and sides of the pan you will be using for the deep-dish pizza with a uniform coating of solid vegetable shortening or margarine.

2. Make sure the pan is coated with an even layer of fat to avoid excess oil and moisture under the dough, which will make it soft and soggy.

3. Lay the dough on the bottom of the pan and, using your fingers, press it from the center outward to cover the bottom evenly. Next, still using your fingers, push the bottom edges up the sides to make a uniform layer of dough all the way around the pan. Avoid any thick or thin spots as they can cause uneven baking.

4. Cover pan with plastic wrap. Let it proof for 30 minutes.

5. Spread mozzarella slices across the dough, starting at the outer edge and allowing the cheese to touch the top of the dough then hang down the sides and onto the base. Try not to overlap the slices too much. The base does not need to be filled in completely. Gaps are okay.

6. Apply any toppings over the mozzarella and then add the sauce directly on top of everything. Finish with a sprinkle of grated Parmigiano-Reggiano.

PANNING DETROIT PAN PIZZA

1. Grease the bottom and sides of the pan you will be using for the pan pizza with a uniform coating of solid vegetable shortening.

2. Make sure the pan is coated with an even layer of fat to avoid excess oil and moisture under the dough, which will make it soft and soggy.

3. Lay the dough on the bottom of the pan and, using your fingers, press it from the center outward to cover the bottom evenly, trying to get to the edge of the pan. Don't worry if it doesn't make it to the corners at this point. Avoid any thick or thin spots as they can cause uneven baking.

4. Cover the pan with plastic wrap. Let it proof for 30 minutes.

5. Uncover. Press the dough again with your fingers. Dimple it all the way across, and the dough should reach the corners. Cover again. Proof for another 30 minutes.

6. Follow directions for Par-Baking Pan Doughs on page 47, beginning with step 3.

PANNING NEW YORK PAN PIZZA

1. Grease the bottom and sides of the pan you will be using for the pizza with a uniform coating of solid vegetable shortening.

2. Make sure the pan is coated with an even layer of fat to avoid excess oil and moisture under the dough, which will make it soft and soggy.

3. Lay the dough on the bottom of the pan and, using your fingers, press it from the center outward to cover the bottom evenly, trying to get to the edge of the pan. Don't worry if it doesn't make it to the corners at this point. Avoid any thick or thin spots as they can cause uneven baking.

4. Cover the pan with plastic wrap. Let it proof for 30 minutes.

5. Uncover. Press the dough again with your fingers. Dimple it all the way across and the dough should reach the corners. Cover again. Proof for another 30 minutes.

6. Follow the directions for topping the specific pizza you're making.

PANNING ROMAN PAN PIZZA

Before removing the dough from its container, liberally sprinkle your work surface with flour. I prefer semola rimacinata or the flour that is in the dough.

1. Dust the dough ball with more flour and gently lift it, taking care to keep all the air inside the dough ball, and set it on the floured work surface.

2. Begin by dimpling the dough around the edges. This locks the fermentation gases into the dough.

3. Continue dimpling the center of the dough, creating uniform rows with your fingers, until the dough is roughly an 8-by-12-inch (20 by 30 cm) rectangle.

4. Starting at the inside edge of a 12-by-16-inch (30 by 40 cm) pan, apply a roughly 4-inch-wide (10 cm wide) border of sunflower or vegetable oil or solid vegetable shortening around the bottom of the pan.

5. Gently lift the dough onto the back of your hands and lay the dough onto the center of the pan, placing it on the area that has not been greased. Adjust the dough so it is centered, then gently pull the edges up and out, stretching them to the edges of the pan. The dough should stick to the greased border.

6. Cover the pan with plastic wrap. Let it proof for 30 minutes.

7. Follow directions for Par-Baking Pan Doughs on page 47, beginning with step 3.

Par-Baking Pan Dough

Par-baking pan pizza dough has a few advantages over simply proofing the dough in a pan, topping it, and baking it. First, it gives you a crispier and flakier bottom and a light, airy interior because the crust actually bakes twice and almost fries in the bottom of the pan as it bakes. Plus, par-baking allows you to make your crusts ahead of time, saving prep time on serving day and cutting your final baking time in half.

Pan doughs bake at a lower temperature for a longer time than other pizza doughs. To keep the crumb structure moist during the longer bake, the dough is made with more oil. Because of the increased oil content, par-baked crusts can be wrapped in plastic wrap and stored in the freezer until you need them, which makes them a great option if you decide you have more par-baked crusts than you need that day. These crusts will also stay soft when wrapped and stored in the refrigerator for a few days, so you can plan a pizza party for the weekend but bake the crusts a few days in advance. That will give you more time to enjoy with friends rather than slaving away in the kitchen.

Par-baked crusts also make great bread for sandwiches. Just grab a serrated knife, split the crust open horizontally, line it with your favorite sandwich filling, and serve.

Follow these simple steps to par-bake any of the pan doughs in this book.

Step 1: Follow the master dough mixing process for your chosen pan dough.

Step 2: Follow panning directions for your chosen pan dough.

Step 3: Prepare your oven for baking. Position one oven rack in the lowest position of your oven and another near the middle, leaving about 6 to 8 inches (15 to 20 cm) between the racks. Place a pizza stone or steel on each oven rack. I like to use large rectangular stones to cover as much of each rack as possible. Once the stones are in place, preheat the oven to 500°F (260°C). Because the stones add a lot of mass to the oven, it could take an hour or even longer, depending on your oven, to preheat the oven. To ensure both the oven and the stones are preheated to 500°F (260°C), use an infrared laser thermometer to test the temperature of the stones.

Step 4: Once the dough in each pan has proofed, uncover one of the pans. Place the pan on the stone on the lower oven rack. The stone on the upper rack creates a brick-oven effect and will provide consistent heat throughout the bake. Close the oven door and allow the crust to bake for 8 to 10 minutes, rotating the pan 180 degrees halfway through the bake. The crust is done when it has turned a nice golden brown. Carefully remove the hot pan from the oven and, using an offset spatula, transfer the crust to a cooling rack until it is cool enough to handle. You can then proceed to the final baking step as directed in your chosen recipe, or you can let the crust cool completely, wrap it in plastic wrap, and either store it in the refrigerator for up to 3 days or place it in the freezer for up to 1 month. Be sure to bring a refrigerated or frozen par-baked crust to room temperature before topping.

Hand-Spreading Pizza Sauce

1. With your stretched dough or a par-baked crust in the pan, ladle the sauce onto the pizza base and spread it over the surface with the back of the ladle, leaving a 1-inch (2.5) border around the edges.

2. Using your fingers, gently ease the sauce into any nooks and crevices in the dough or crust.

3. Continue to spread the sauce with your fingers until the base is evenly covered.

Cutting Fior di Latte Mozzarella

1. Fior di latte (milk flower) mozzarella cheese is fresh, soft, creamy mozzarella made from cow's milk. Low-moisture mozzarella is firmer, saltier, and tangier and has a longer shelf life. Fior de latte is typically sold in either a water brine in a tub or in a vacuum-sealed package. Always drain off the water and dry the mozzarella well with a paper towel before cutting it.

2. Then, cut the mozzarella ball in half lengthwise.

3. Lay the two halves flat sides down and cut them vertically into slices about ½ inch (12 mm) thick.

4. Arrange the slices in stacks and cut the stacks lengthwise into strips about ½ inch (12 mm) thick.

5. Once you have a pile of ½-inch-thick (12 mm) matchstick pieces, bunch them together for the next step.

6. Arrange the matchsticks horizontally and cut them crosswise into ½-inch (12 mm) cubes.

7. Repeat the process with the remaining mozzarella.

8. The end result is a pile of perfectly cut fresh mozzarella.

Cutting Cherry Tomatoes

1. Place the shallow lid of a resealable container bottom-side up on a work surface and fill it with a single layer of cherry tomatoes.

2. Place a matching lid bottom-side down on top to hold the tomatoes in place.

3. Using a sharp knife, slowly cut horizontally through the tomatoes, using the container lids as a guide.

4. Perfectly cut tomatoes every time!

Using a Food Mill to Make Tomato Sauce

My grandmother always had a food mill in her kitchen and used it for making everything from mashed potatoes to tomato sauce. It's a great tool to have because it allows you to create a variety of different textures using the interchangeable disks that come with it. The disks have different-sized holes, ranging from fine to coarse, that will change the texture of whatever you're passing through them. If you don't already have a food mill, I encourage you to invest in one (see page 33). Once you use it, you'll agree that it's a game changer.

1. Fit your food mill with the disk with medium-size holes, then place the mill on top of a bowl large enough to catch the amount of tomatoes you'll be passing through it.

2. Next, add your tomatoes to the mill and slowly turn the handle to begin moving the tomatoes through the disk.

3. Continue grinding the tomatoes until all the large chunks have gone through. Remember to turn the crank counterclockwise occasionally to allow the blades to pick up any large pieces left behind, then continue turning the handle clockwise until all that's left in the top section of the mill is under-ripe pieces, tomato seeds, and, if using fresh rather than canned tomatoes, skins.

4. When everything has passed through the mill, turn it over and, using a spoon or rubber spatula, scrape off any pulp clinging to the bottom of the disk into the bowl.

MASTER DOUGH RECIPES

Ever since I was a kid, it has been obvious that pizza is more to me than just sauce and cheese. I'd watch my grandmother, mother, and literally every Italian woman in a kitchen around me make pizza dough. There were no scales, specialty flours, or even measuring cups.

I can remember seeing my grandmother make dough with just a big bowl and her hands. She used warm tap water, always. I'd watch her place her wrist under the water, similar to the way a mother would test the milk in a baby bottle. I'd ask, "How do you know the temperature is right?" She said she wanted the water to be the same temperature as her skin. I had no idea what that meant until she grabbed my arm and put it under the water. "Run the water and move the handle on the faucet on the hot side until you can't feel the water anymore," she instructed. It was incredible to see this work, and I mean, it really works! This is what we call in Italian *acqua tepida,* or "tepid water."

Many years later, I traveled to Napoli where I took my first Neapolitan pizza course at the headquarters of the Associazione Verace Pizza Napoletana, the governing body that promotes and protects true Neapolitan pizza all over the world. On the day that we made our first batches of dough, we did the work by hand, and when we got to the water, I was floored. The instructor rolled up his sleeve, went to the tap, and adjusted the water in exactly the same way my grandmother had shown me so many years earlier.

As you explore the doughs in this book, go with it using my advice. The doughs are perfect, so trust the formulas. These are my personal formulas that I've used for years. They have been tested by me in literally every possible scenario. No matter if I am baking at home or making pizzas for a trade show, these are my go-to recipes. Trust the ingredients. You'll never hear me say, "If the dough feels sticky, add more flour." I repeat, trust the formula and the process!

Making dough like my grandmother is easy. You'll need to take some time to gather a few proper ingredients, a couple of bowls, and occasionally a mixer. Then you can focus on the art of making dough that we pizzaioli call *l'arte bianca,* "the white art."

You will soon find out that time and temperature are everything when it comes to making dough. Was my grandmother wrong for wanting to use warm water to make her dough? No, actually, because she knew that if she used warm water the yeast would work more quickly. She would start making dough in the morning, and after it was mixed, she would put it in a bowl, cover the bowl with a damp towel, and let the dough rise. Once the dough hit the towel, she would punch it down and do the process again. After three or four rounds of this, she would say that the dough was ready to use. In my grandmother's kitchen that meant that she would usually have pizzas in the oven within four hours.

As I started diving into making dough at the professional level, it wasn't about how fast I could make it. It was more about how light and airy my crust could be or the flavors that develop over time in the refrigerator.

In this chapter, you'll find eight dough formulas, two of which include a preferment variation. I'm giving you a dough for every style of pizza, and some of the doughs can be turned into more than just pizza. Focus on making one dough style at a time, then put that dough to work making some of my favorite recipes that use the dough—recipes that I've gathered through the years during my travels all around the world.

Note: Most of the doughs in this book can be stored for up to 48 hours in the refrigerator, but it depends on the flour used in the formula. If the primary flour is lower in protein, like Caputo 00 Pizzeria flour or King Arthur all-purpose, the dough will be good for 24 hours. But if Caputo Chef's flour or King Arthur bread flour is used, the dough will keep for up to 48 hours.

Preferments

Certain types of dough involve making a dough preparation the day before you begin making the actual dough. This preparation, known as a preferment, is allowed to ferment at ambient temperature for a certain amount of time, after which it becomes an ingredient in the final dough. Doughs made with preferments use what is known as the indirect method.

The two most common preferments used in pizza doughs are the biga and the poolish. Each one is used to achieve specific results in your final crust. The most popular of the two preferments is the biga. A biga dough will yield a crust with larger, irregular pockets or cell structure, while a poolish dough will produce a crust with more uniform, pinhole bubbles.

I've standardized the recipes for these preferments to make them simpler to use. The two dough formulas in this book that call for them are my Roman pan dough (page 61), which calls for a biga, and my Contemporary Detroit Pan dough (page 70), which calls for a poolish. In both cases, the preferment is added as an ingredient to finish the dough.

As you gather your ingredients, you'll need to source a stronger flour with a protein percentage ranging from 13 to 14 percent. The flours I use the most for my preferments are Caputo Saccorosso (13 percent protein), Caputo Chef's Flour in the retail size, and King Arthur Sir Lancelot (14 percent protein). A preferment is going to go through some stress while doing its thing over the first part of its life, and a high-protein flour will allow it to rise and retain the gases that are developing. This will not only give your dough a better structure but also more flavor. If you cannot get your hands on one of these flours, you can substitute King Arthur bread flour, which is 12.7 percent protein. The result will not be 100 percent the same, but it will get you in the ballpark or at least close enough for city work or horseshoes.

Besides flour strength, you'll need to manage two important temperatures: the water temperature and the ambient temperature where the preferment will be held. Both the biga and poolish call for water at a temperature of 62°F (17°C) to 66°F (19°C). Once you have finished mixing the preferment, you'll store it in a spot that has a consistent temperature of 66°F (19°C) to 68°F (20°C).

You might need to get creative to ensure your preferment stays at the target temperature for 14 to 16 hours. In my house, my basement is usually always in that range, but I also have a small wine fridge that can be set in that range, so it holds my preferment just fine too. Believe me, you wouldn't sound ridiculous if you told me you walked around your house holding a digital instant-read thermometer in the air until you found a good spot for the job.

Lastly, when we mix preferments, we are just looking to combine ingredients and then stand back and let Mother Nature take over the rest of the process. Since my biga is much lower in hydration than my poolish, always add the yeast to the water first and stir it up until it's dissolved. Then go ahead and start your mixing by hand to finish it. The amount of preferment used in each dough formula is small, so it is easy to mix both preferments by hand. You're investing about 3 minutes of hand mixing and 14 to 16 hours of inactive ambient temperature storage before mixing the final dough. But when you eat the pizzas made with these two additions, you'll know by the taste and texture that your time investment was well spent.

BIGA

180 grams water at 62°F (17°C) to 66°F (19°C)

1.5 grams instant dry yeast

400 grams Caputo Chef's Flour or King Arthur Sir Lancelot high-gluten flour

Lightly coat the bottom and sides of a large, tall, narrow container, preferably food grade plastic with a sealable lid, with oil and set to the side. Any kind of oil or even nonstick cooking spray can be used. It will be acting only as lubricant, allowing the preferment to rise without restriction.

Pour the water into a large bowl, then add the yeast. Whisk until the yeast is fully dissolved.

Add the flour to the yeast-water mixture. Using your hands, combine the ingredients until a shaggy mass forms. Do not overmix. A properly made biga will look ragged rather than smooth and small traces of flour will be visible. Use a bowl scraper along the bottom of the bowl to help incorporate all the flour. Continue mixing with your hands until large clumps form.

Scrape the biga and any flour remaining in the bowl into the prepared container. Cover loosely with a lid and store at 66°F (19°C) to 68°F (20°C) for 14 to 16 hours. The biga is ready when it appears bubbly and sponge-like, with a sweet acidic aroma, and has roughly doubled in size.

POOLISH

400 grams water at 62°F (17°C) to 66°F (19°C)

0.2 gram instant dry yeast

400 grams Caputo Chef's Flour or King Arthur Sir Lancelot high-gluten flour

Lightly coat the bottom and sides of a large, tall, narrow container, preferably food grade plastic, with oil and set to the side. Any kind of oil or even nonstick cooking spray can be used. It will be acting only as lubricant, allowing the preferment to rise without restriction.

Pour the water into a large bowl, then add the yeast. Whisk until the yeast is fully dissolved.

Add the flour to the yeast-water mixture. Using a rubber spatula, mix until blended. A properly made poolish will have the consistency of lumpy pancake batter. It should not be smooth, but if large lumps are visible, try to break them up with your fingers, as they are signs of undermixing.

Scrape the poolish and any flour remaining in the bowl into the prepared container. Loosely cover with a lid and store at 66°F (19°C) to 68°F (20°C) for 14 to 16 hours. The poolish is ready when it has a dairy or yogurt-like smell and has roughly doubled in size.

NEAPOLITAN

The mother of all pizza doughs, Neapolitan dough is perhaps the simplest to assemble and requires nothing more than water, salt, flour, and yeast. This dough was traditionally mixed by hand, as there was no electricity to power a mixer. As I noted earlier, I love to teach this dough with hand mixing because it helps the maker understand how dough develops over a series of stages as it comes together.

I learned to make this dough on my first trip to Napoli, so it is very special to me. That trip marked the beginning of my pizza-school journey to becoming a maestro-certified pizzaiolo nearly twenty years later. The process allows you to add a lot of air to the dough, which is the key to developing the appealingly light texture of the crust, the puff of the *cornicione*, and the signature "leopard spotting"—small charred spots—that make pizzas like the Margherita and *capricciosa* so popular. (In Italian, *cornicione* refers to a cornice, molding, or frame. In pizza, the *cornicione* is the raised outer edge—essentially the picture frame—of the pizza crust.)

Neapolitan pizza is all about the balance of ingredients and toppings, so resist the urge to add more sauce and cheese. This less-is-more approach will ensure that the crust will not become soggy so the texture can really shine. I also recommend using the broiler method (see page 42) if you plan to bake the pizzas in the Neapolitan chapter in your home oven. It will provide you with much more heat inside your oven and re-create the effects of a rolling fire inside a professional wood-fired oven.

With the many options for indoor and outdoor portable pizza ovens now, you can easily move the fun outdoors and bake any of my Neapolitan pizzas with great success. However, if you do choose to use a portable oven, I suggest you remove the honey from the dough formula. It's there to help give the crust some color in a lower-temperature conventional home oven.

My favorite brand of flour for Neapolitan pizza is Caputo 00 Pizzeria Flour. It is pretty easy to find online and in specialty markets. If you need to substitute another flour for Italian 00 flour, I suggest King Arthur all-purpose flour, which has a similar protein content. You may notice a textural difference between the Caputo and King Arthur flours. The 00 flour has a finer grind, which results in a pizza crust that's lighter and eats less bready.

CONTINUED

210 grams water at 70°F (21°C), divided

10 grams fine sea salt

2 grams instant dry yeast

3 grams honey

350 grams Caputo 00 Pizzeria flour or King-Arthur all-purpose flour

Put 150 grams of the water in a small bowl, add the salt, and stir to dissolve. Put the remaining 60 grams water in a second small bowl, add the yeast and honey, and stir to dissolve.

In a bowl large enough to hold all the ingredients, combine all the salted water and half of the flour. Using your hand or a large spoon, mix together until the water is absorbed. Once the water is absorbed, add the yeast mixture with half of the remaining flour. Continue mixing, making sure to scrape the sides and bottom of the bowl with a bowl scraper or rubber spatula to ensure all the flour is incorporated. As soon as no traces of flour remain, add the last of the flour and continue mixing with your hand or the spoon until all the flour has been incorporated into the dough. The dough will not be smooth at this point.

Cover the bowl with a damp kitchen towel and allow the dough to rest for 20 minutes. Remove the towel and, with slightly wet fingers, grab the dough on one side from the bottom of the bowl, then pull the dough toward you and press it onto the center. Use a bowl scraper if you have a problem getting the dough unstuck from the bottom of the bowl. Do this four times so all the dough has been folded to the center. Re-cover the bowl and repeat two more times, with a 20-minute rest after each fold.

Divide the dough into two equal portions. They should each weigh about 290 grams. Form each portion into a round ball as described on page 41. Place each ball into an individual covered storage container and refrigerate for 24 hours to cold ferment before using.

Note: If you want to use the dough the same day you make it, after the last fold and 20-minute rest and before dividing it in half, re-cover the bowl with the damp towel and bulk ferment the dough at ambient temperature, about 68°F to 70°F (20°C to 21°C), for 2 hours. Then divide the dough as directed, form into balls, and proof in covered containers at ambient temperature for up to 4 hours, or until doubled in size.

ITALIAN ARTISAN

While pizza as we know it today started in Napoli, as you travel throughout Italy, the round pizza that's most commonly eaten is called *pizza classica*. With Neapolitan pizza, there are very specific rules that need to be respected when both making the dough and baking it in a very hot wood-fired oven. As you travel north, things begin to change, like the ingredients for toppings and the type of oven used. *Pizza classica* is baked at lower temperatures, which allows for a broader spectrum of toppings. The baking times are longer too, and to keep the interior crumb moist, light, and airy in these lower, longer bakes, olive oil is added to the dough. This is my go-to dough for these Italian artisan pizzas. It's easy to put together and consistent every time.

210 grams water at 62°F (17°C) to 66°F (19°C)

3.5 grams honey

350 grams Caputo Chef's Flour

2 grams instant dry yeast

8 grams fine sea salt

9 grams extra-virgin olive oil

Extra-virgin olive oil for the work surface, brushing the dough, and the storage containers

In the bowl of a stand mixer fitted with the paddle attachment, combine the water and honey. Whisk until the honey dissolves.

Add the flour and yeast to the mixer bowl and begin mixing on speed 1 for 3 minutes. After 1 minute has elapsed, stop the mixer and, using a bowl scraper, scrape down the sides of the bowl and along the bottom to ensure all the flour is being incorporated. Continue to mix on speed 1 for the remaining 2 minutes.

Stop the mixer and add the salt. Turn on the mixer to speed 2 and mix for 2 minutes. Stop the mixer and check to make sure there is no loose flour or salt remaining in the bowl before proceeding. If you find either, use the bowl scraper to scrape down the sides of the bowl, then turn on the mixer to speed 2 and mix for 1 minute.

Stop the mixer and replace the paddle attachment with the dough hook. Turn on the mixer to speed 3 and slowly drizzle in the oil. Continue mixing for 2 to 3 minutes, or until the bowl is clean and the dough is smooth and elastic. Stop the mixer.

Lightly oil your work surface. Using the bowl scraper, transfer the dough to the oiled work surface. Using a pastry brush, brush the top of the dough with a little oil, then cover the dough with plastic wrap and let rest at ambient temperature for 15 minutes.

Divide into two equal portions. They should each weigh about 290 grams. Form each portion into a round ball as described on page 41. Lightly oil two storage containers with lids. Place a ball into each oiled container, cover, and refrigerate for a minimum of 24 hours to cold ferment and a maximum of 48 hours before using.

TRADITIONAL
ROMAN PAN

While the contemporary Roman dough is my go-to formula when making this style of pizza, the reality is that I sometimes find myself in a pinch where I need to make a dough to use quickly and I don't have the time to invest in making a biga. This is a process that I have developed over the years to create a beautiful Roman crust that is still open and airy with a result that you're sure to love, without the investment of sixteen additional hours to create the biga.

508 grams water, made by combining 465 grams cold water and 43 grams ice

4 grams non-diastatic malt powder, or 7 grams honey

630 grams Caputo Chef's Flour or King Arthur bread flour

70 grams semola rimacinata (fine semolina flour)

4.5 grams instant dry yeast

18 grams fine sea salt

21 grams extra-virgin olive oil

Extra-virgin olive oil for the work surface, your hands, and the storage containers

In the bowl of a stand mixer fitted with the paddle attachment, combine the water and malt powder. Whisk until the malt dissolves.

In a large bowl, combine both flours and the yeast and stir to blend well. Add the flour mixture to the mixer bowl and begin mixing on speed 1 for 2 to 3 minutes, or until the dough starts to come together in a solid mass. Then increase the mixer speed to speed 2 and mix for 3 to 4 minutes, or until the dough starts to pull away from the bowl. If the dough climbs up the paddle during mixing, stop the mixer and, using a bowl scraper, push the dough down, then scrape down the sides of the bowl and along the bottom to ensure all the ingredients are being incorporated.

Replace the paddle attachment with the dough hook. Add the salt to the bowl and start mixing on speed 2 for 2 minutes. Then slowly drizzle in the oil and continue mixing on speed 2 for about 2 minutes, or until dough starts to pull away from the bowl. Stop the mixer.

Lightly oil your work surface and both hands. Use a bowl scraper and your hands to transfer the dough to the oiled work surface. Drizzle a small amount of oil onto the top of the dough, cover the dough with plastic wrap, and let rest at ambient temperature for 20 minutes.

Uncover the dough and slip the bowl scraper or a bench scraper under the dough to make sure it is not stuck to the work surface. Then, using oiled hands, lift the dough from the center until it releases from the work surface and fold it onto itself, which will give the dough some volume and strength. Re-cover the dough with plastic wrap and let rest for 20 minutes. Repeat this step two more times for a total of three folds and 60 minutes.

Divide the dough into two equal portions. They should each weigh about 627 grams. Form each portion into an oval ball as described on page 41. Lightly oil two storage containers with lids. Place a ball into each oiled container, cover, and refrigerate for a minimum of 24 hours to cold ferment, and a maximum of 48 hours total before using.

YIELD: TWO 627-GRAM DOUGH BALLS, ENOUGH FOR TWO 12-BY-16-INCH (30 BY 40 CM) PANS
TIME: ABOUT 17 HOURS (INCLUDES 3 MINUTES MIXING AND UP TO 16 HOURS REST FOR
THE BIGA, 15 MINUTES FOR MIXING THE FINAL DOUGH, AND 1 HOUR FOR FOLDING)
PLUS 24-HOUR COLD FERMENT IN THE REFRIGERATOR

CONTEMPORARY
ROMAN PAN
WITH BIGA

This pizza is seen throughout Rome, where it is called *pizza in teglia*, which refers to the pan in which it is baked. When you walk into a shop selling *pizza in teglia*, it is displayed on a counter behind glass for viewing. To order, you will be asked which variety you would like by the server, who then holds a spatula to your pizza of choice so you can indicate how much you want. At that point, the pizza is cut with a long pair of offset scissors, placed on a scale, and you are charged by the weight of the slice. This type of counter service is called *al taglio*, literally pizza "by the cut." So when in Rome, ask for *pizza in teglia al taglio* and you'll sound like a local!

This dough is beautiful but takes some practice to execute perfectly. It is wet due to its high hydration and calls for a biga preferment. Once you master the dough and the stretching to get it into the pan, the result is an incredibly light and airy base full of bubbles that can be topped like a pizza or served *bianco* (without tomato sauce) and used as an amazing flatbread for sandwiches. Since the dough contains so much water, as it bakes, the water turns to steam, and all that's left at the end of baking is the structure of gluten that holds it up. The goal is to retain as much of the gases created through fermentation as possible, both by the biga and the final dough, to ensure the crust is bubbly and light.

1 recipe Biga (page 53)

328 grams water, made by combining 300 grams cold water and 28 grams ice, divided

4 grams non-diastatic malt powder, or 7 grams honey

230 grams Caputo Chef's Flour or King Arthur bread flour

70 grams semola rimacinata (fine semolina flour)

1 gram instant dry yeast

Remove the biga from its container, cut it into small chunks, and add them to the bowl of a stand mixer fitted with the paddle attachment. Add half of the water and begin mixing on speed 1 for 1 minute.

Stop the mixer and add the malt powder, both flours, and the yeast. Turn on the mixer to speed 1 and continue mixing for 3 to 4 minutes, or until the dough starts to come together in a solid mass. Then slowly add about half of the remaining water plus any remaining ice and increase the mixer speed to speed 2. Once the dough pulls away from the bowl, 2 to 3 minutes, add the salt and continue to slowly add half of the remaining water.

CONTINUED

18 grams fine sea salt

21 grams extra-virgin olive oil

Extra-virgin olive oil for the work surface, your hands, and the storage containers

Once the dough pulls away from the bowl again, slowly add the oil and the remaining water and mix. Increase the mixer speed to speed 3 and continue mixing until dough pulls away from the bowl. The dough is going to be very loose at first, then it will come together, and then it will spread and stick to the sides of the bowl each time you add something, and then tighten again after more mixing. The whole mixing should take about 8 to 12 minutes.

Stop the mixer and check the dough. At this point, you should be able to pull on the dough with little tearing. If the dough feels weak, detach the paddle and set it into the bowl, then remove the bowl with the dough and paddle from the mixer stand. Cover and place the bowl in the refrigerator for 10 minutes. After 10 minutes of rest, return the bowl to the mixer stand, reset the paddle attachment, and mix on speed 3 until the dough pulls away from the bowl. Recheck the dough. If it still tears, place the bowl with the dough and paddle in the refrigerator for another 10-minute rest and then mix again on speed 3 until the dough pulls away from the bowl. Once the dough feels smooth and elastic, proceed to the next step.

Lightly oil your work surface and both hands (which will make it much easier to handle the dough). Use a bowl scraper and your hands to transfer the dough to the oiled work surface. Drizzle a small amount of oil onto the top of the dough (which will prevent it from sticking to the plastic wrap), cover the dough with plastic wrap, and let rest at ambient temperature for 20 minutes.

Uncover the dough and slip the bowl scraper or a bench scraper under the dough to make sure it is not stuck to the work surface. Repeat the step of oiling work surface and hands. Then, using your hands, lift the dough from the center until it releases from the work surface and fold it on itself, which will give the dough some volume and strength. Re-cover the dough with plastic wrap and let rest for 20 minutes. Repeat this step two more times for a total of three folds and 60 minutes.

Divide the dough into two equal portions. They should each weigh about 627 grams. Form each portion into an oval ball as described on page 41. Lightly oil two storage containers with lids. Place a ball into each oiled container, cover, and refrigerate for a minimum of 24 hours to cold ferment and a maximum of 48 hours total before using.

CHICAGO PAN

The pan pizza in Chicago has many variations based on which neighborhood you're in. Sometimes it is something that is hand tossed and then baked in a pan, but most of the time, it's the classic deep dish for which Chicago is known. There's another local pan pizza that's often called deep dish, but it isn't. That's the Chicago stuffed pizza, which has two layers of dough like a double-crust pie, with fillings and mozzarella between them and tomato sauce baked on the top crust. The Chicago Pan Pizzas chapter (page 189) includes both deep dish and stuffed recipes, with the former calling for this dough and the latter calling for my Chicago Tavern dough (page 66).

In my Chicago doughs, I trade out cornmeal for toasted corn flour (see Note, page 65), which imparts a beautiful flavor and sweetness to the pizzas. Just be careful to keep stirring the corn flour until it turns chocolate brown to prevent burning. You can even toast the corn flour ahead of time, so you'll always have it ready when you need it.

Both this dough and my tavern dough are super simple to make and each has its own identity. The only question is: Do you call these pizzas or are you like my friends on the East Coast who call them casseroles?

390 grams water at 62°F (17°C) to 66°F (19°C)

6 grams sugar

540 grams all-purpose flour, preferably Ceresota or King Arthur

60 grams toasted corn flour (see note, next page)

9 grams instant dry yeast

15 grams iodized table salt

48 grams corn oil

Corn oil for the work surface, dough, and storage containers

In the bowl of a stand mixer fitted with the paddle attachment, combine the water and sugar. Whisk until the sugar dissolves.

In a large bowl, combine both flours and the yeast and stir to blend well. Add the flour mixture to the mixer bowl and begin mixing on speed 1 for 2 to 3 minutes, or until the dough starts to come together in a solid mass. Then increase the mixer speed to speed 2 and mix for 3 to 4 minutes, or until dough starts to pull away from the bowl. If the dough climbs up the paddle during mixing, stop the mixer and, using a bowl scraper, push the dough down, then scrape down the sides of the bowl and along the bottom to ensure all ingredients are being incorporated.

Replace the paddle attachment with the dough hook. Add the salt to the bowl and start mixing on speed 2 for 2 minutes. Then slowly drizzle in the oil and continue mixing on speed 2 for about 2 minutes, or until the dough starts to pull away from the bowl. Stop the mixer.

CONTINUED

Lightly oil your work surface. Use the bowl scraper to transfer the dough to the oiled work surface. Using a pastry brush, lightly coat the top of the dough with oil, then cover the dough with plastic wrap and let rest at ambient temperature for 15 minutes.

Uncover the dough and slip the bowl scraper or a bench scraper under the dough to make sure it is not stuck to the work surface. Then, using oiled hands, lift the dough from the center until it releases from the work surface and fold it onto itself, which will give the dough some volume and strength. Re-cover the dough with plastic wrap and let rest for 20 minutes. Repeat this step two more times for a total of three folds and 60 minutes.

Divide the dough into two equal portions. They should each weigh about 530 grams. Form each portion into a round ball as described on page 41. Lightly oil two storage containers with lids. Place a ball into each oiled container, cover, and refrigerate for 24 hours to cold ferment before using.

Note: *To toast corn flour, add the flour to a sauté pan and place over medium heat. Then, using a wooden spoon, stir constantly until the flour turns chocolate brown. Don't walk away from the stove, or the flour will burn and be good only for the garbage can. Let cool completely before using. It will keep in an airtight container in the pantry for up to 6 months. If you are unable to obtain the corn flour, or choose not to use it, simply increase the amount of all-purpose flour so the total flour is the same (600g for Chicago Pan and 350g for Chicago Tavern).*

CONTINUED

CHICAGO TAVERN

Tavern pizza got its name from the days when pizza was baked in the back kitchen of a neighborhood bar and then set out for customers to snack on. The crust was thin and crisp and was typically loaded up with Italian sausage and other saltier ingredients like pepperoni, and the pizza was cut into small squares so it could be served on a cocktail napkin. This was genius marketing: you could hold a piece of pizza in one hand and a beer in the other. Then after all that salty pizza, you'd be extra thirsty and keep buying beers! Although deep dish is widely regarded as the Chicago favorite, this thin and crispy pizza is the first choice of Chicagoans, who usually only eat deep dish when they have visitors from out of town.

A few key points about this dough: First, it is meant to be dry, almost biscuit-like. I have increased the amount of water a bit because your KitchenAid mixer would never be able to handle the dough. You'd end up destroying your machine. Second, milk has long been added because its fat content keeps the crust moist and gives it a really nice brown color. Third, the addition of lard is traditional, which contributes both great texture and flavor. If you're concerned about turning off a vegan, you can swap out the lard for corn oil, which is also traditional and has good flavor. Lastly, speaking of corn, we Chicagoans use a lot of cornmeal in our pizzerias, both in the dough and on the peel to help pizzas slide smoothly into the oven. Cornmeal adds considerable texture to the dough, sometimes even tricking eaters into thinking they are consuming a crispy pizza rather than experiencing gritty cornmeal in their teeth. I've never been a big fan of cornmeal in my dough, but I do love the sweetness it brings. My trick is to use corn flour, which I toast before I add it to the dough. It contributes great flavor, plus your whole house will smell like popcorn when you're toasting it.

I like to use Ceresota brand all-purpose flour for this dough. The flour is widely used in and around Chicago but is hard to find outside the Midwest. King Arthur all-purpose flour is a good substitute.

182 grams water at 62°F (17°C)
to 66°F (19°C)

18 grams whole milk

1.75 grams sugar

2 grams instant dry yeast

315 grams all-purpose flour,
preferably Ceresota or
King Arthur

35 grams toasted corn flour
(see Note, page 65)

5.25 grams iodized table salt

18 grams lard or corn oil

Corn oil for the work surface,
brushing the dough, and the
storage containers

In the bowl of a stand mixer fitted with the dough hook, combine the water, milk, sugar, and yeast. Whisk until the sugar and yeast dissolve.

In a medium bowl, combine both flours and stir to blend well. Add the flour mixture to the mixer bowl and begin mixing on speed 1 for 3 minutes. After 2 minutes have elapsed, stop the mixer and, using a bowl scraper, scrape down the sides of the bowl and along the bottom to ensure all the ingredients are being incorporated. Add the salt and continue to mix on speed 1 for the remaining 1 minute.

Increase the mixer speed to speed 2 and mix for 2 minutes. Now, increase to speed 3 and slowly add the lard in chunks or drizzle in the oil. Continue mixing for up to 3 more minutes, or until the bowl is clean and the dough is smooth and elastic. Stop the mixer.

Lightly oil your work surface. Using the bowl scraper, transfer the dough to the oiled work surface. Using a pastry brush, brush the top of the dough with a little oil, then cover the dough with plastic wrap and let rest at ambient temperature for 15 minutes.

Divide the dough into two equal portions. They should each weigh about 290 grams. Form each portion into a round ball as described on page 41. Lightly oil two storage containers with lids. Place a ball into each oiled container, brush the top of each ball with more oil, cover the containers, and refrigerate for 24 hours to cold ferment before using.

CLASSIC
NEW YORK

When pizza first arrived in America, as much as it tried to stay true to its Italian roots, some things simply weren't available. Ingredients, such as flour, and equipment, like the planetary mixer, were different. Such differences meant that American pizza makers had to create their own style. If you compare this dough formula and the Italian Artisan formula on page 58, you'll find many similarities and a few small changes. The latter are mainly due to the switch from higher-temperature wood-fired ovens to lower-temperature gas deck ovens. As a kid growing up in Chicago, my pizza love started with the thin and crispy square-cut tavern pizza, like the one on page 66. But I can clearly remember my first New York slice. It changed my views of what pizza could be, and I immediately professed my love for it.

203 grams water at
62°F (17°C) to 66°F (19°C)

3 grams honey

312 grams King Arthur
bread flour

13 grams Caputo Semola
Rimacinata (or similar flour)

2 grams instant dry yeast

7 grams fine sea salt

5 grams extra-virgin olive oil

Extra-virgin olive oil
for the work surface,
brushing the dough, and
the storage containers

In the bowl of a stand mixer fitted with the paddle attachment, combine the water and honey. Whisk until the honey dissolves.

Add the flour and yeast to the mixer bowl and begin mixing on speed 1 for 3 minutes. After 1 minute has elapsed, stop the mixer and, using a bowl scraper, scrape down the sides of the bowl and along the bottom to ensure all the flour is being incorporated. Continue to mix on speed 1 for the remaining 2 minutes.

Stop the mixer and add the salt. Turn on the mixer to speed 2 and mix for 2 minutes. Stop the mixer and check to make sure there is no loose flour or salt remaining in the bowl before proceeding. If you find either, use the bowl scraper to scrape down the sides of the bowl, then turn on the mixer to speed 2 and mix for 1 minute.

Stop the mixer and replace the paddle attachment with the dough hook. Turn on the mixer to speed 3 and slowly drizzle in the oil. Continue mixing for 2 to 3 minutes, until the bowl is clean and the dough is smooth and elastic. Stop the mixer.

Lightly oil your work surface. Using the bowl scraper, transfer the dough to the oiled work surface. Using a pastry brush, brush the top of the dough with a little oil, then cover the dough with plastic wrap and let rest at ambient temperature for 15 minutes.

Divide the dough into two equal portions. They should each weigh about 270 grams. Alternatively, divide the dough into two portions, one weighing 320 grams and one weighing 220 grams. Form each portion into a round ball as described on page 41. Lightly oil two storage containers with lids. Place a ball into each oiled container, cover, and refrigerate for a minimum of 24 hours to cold ferment and a maximum of 48 hours total before using.

NEW YORK PAN

Commonly known as a "square" in a New York slice shop, the pan pizza is a Big Apple tradition. The pizza is baked almost all the way through before it is displayed on the counter, then when you find the slice you want, that slice goes back into the oven to be warmed, which makes the bottom so crispy that, when you bite into it, it shatters like glass while the middle remains soft and airy. The difference between a Sicilian and a grandma is the amount of dough and its thickness after baking. The grandma is much thinner, giving the pizza a totally different bite from the more bread-like Sicilian, which is close to focaccia. Depending on which New York borough you're in, the texture and amount of dough will change.

585 grams water at 62°F (17°C) to 66°F (19°C)

14 grams honey

810 grams King Arthur bread flour

90 grams semola rimacinata (fine semolina flour)

7 grams instant dry yeast

17 grams fine sea salt

18 grams extra-virgin olive oil

Extra-virgin olive oil for the work surface, brushing the dough, and the storage containers

In the bowl of a stand mixer fitted with the paddle attachment, combine the water and honey. Whisk until the honey dissolves.

In a large bowl, combine both flours and the yeast and stir to blend well. Add the flour mixture to the mixer bowl and begin mixing on speed 1 for 2 to 3 minutes, or until the dough starts to come together in a solid mass. Then increase the mixer speed to speed 2 for 3 to 4 minutes, or until the dough starts to pull away from the bowl. If dough climbs up the paddle during mixing, stop the mixer and, using a bowl scraper, push the dough down, then scrape down the sides of the bowl and along the bottom to ensure all the ingredients are being incorporated.

Stop the mixer and replace the paddle attachment with the dough hook. Add the salt to the bowl, then start mixing on speed 2 for 2 minutes. Then slowly drizzle in the oil and continue mixing on speed 2 for 2 minutes, or until dough starts to pull away from the bowl. Stop the mixer.

Lightly oil your work surface. Using the bowl scraper, transfer the dough to the oiled work surface. Using a pastry brush, lightly brush the top of the dough with oil, then cover the dough with plastic wrap and let rest at ambient temperature for 15 minutes.

Divide the dough into two 770-gram portions if making Sicilian pan pizzas or three 510-gram portions if making grandma pizzas. Form each portion into a oval ball as described on page 41. Lightly oil two or three storage containers with lids. Place a ball into each oiled container, cover, and refrigerate for a minimum of 24 hours to cold ferment and a maximum of 48 hours total before using.

YIELD: TWO 700-GRAM DOUGH BALLS, ENOUGH FOR TWO 10-BY-14-INCH (25 BY 35 CM) PANS
TIME: ABOUT 17 HOURS TOTAL (INCLUDES 11 MINUTES MIXING, UP TO 16 HOURS REST FOR THE POOLISH, 1 HOUR BENCH REST) PLUS 24-HOUR COLD FERMENT IN THE REFRIGERATOR

CONTEMPORARY
DETROIT PAN
WITH POOLISH

The Detroit pizza started out in the mid to late 1940s when US troops were returning from World War II and industrial plants were going back to building cars instead of M5 tanks and B-24 bombers. The story goes that Gus Guerra found a gap that needed to be filled. Soldiers returning home from oversees were looking for European-inspired cuisine, so Gus, together with his wife, whose mother was Sicilian, recreated an old-world dough recipe and baked it in a blue steel pan that was used on the automobile assembly lines. Gus began serving this new type of pizza pie in his Detroit restaurant, Buddy's Rendezvous Pizzeria, and it soon became a neighborhood favorite. In the early 1950s, Gus sold his restaurant, and the new owners shortened the name to Buddy's. Today, Buddy's has several locations in the Detroit metro area. Once you see how delicious this pizza is, you'll understand why Detroit pizza can now be found across the United States and around the world.

1 recipe Poolish (page 54)

160 grams water at 62°F (17°C) to 66°F (19°C)

320 grams King Arthur Sir Lancelot high-gluten flour or King Arthur bread flour

80 semola rimacinata (fine semolina flour)

7 grams non-diastatic malt powder or 10 grams honey

2 grams instant dry yeast

15 grams fine sea salt

15 grams corn oil

Corn oil for the storage containers

In the bowl of a stand mixer, combine the poolish and water. Stir until the poolish breaks down and is well mixed.

In a large bowl, combine both flours, the malt powder, and the yeast and stir to blend well. Add the flour mixture to the mixer bowl. Fit the mixer with the paddle attachment and begin mixing on speed 1 for 2 to 3 minutes, or until the dough starts to come together in a solid mass. Then increase the mixer speed to speed 2 and mix for 3 to 4 minutes, or until the dough starts to pull away from the bowl.

Stop the mixer and replace the paddle attachment with the dough hook. Add the salt to the bowl, then start mixing on speed 2 for 2 minutes. Then slowly drizzle in the oil and continue mixing on speed 2 for 2 minutes.

Stop the mixer. Divide the dough into two equal oval dough balls (page 41). They should each weigh about 700 grams. Lightly oil two storage containers with lids. Place a dough ball in each oiled container, cover, and refrigerate for a minimum of 24 hours to cold ferment and a maximum of 48 hours total before using.

TRADITIONAL

DETROIT PAN

The difference between the traditional and contemporary doughs, for both the Detroit and the Roman, is that the traditional dough is a quick method that produces gas during the proofing stage. Not much flavor is developed due to the process. However, with the Contemporary versions, the Biga and Poolish provide their own flavors in the initial fermentation steps of the preferment. There is an initial investment of time in the contemporary doughs but the reward is a more open structure and complex flavor to the crust.

560 grams water at 62°F (17°C) to 66°F (19°C)

7 grams non-diastatic malt powder or 10 grams honey

720 grams King Arthur Sir Lancelot high-gluten or bread flour

80 grams semola rimacinata (fine semolina flour)

4 grams instant dry yeast

15 grams fine sea salt

15 grams corn oil

Corn oil for the work surface, your hands, and the storage containers

In the bowl of a stand mixer fitted with the paddle attachment, combine the water and malt. Whisk until the malt dissolves.

In a large bowl, combine both flours and the yeast and stir to blend well. Add the flour mixture to the mixer bowl and begin mixing on speed 1 for 2 to 3 minutes, or until the dough starts to come together in a solid mass. Increase the mixer speed to speed 2 and mix for 3 to 4 minutes, or until the dough starts to pull away from the bowl. If the dough climbs up the paddle during mixing, stop the mixer and, using a bowl scraper, push the dough down, then scrape down the sides of the bowl and along the bottom to ensure all the ingredients are being incorporated.

Replace the paddle attachment with the dough hook. Add the salt to the bowl, then start mixing on speed 2 for 2 minutes. Slowly drizzle in the oil and continue mixing on speed 2 for 2 minutes, or until dough starts to pull away from the bowl.

Lightly oil your work surface and both hands. Use a bowl scraper and your hands to transfer the dough to the oiled work surface. Drizzle a small amount of oil onto the top of the dough, cover the dough with plastic wrap, and let rest at ambient temperature for 20 minutes.

Uncover the dough and slip the bowl scraper or a bench scraper under the dough to make sure it is not stuck to the work surface. Then, using oiled hands, lift the dough from the center until it releases from the work surface and fold it on itself, which will give the dough some volume and strength. Re-cover the dough with plastic wrap and let rest for 20 minutes. Repeat this step two more times for a total of three folds and 60 minutes.

Divide the dough into two equal oval dough balls (page 41). They should each weigh about 700 grams. Lightly oil two storage containers with lids. Place a dough ball in each oiled container, cover, and refrigerate for a minimum of 24 hours to cold ferment and a maximum of 48 hours total before using.

THE ART OF THE SAUCE

After years of traveling back and forth between the United States and Italy, I learned one very important thing about making pizza sauce. Whatever ends up in your sauce will end up on your pizza. Although that seems obvious, the implications of it took some time for me to grasp. That's because I grew up in Chicago where pizza sauce has typically included a lot of dried herbs, cheese, and other things, so I always felt the need to doctor up a can of tomatoes to give my sauce maximum flavor. It wasn't until I did a deep dive into the traditions of Italian pizza making that I realized the beauty of clean sauces. For example, for my Classic Italian Sauce (page 76), I add only sea salt, olive oil, fresh basil, and garlic to the tomatoes. The simplicity of the sauce is what makes it so great.

Not all sauces are that simple—and the Neapolitan Sauce (page 75) is even simpler—but they are all great examples of how the sauce can complement and truly make your pizza shine.

NEAPOLITAN SAUCE

It wasn't until my first trip to Napoli that my understanding of tomato sauce as an ingredient, not a condiment, became crystal clear and changed my thinking forever. In Napoli, tomato sauce for pizza is seasoned with only sea salt. I remember thinking that the sauce was going to be very bland, but what I didn't account for was the quality of the tomatoes themselves. Grown in the shadow of Mount Vesuvius, the San Marzano tomatoes of the Agro Sarnese–Nocerino area of Campania are widely regarded as among the world's best tomatoes for canning. They are sweet with a slight finish of acidity due to the volcanic soil and the extreme heat of the region. Their naturally bold flavor needs only sea salt to heighten it.

Here's how the role of tomato sauce was explained to me long ago. The two red-sauce pizzas that date back to the origins of Neapolitan pizza are the Margherita (page 88) and the marinara. They each have distinct ingredients. The Margherita is topped with tomato sauce, fresh basil, Parmigiano-Reggiano, and olive oil. The marinara is topped with tomato sauce, dried oregano, fresh garlic, and olive oil. These important distinctions reflect the traditions of the original Neapolitan pizzaioli. Over the years, as new generations of pizzaioli have come on the scene, it is common to see variations of the Margherita and marinara, like my tribute to Maestro Antonio Starita and his version of the marinara that I call Marinara alla Starita (page 97), which features basil, garlic, cherry tomatoes, pecorino romano, and olive oil.

One 28-ounce (794 g) can whole peeled tomatoes, preferably San Marzano

1 teaspoon fine sea salt

In a medium bowl, combine the tomatoes and salt.

Using your hands, crush the tomatoes to a coarse pulp, discarding any stringy bits from the center of a tomato and any firm pieces from the stem end.

Use immediately, or store in an airtight container in the refrigerator for up to 5 days.

CLASSIC
ITALIAN SAUCE

As I traveled throughout Italy absorbing as much pizza knowledge as possible, I noticed that pizzas in the north were different from pizzas in the south. The origins of pizza are rooted in the region of Campania and its capital, Napoli, as the Neapolitan sauce recipe on page 75, in which only San Marzano tomatoes and sea salt are used, illustrates. As you travel north to the region of Emilia-Romagna and specifically to its second largest city, Parma, the tomato variety changes. That's because the climate and soil around Parma produce tomatoes that are a bit sweeter than those grown in the high temperatures and volcanic soil of Campania.

This sauce is more robust than the Neapolitan sauce due to the addition of garlic and fresh basil. You still must start with a really good tomato. If you do, I promise that you won't need to add any sugar or dried herbs to make a delicious sauce.

One 28-ounce (794 g) can Italian whole peeled tomatoes

1 teaspoon fine sea salt

½ garlic clove, crushed

2 fresh basil leaves, torn

1 tablespoon extra-virgin olive oil

Fit a food mill with the disk with medium-size holes and place the mill on top of a medium bowl. Add the tomatoes to the mill and pass them through as described on page 48, being careful to scrape every last bit of pulp clinging to the bottom of the mill into the bowl.

Add the salt, garlic, basil, and oil to the pureed tomatoes and stir until well blended. Use immediately, or store in an airtight container in the refrigerator for up to 5 days.

OGNI
STRUNZ
È MARENARO

RUSTIC

HAND-CRUSHED SAUCE

When I was growing up, this cooked sauce was a staple in my mom's and my grandmothers' kitchens. They would use whole canned tomatoes and cook them down a bit until the sauce became concentrated and sweet. I love the way the garlic permeates the oil to provide a beautiful depth of flavor. I use this sauce in many different recipes, but my favorite way to use it is on top of the pizzas in the Chicago pan chapter (page 189) and as the sauce for my meatballs (page 223).

2 tablespoons extra-virgin olive oil

1 garlic clove, crushed

One 28-ounce (794 g) can Italian whole peeled tomatoes, crushed by hand

1 teaspoon fine sea salt

¼ teaspoon dried oregano

3 fresh basil leaves, torn

In a small-medium saucepan over low heat, warm the oil and garlic for about 1 to 2 minutes, or until the garlic is golden brown. Be careful the garlic does not burn. Add the tomatoes, salt, and oregano, stir well, and raise the heat to medium. When the mixture begins to simmer, turn down the heat to low and cook, stirring occasionally, for 15 to 20 minutes, or until the sauce reduces a bit.

Remove the pan from the heat, stir in the basil, and let the sauce cool completely. Use immediately, or transfer to an airtight container and store in the refrigerator for up to 5 days.

SPICY
WHITE SAUCE

This spicy cream sauce can be used as a base sauce and makes a great drizzle atop anything that needs a creamy kick.

1 cup (240 ml) Creamy White Sauce (page 81)

2 tablespoons drained and chopped pepperoncini in brine

2 tablespoons brine from pepperoncini jar

2 tablespoons hot honey, preferably Mike's Hot Honey

1 teaspoon red pepper flakes

About 1 tablespoon warm water if needed

Pinch kosher salt

In a medium bowl, combine the white sauce, pepperoncini, brine, honey, and red pepper flakes. Using an immersion blender, pulse until smooth.

If the sauce is too thick, slowly drizzle in the water while continuing to pulse, adding only as much as needed to achieve the desired consistency. Salt to taste, being careful not to oversalt, as the pepperoncini brine is salty.

Use immediately, or transfer to an airtight container and store in the refrigerator for up to 5 days.

CLASSIC NEAPOLITAN PIZZAS

Classic Neapolitan pizza is traditionally baked in a very hot wood-fired oven. I'm talking 850°F (450°C) plus. Since most home cooks don't have an oven capable of heating beyond 500°F to 550°F (260°C to 288°C), I've created a method using your stovetop and oven that will give you a bunch of the characteristics you'd get baking a Neapolitan pizza in a professional pizzeria oven. However, if you have a portable pizza oven, such as one of the models described on page 33, these pizzas will really shine. Use as much heat as possible and bake for as little time as possible. For a real Neapolitan pizza, your goal is a superfast bake—in and out in just ninety seconds.

PROSCIUTTO
CRUDO E RUCOLA

This pizza is seen in nearly every region in Italy and in many bastardized versions throughout the rest of the world. First, the prosciutto (a.k.a. *prosciutto crudo*, or dry-cured ham) goes on the pizza after baking and never before it goes in the oven. Next, before you finish the pizza with prosciutto and arugula, cut it into slices. Topping the pizza with these ingredients and then cutting it will cause the arugula to wilt. The idea here is to use the baked pizza base as a canvas, with the prosciutto and arugula becoming three-dimensional additions. I like to use *prosciutto di Parma*, but if you cannot find it, a good-quality domestic prosciutto can be substituted.

One 290-gram ball Neapolitan dough (page 55)

4 fresh basil leaves, torn in half

3 ounces (90 g) fior di latte mozzarella cheese, cubed (scant 1 cup; see page 48)

10 cherry tomatoes, halved (see page 48)

1 cup loosely packed arugula (½ ounce [15 g])

6 thin slices prosciutto di Parma (about 3 ounces [90 g])

¼ cup (30 g) grated Parmesan cheese, preferably Parmigiano-Reggiano

Lemon-infused extra-virgin olive oil, preferably Partanna from Sicily, for drizzling

Remove the dough from the refrigerator and place it on the counter to proof until the dough temperature reads 55 to 60°F (13 to 16°C) using an instant-read thermometer, typically about 2 hours, or until dough has doubled in size.

One hour before baking the pizza, slide a rack into the top position of the oven (about 4 inches [10 cm] from the heat source), place a pizza stone or steel on the rack, and preheat the oven to 500°F (260°C) or the highest setting.

When ready to bake, place a 12-inch (30 cm) sauté pan on the stovetop and turn on the heat to high.

While the pan heats, using the method on page 42, gently remove the dough ball from its container, dredge it in flour, place it on a well-floured work surface, and stretch it into a 12-inch (30 cm) round.

Carefully and gently lay the dough in an even layer in the hot sauté pan, then cover the pan with a lid and bake the dough on the stovetop over high heat for 5 minutes.

Remove the pan from the stove, then remove the lid. Spread the basil and mozzarella evenly over the surface of the dough followed by the cherry tomatoes, leaving a 1-inch (2.5 cm) border around the edges.

Turn the oven setting to broil. If your broiler has temperature settings, set it on high. Place the sauté pan on the stone or steel and bake the pizza for 3 to 4 minutes, or until the crust is blistered with black leopard spots and slightly browned.

Remove the pan from the oven and, using an offset spatula, lift the pizza out of the pan and transfer the pizza to a cooling rack.

After a few minutes, transfer the pizza to a clean cutting board and cut into six slices. Scatter the arugula evenly over the pizza and then place a slice of prosciutto on each slice. Finish with a dusting of Parmesan and a drizzle of lemon oil. Serve.

MARGHERITA CLASSICA

I fell in love with the Margherita pizza on my first trip to Napoli, so it has always held a special place in my heart. Its ingredients are so clean and simple that it is often the pizza that pizzaioli are judged by because it offers nowhere to hide. Everything has to be spot on, from the dough to the bake and everywhere in between. The history of this pizza (see page 13) is part of the fabric of Neapolitan pizza making, and mastering this classic will win the hearts of your family and friends.

One 290-gram ball Neapolitan dough (page 55)

⅓ cup (80 ml) Neapolitan Sauce (page 75)

4 fresh basil leaves, torn in half

3 ounces (90 g) fior di latte mozzarella cheese, cubed (scant 1 cup; see page 48)

¼ cup (30 g) grated Parmesan cheese, preferably Parmigiano-Reggiano

1 tablespoon extra-virgin olive oil

Pinch fine sea salt

Remove the dough from the refrigerator and place it on the counter to proof until the dough temperature reads 55 to 60°F (13 to 16°C) using an instant-read thermometer, typically about 2 hours, or until dough has doubled in size.

One hour before baking the pizza, position a rack in the top of the oven (about 4 inches [10 cm] from the heat source), place a pizza stone or steel on the rack, and preheat the oven to 500°F (260°C) or the highest setting.

When ready to bake, place a 12-inch (30 cm) sauté pan on the stovetop and turn on the heat to high.

While the pan heats, using the method on page 42, gently remove the dough ball from its container, dredge it in flour, place it on a well-floured work surface, and stretch it into a 12-inch (30 cm) round.

Carefully and gently lay the dough in an even layer in the hot sauté pan, then cover the pan with a lid and bake the dough on the stovetop over high heat for 5 minutes.

Remove the pan from the stove, then remove the lid. Using a ladle, top the dough with the sauce, spreading it evenly over the surface and leaving a 1-inch (2.5 cm) border around the edges. Scatter the basil and then the mozzarella evenly over the sauce. Dust with the Parmesan, then drizzle evenly with the oil and sprinkle with the salt.

Turn the oven setting to broil. If your broiler has temperature settings, set it on high. Place the sauté pan on the stone or steel and bake the pizza for 3 to 4 minutes, or until the crust is blistered with black leopard spots and slightly browned.

Remove the pan from the oven and, using an offset spatula, lift the pizza out of the pan and transfer the pizza to a cooling rack. After a few minutes, transfer to a clean cutting board. Cut and serve.

PIZZA ALLA
DIAVOLA

> **Although *alla diavola* means "devil's style," this pizza gets its name because of the romance of fire and smoke and not because it's evil. Baked in an oven that is often compared to Dante's *inferno*, it receives an extra kiss of smokiness from the addition of smoked mozzarella. To take this pizza over the top, trade out the smoked mozzarella for smoked scamorza, which is a stretched-curd cheese from southern Italy similar to mozzarella but drier and denser. Both spicy soppressata and a healthy pinch of red pepper flakes bring some heat to the party.**

One 290-gram ball Neapolitan dough (page 55)

⅓ cup (80 ml) Neapolitan Sauce (page 75)

4 fresh basil leaves, torn in half

¼ cup shredded smoked mozzarella or smoked scamorza cheese (1 ounce [30 g])

3 ounces (90 g) fior di latte mozzarella cheese, cubed (scant 1 cup; see page 48)

1 ounce (30 g) spicy soppressata, thinly sliced and each slice halved

½ teaspoon red pepper flakes, preferably peperoncini from Calabria

¼ cup (30 g) grated Parmesan cheese, preferably Parmigiano-Reggiano

1 tablespoon extra-virgin olive oil

Remove the dough from the refrigerator and place it on the counter to proof until the dough temperature reads 55 to 60°F (13 to 16°C) using an instant-read thermometer, typically about 2 hours, or until dough has doubled in size.

One hour before baking the pizza, position a rack in the top of the oven (about 4 inches [10 cm] from the heat source), place a pizza stone or steel on the rack, and preheat the oven to 500°F (260°C) or the highest setting.

When ready to bake, place a 12-inch (30 cm) sauté pan on the stovetop and turn on the heat to high.

While the pan heats, using the method on page 42, gently remove the dough ball from its container, dredge it in flour, place it on a well-floured work surface, and stretch it into a 12-inch (30 cm) round.

Carefully and gently lay the dough in an even layer in the hot sauté pan, then cover the pan with a lid and bake the dough on the stovetop over high heat for 5 minutes.

Remove the pan from the stove, then remove the lid. Using a ladle, top the dough with the sauce, spreading it evenly over the surface and leaving a 1-inch (2.5 cm) border around the edges. Scatter the basil and then both mozzarellas evenly over the sauce. Next add the soppressata, laying it flat and trying to overlap the slices, and then sprinkle on the red pepper flakes. Dust with the Parmesan and drizzle with the oil.

Turn the oven setting to broil. If your broiler has temperature settings, set it on high. Place the sauté pan on the stone or steel and bake the pizza for 3 to 4 minutes, or until the crust is blistered with black leopard spots and slightly browned.

Remove the pan from the oven and, using an offset spatula, lift the pizza out of the pan and transfer the pizza to a cooling rack. After a few minutes, transfer to a clean cutting board. Cut and serve.

QUATTRO STAGIONI

This pizza is a showstopper with a big wow factor. It is divided into four quadrants, each of which contains different ingredients representing one of the four seasons. I learned the method for making the quadrants during one of my earliest trips to Napoli, and I still use it today. There are a few ways to create the dough strips that mark the sections, however. For example, you can cut a very narrow strip of dough from around the entire edge of the stretched dough, cut it into two equal pieces, and arrange them in a cross on the dough. Any way you do it, this pizza is awesome. And if you are at a pizzeria, I like to say that this is the perfect pizza for someone who can't decide what they want to eat!

One 290-gram ball Neapolitan dough (page 55)

1 tablespoon extra-virgin olive oil

¼ cup (30 g) grated Parmesan cheese, preferably Parmigiano-Reggiano

Remove the dough from the refrigerator and place it on the counter to proof until the dough temperature reads 55 to 60°F (13 to 16°C) using an instant-read thermometer, typically about 2 hours, or until dough has doubled in size.

One hour before baking the pizza, position a rack in the middle of the oven (8 to 10 inches [15 to 20 cm] from the heat source), place a pizza stone or steel on the rack, and preheat the oven to 500°F (260°C) or the highest setting.

When ready to bake, lightly dust a pizza peel with flour and set to the side. Using the method on page 42, gently remove the dough ball from its container, dredge it in flour, place it on a well-floured work surface, and stretch it into a 12-inch (30 cm) round, pressing the dough to the edges to make a flat, uniform surface. Transfer the stretched dough to the peel.

Using a pizza cutter, and starting at the edge of the dough, make narrow cuts from 3 o'clock to 12 o'clock, 6 o'clock to 3 o'clock, 9 o'clock to 6 o'clock, and 12 o'clock to 9 o'clock. Make sure not to cut all the way through when you get to the end of each section. Lift a dough strip at the cut end, bring it to the center of the dough circle, and press down to secure. Repeat with each of the remaining dough strips until you have four individual sections.

CONTINUED

QUADRANT 1

Scant ¼ cup cubed fior di latte mozzarella cheese (about 1 ounce [30g]; see page 48)

3 cherry tomatoes, halved (see page 48)

1 fresh basil leaf, torn

QUADRANT 2

2 tablespoons Neapolitan Sauce (page 75)

3 thin slices prosciutto cotto (cooked ham), julienned

2 slices Neapolitan salami, thinly sliced, julienned (¼ ounce [10 g])

Scant ¼ cup cubed fior di latte mozzarella cheese (about 1 ounce [30 g]; see page 48)

QUADRANT 3

Scant ¼ cup (60 ml) Neapolitan pizza sauce (page 75)

2 tablespoons artichoke hearts, quartered

Scant ¼ cup cubed fior di latte mozzarella cheese (about 1 ounce [30g]; see page 48)

QUADRANT 4

Scant ¼ cup cubed fior di latte mozzarella cheese (about 1 ounce [30g]; see page 48)

¼ cup sliced roasted mushrooms (about ½ ounce [15 g])

Starting at the top left for Quadrant 1, scatter the mozzarella over the quadrant and then top with the cherry tomatoes and basil. Next, fill Quadrant 2, which lies to the right of Quadrant 1. First spread the dough with the sauce, then top with the ham and salami and finally the mozzarella. To fill Quadrant 3, which lies below Quadrant 1, first spread the dough with the sauce, then top with the artichoke hearts followed by the mozzarella. For Quadrant 4, the last section, scatter the mozzarella over the dough and top with the mushrooms. Drizzle the oil evenly over all the quadrants and then dust evenly with the Parmesan.

Turn the oven setting to broil. If your broiler has temperature settings, set it on high. Slide the pizza off the peel onto the stone or steel (see page 42) and bake the pizza for 8 to 10 minutes, or until the crust is blistered with black leopard spots and slightly browned and the toppings are done.

Using the peel, remove the pizza from the oven and transfer to a cooling rack. After a few minutes, transfer to a clean cutting board to cut and serve. I like to cut this pizza into four pieces with each quadrant as a slice. This keeps the integrity of the ingredients. If you want to cut each quadrant in half, try to reposition ingredients that get in the way of your cutting so they don't act as a squeegee and wipe the base
clean of toppings.

QUATTRO FORMAGGI

Think of the *pizza quattro formaggi* (four cheeses) as a big kid's cheese pizza. The cheese selections often leave people scratching their heads as to whether they'll work together, but my version is steeped in Italian tradition. Most grocery stores will have these cheeses in their deli case. Buy them in chunks (ask a clerk if you see them only sliced or crumbled) and go home and shred (with a box grater) and crumble them yourself. While I'll always encourage you to be creative in the kitchen, which in this case means substituting other cheeses, please do me a favor and make the pizza the traditional way at least once. I promise it's awesome!

One 290-gram ball Neapolitan dough (page 55)

3 ounces (90 g) fior di latte mozzarella cheese, cubed (scant 1 cup; see page 48)

4 fresh basil leaves, torn in half

2 tablespoons shredded fontina cheese

2 tablespoons shredded Emmental cheese

1 tablespoon crumbled Gorgonzola cheese

Remove the dough from the refrigerator and place it on the counter to proof until the dough temperature reads 55 to 60°F (13 to 16°C) using an instant-read thermometer, typically about 2 hours, or until dough has doubled in size.

One hour before baking the pizza, slide a rack into the top position of the oven (about 4 inches [10 cm] from the heat source), place a pizza stone or steel on the rack, and preheat the oven to 500°F (260°C) or the highest setting.

When ready to bake, place a 12-inch (30 cm) sauté pan on the stovetop and turn on the heat to high.

While the pan heats, using the method on page 42, gently remove the dough ball from its container, dredge it in flour, place it on a well-floured work surface, and stretch it into a 12-inch (30 cm) round.

Carefully and gently lay the dough in an even layer in the hot sauté pan, then cover the pan with a lid and bake the dough on the stovetop over high heat for 5 minutes.

Remove the pan from the stove, then remove the lid. Scatter the mozzarella, basil, fontina, Emmental, and Gorgonzola evenly over the surface of the dough, leaving a 1-inch (2.5 cm) border around the edges.

Turn the oven setting to broil. If your broiler has temperature settings, set it on high. Place the sauté pan on the stone or steel and bake the pizza for 3 to 4 minutes, or until the crust is blistered with black leopard spots and slightly browned.

Remove the pan from the oven and, using an offset spatula, lift the pizza out of the pan and transfer the pizza to a cooling rack. After a few minutes, transfer to a clean cutting board. Cut and serve.

SOLE NEL PIATTO

The *sole nel piatto* (sun on a plate) has long been popular in Napoli and has now spread around the world. Like the Quattro Stagioni on page 91, this is a showstopper. Shaping it takes a little practice, but once you figure out how to make the cuts on the edge of the dough and then how to crimp them, the sky is the limit when it comes to what you can stuff into each point. The same goes for the center toppings. I like to top the center as a classic Margherita because the stuffed ricotta points are so rich.

One 290-gram ball Neapolitan dough (page 55)

½ cup (115 g) whole-milk ricotta cheese, divided into eight 1-tablespoon dollops

⅓ cup (80 ml) Neapolitan sauce (page 75)

3 ounces (90 g) fior di latte mozzarella cheese, cubed (scant 1 cup; see page 48)

¼ cup (30 g) grated Parmesan cheese, preferably Parmigiano-Reggiano

4 fresh basil leaves, torn in half

1 tablespoon extra-virgin olive oil

Remove the dough from the refrigerator and place it on the counter to proof until the dough temperature reads 55 to 60°F (13 to 16°C) using an instant-read thermometer, typically about 2 hours, or until dough has doubled in size.

One hour before baking the pizza, position a rack in the middle of the oven (8 to 10 inches [20 to 25 cm] from the heat source), place a pizza stone or steel on the rack, and preheat the oven to 500°F (260°C) or the highest setting.

When ready to bake, using the method on page 42, gently remove the dough ball from its container, dredge it in flour, place it on a well-floured work surface, and stretch it into a 12-inch (30 cm) round, pressing the dough to the edges to make a flat, uniform surface.

Lightly dust a sheet pan with flour and transfer the stretched dough to the pan.

Using a pizza cutter, and starting at the edge of the dough, make a 1½-inch-long (4 cm) cut at 12 o'clock, 3 o'clock, 6 o'clock, and 9 o'clock. Then make the same size cut between 1 and 2 o'clock, 4 and 5 o'clock, 7 and 8 o'clock, and 10 and 11 o'clock. Working quickly, place a ricotta dollop on the center of each dough cut. Once each dough cut has ricotta, grab the two outer edges of a dough cut and crimp them together in the center, creating a cone shape. Repeat until all eight points are crimped.

Using a ladle or large spoon, top the center of the dough with the sauce, spreading it evenly over the surface and leaving the eight points uncovered. Scatter the mozzarella evenly over the sauce, then dust with the Parmesan, top with the basil, and drizzle with the oil.

Turn the oven setting to broil. If your broiler has temperature settings, set it on high. Place the sheet pan on the stone or steel and bake the pizza for 8 to 10 minutes, or until the crust is blistered with black leopard spots and slightly browned.

Remove the pan from the oven and, using an offset spatula, lift the pizza out of the pan and transfer the pizza to a cooling rack. After a few minutes, transfer to a clean cutting board to cut and serve. I like to cut this pizza so each point can act as a handle when it's time to pick up a slice and eat.

MARINARA ALLA
STARITA

Many years ago, I met Maestro Antonio Starita, or "Don Antonio," in Las Vegas at the International Pizza Expo. It was so long ago that I don't have a single tattoo in the photo commemorating the occasion. Over the years, I have been very fortunate to have been able to work alongside him and closely observe his methods, which come from a time when learning a craft was generational. Few people have influenced me in my pursuit of the art and traditions of Neapolitan pizza as much as Don Antonio has. His pizzeria in Napoli is one of the oldest in the city. Started in 1901 by his grandfather, Starita a Materdei has people lining the street for a pizza that seems to come from another time. The respect Don Antonio has for ingredients and the true Neapolitan pizza inspires me every time my hands touch flour.

One 290-gram ball Neapolitan dough (page 55)

½ cup (120 ml) Neapolitan Sauce (page 75)

4 fresh basil leaves, torn in half

1 teaspoon dried oregano

1 garlic clove, chopped

10 cherry tomatoes, halved (see page 48)

¼ cup (30g) grated romano cheese, preferably pecorino romano

2 tablespoons extra-virgin olive oil

Remove the dough from the refrigerator and place it on the counter to proof until the dough temperature reads 55 to 60°F (13 to 16°C) using an instant-read thermometer, typically about 2 hours, or until dough has doubled in size.

One hour before baking the pizza, position a rack in the top of the oven (about 4 inches [10 cm] from the heat source), place a pizza stone or steel on the rack, and preheat the oven to 500°F (260°C) or the highest setting.

When ready to bake, place a 12-inch (30 cm) sauté pan on the stovetop and turn on the heat to high.

While the pan heats, using the method on page 42, gently remove the dough ball from its container, dredge it in flour, place it on a well-floured work surface, and stretch it into a 12-inch (30 cm) round.

Carefully and gently lay the dough in an even layer in the hot sauté pan, then cover the pan with a lid and bake the dough on the stovetop over high heat for 5 minutes.

Remove the pan from the stove, then remove the lid. Using a ladle, top the dough with the sauce, spreading it evenly over the surface and leaving a 1-inch (2.5 cm) border around the edges. Scatter the basil, oregano and then garlic and tomatoes evenly over the pizza. Dust with the cheese, then drizzle evenly with the oil.

Turn the oven setting to broil. If your broiler has temperature settings, set it on high. Place the sauté pan on the stone or steel and bake the pizza for 3 to 4 minutes, or until the crust is blistered with black leopard spots and slightly browned. Remove the pan from the oven and, using an offset spatula, lift the pizza out of the pan and transfer the pizza to a cooling rack. After a few minutes, transfer to a clean cutting board. Cut and serve.

MARRUZU E MINNUZU

I named this pizza after my dad and uncle, using their Calabrese dialect nicknames: Marruzu for Mario, my father, and Minnuzu for my uncle Carmine. I remember making this pizza for them when I was younger, and they loved it. Broccoli rabe and Italian sausage are a classic southern Italian combination. Here, I top this family-favorite pizza with Spicy Rapini, which is traditionally sautéed with garlic, red pepper flakes, and *'nduja*, a soft, spreadable spicy cured pork sausage (salami) from Calabria. If you cannot find *'nduja*, spicy chili paste can be substituted.

One 290-gram ball Neapolitan dough (page 55)

¼ cup (60 ml) Neapolitan Sauce (page 75)

¼ cup shredded smoked mozzarella or smoked scamorza cheese (1 ounce [30 g])

3 ounces (90 g) fior di latte mozzarella cheese, cubed (scant 1 cup; see page 48)

½ cup Spicy Rapini (2 ounces [60 g]; page 99)

3 ounces cooked Italian sausage, crumbled

Pinch red pepper flakes

¼ cup (30 g) grated Parmesan cheese, preferably Parmigiano-Reggiano

Remove the dough from the refrigerator and place it on the counter to proof until the dough temperature reads 55 to 60°F (13 to 16°C) using an instant-read thermometer, typically about 2 hours, or until dough has doubled in size.

One hour before baking the pizza, slide a rack into the top position of the oven (about 4 inches [10 cm] from the heat source), place a pizza stone or steel on the rack, and preheat the oven to 500°F (260°C) or the highest setting.

When ready to bake, place a 12-inch (30 cm) sauté pan on the stovetop and turn on the heat to high.

While the pan heats, using the method on page 42, gently remove the dough ball from its container, dredge it in flour, place it on a well-floured work surface, and stretch it into a 12-inch (30 cm) round.

Carefully and gently lay the dough in an even layer in the hot sauté pan, then cover the pan with a lid and bake the dough on the stovetop over high heat for 5 minutes.

Remove the pan from the stove, then remove the lid. Using a ladle, top the dough with the sauce, spreading it evenly over the surface and leaving a 1-inch (2.5 cm) border around the edges. Scatter both mozzarellas, then the Spicy Rapini and the Italian sausage evenly over the pizza.

Turn the oven setting to broil. If your broiler has temperature settings, set it on high. Place the sauté pan on the stone or steel and bake the pizza for 3 to 4 minutes, or until the crust is blistered with black leopard spots and slightly browned.

Remove the pan from the oven and, using an offset spatula, remove the pizza from the pan and place on a cooling rack. After a few minutes, transfer to a clean cutting board. Finish with the red pepper flakes and Parmesan. Cut and serve.

CONTINUED

SPICY RAPINI

In my house, we eat this as a side dish. But it works great as a spicy pizza topping too.

1 cup (240 ml) water

½ cup (150 g) 'nduja (you can substitute Calabrian chili paste)

1 bunch of Broccoli Rabe, chopped

¼ cup (60 ml) extra-virgin olive oil

2 cloves fresh garlic, sliced

Preheat a 12-inch (30 cm) sauté pan on high.

Add the water and 'nduja. Using a wood spoon, begin to break up the 'nduja until it is incorporated into the water.

Add the broccoli rabe and cover. Cook for 3 minutes.

Uncover and add the oil and garlic. Sauté for 4 minutes, stirring frequently.

Remove the pan from the heat and allow the broccoli to cool. If not using right away, store in the refrigerator in an airtight container for up to 3 days.

When you're ready to use it, it can be warmed in a sauté pan until heated through, or used cold as a pizza topping.

REGIONAL ITALIAN ARTISAN PIZZAS

As pizza left Napoli and the borders of Campania and spread throughout the rest of Italy, it evolved with changes in ovens and ingredients. The Italian artisan pizza has fewer restrictions when it comes to rules and guidelines than the Neapolitan pizza. Because it bakes at a lower temperature, it can spend more time in the oven, giving you a nicely browned crust with a crispy bottom. This is the pizza that most Italians eat.

COTTO E FUNGHI

When speaking of prosciutto, it's important to remember there are two types: *crudo* (raw) and *cotto* (cooked). *Prosciutto crudo* is air-cured ham that is typically thinly sliced and should only be added to a pizza after baking, while *prosciutto cotto* is cooked ham that is cut in various ways—sliced, julienned, cubed—and can be added to a pizza before baking. *Cotto e funghi* is a classic pizza found throughout Italy and is as popular as pepperoni pizza is in the United States. Cooked ham can be added to this pizza after the bake as well, and I like to do that when I find a particularly good imported *prosciutto cotto*. I know that it will be gently warmed in the residual heat, which will open up its flavor, giving the diner a fuller appreciation of its high quality.

One 290-gram ball Italian Artisan dough (page 58)

⅓ cup (80 ml) Classic Italian Sauce (page 76)

1 garlic clove, chopped

3 fresh basil leaves, torn

3 ounces (90 g) fior di latte mozzarella cheese, sliced thin and chopped (see page 48)

¼ cup (25 g) Sautéed Mushrooms (page 223)

2 ounces (60 g) prosciutto cotto (cooked ham), julienned

1 teaspoon grated Parmesan cheese, preferably Parmigiano-Reggiano

Extra-virgin olive oil for drizzling

Remove the dough from the refrigerator and place it on the counter to proof until the dough temperature reads 55 to 60°F (13 to 16°C) using an instant-read thermometer, typically about 2 hours, or until dough has doubled in size.

One hour before baking the pizza, slide one rack into the lowest position of the oven and a second rack into the middle of the oven, leaving 6 to 8 inches (15 to 20 cm) between the racks. Place a pizza stone or steel on each rack and preheat the oven to 500°F (260°C) or the highest setting.

When ready to bake, using the method on page 42, lightly dust a pizza peel with flour and set to the side. Gently remove the dough ball from its container, dredge it in flour, place it on a well-floured work surface, and stretch it into a 12-inch (30 cm) round. Transfer the stretched dough to the peel.

Using a ladle, top the dough with the sauce, spreading it evenly over the surface and leaving a 1-inch (2.5 cm) border around the edges. Sprinkle with the garlic and basil, then spread the mozzarella, mushrooms, and ham evenly over the sauce. Dust with the Parmesan and drizzle with a little oil.

Slide the pizza off the peel onto the stone or steel on the lowest oven rack and bake the pizza for 5 to 6 minutes, or until the crust is golden brown.

Using the peel, remove the pizza from the oven and transfer to a cooling rack. After a few minutes, transfer to a clean cutting board to cut and serve.

CAPRICCIOSA

While this pizza may seem like it's topped with a bunch of random ingredients (hence its name; *capricciosa* means "capricious"), the combination of artichoke, ham, mushrooms, and olives is classic and reminds me of late summer and early fall. Popular all over Italy, this pizza is a core menu item for most pizzerias.

One 290-gram ball Italian Artisan dough (page 58)

⅓ cup (80 ml) Classic Italian Sauce (page 76)

3 ounces (90 g) fior di latte mozzarella cheese, julienned ¼ inch (6 mm) thick (see page 48)

¼ cup (45 g) Marinated Artichoke Hearts (page 227)

2 tablespoons Gaeta or Kalamata olives, pitted

¼ cup (25 g) Sautéed Mushrooms (page 223)

3 thin slices prosciutto cotto (cooked ham)

Extra-virgin olive oil for drizzling

Grated Parmesan cheese, preferably Parmigiano-Reggiano, for finishing

Remove the dough from the refrigerator and place it on the counter to proof until the dough temperature reads 55 to 60°F (13 to 16°C) using an instant-read thermometer, typically about 2 hours, or until dough has doubled in size.

One hour before baking the pizza, slide one rack into the lowest position of the oven and a second rack into the middle of the oven, leaving 6 to 8 inches (15 to 20 cm) between the racks. Place a pizza stone or steel on each rack and preheat the oven to 500°F (260°C) or the highest setting.

When ready to bake, using the method on page 42, lightly dust a pizza peel with flour and set to the side. Using the method on page 42, gently remove the dough ball from its container, dredge it in flour, place it on a well-floured work surface, and stretch it into a 12-inch (30 cm) round. Transfer the stretched dough to the peel.

Using a ladle, top the dough with the sauce, spreading it evenly over the surface and leaving a 1-inch (2.5 cm) border around the edges. Distribute the mozzarella, artichokes, olives, mushrooms, and ham evenly over the sauce. Drizzle with a little oil and sprinkle with a big pinch of Parmesan.

Slide the pizza off the peel onto the stone or steel (see page 42) on the lowest oven rack and bake the pizza for 5 to 6 minutes, or until the crust is golden brown.

Using the peel, remove the pizza from the oven and transfer to a cooling rack. After a few minutes, transfer to a clean cutting board. Drizzle with a little more oil, and add a sprinkle of Parmesan. Cut and serve.

LA REGINA

I fell in love with this pizza during a visit to Rome one late spring. It arrived with chopped peeled tomatoes instead of a tomato sauce base, which proved brilliant. As the pizza baked, the tomatoes cooked, releasing their juice, which married with the melting mozzarella. The combination of the fresh flavors of the tomatoes and basil, the richness of the cheese, and the bright taste of the marinated artichoke hearts was incredible, and as if that wasn't enough, the salty bite of the *prosciutto cotto* sent the whole pie up a notch. Just thinking about this pizza brings back memories of cool breezes on an early morning in Rome.

One 290-gram ball Italian Artisan dough (page 58)

1 cup (250 g) drained canned Italian whole peeled tomatoes, cut into ½-inch (1 cm) chunks

3 ounces (90 g) fior di latte mozzarella cheese, julienned ¼ inch (6 mm) thick (see page 48)

2 fresh basil leaves, torn, plus 2 leaves, cut into chiffonade for garnish

¼ cup (45 g) Marinated Artichoke Hearts (page 227)

3 thin slices prosciutto cotto (cooked ham), cut into large pieces

Pinch grated Parmesan cheese, preferably Parmigiano-Reggiano, plus more to finish

Extra-virgin olive oil for drizzling

Remove the dough from the refrigerator and place it on the counter to proof until the dough temperature reads 55 to 60°F (13 to 16°C) using an instant-read thermometer, typically about 2 hours, or until dough has doubled in size.

One hour before baking the pizza, slide one rack into the lowest position of the oven and a second rack into the middle of the oven, leaving 6 to 8 inches (15 to 20 cm) between the racks. Place a pizza stone or steel on each rack and preheat the oven to 500°F (260°C) or the highest setting.

When ready to bake, using the method on page 42, lightly dust a pizza peel with flour and set to the side. Gently remove the dough ball from its container, dredge it in flour, place it on a well-floured work surface, and stretch it into a 12-inch (30 cm) round. Transfer the stretched dough to the peel.

Spread the tomatoes evenly over the surface of the dough, leaving a 1-inch (2.5 cm) border around the edges. Then scatter the mozzarella, basil, artichoke hearts, ham, and Parmesan evenly over the tomatoes. Drizzle with olive oil.

Slide the pizza off the peel onto the stone or steel on the lowest oven rack and bake the pizza for 5 to 6 minutes, or until the crust is golden brown.

Using the peel, remove the pizza from the oven and transfer to a cooling rack. After a few minutes, transfer to a clean cutting board, sprinkle with the basil chiffonade and Parmesan, and finish with a drizzle of oil. Cut and serve.

CALABRESE

If there was ever a way to put on a plate the first thing that comes to mind when I think of my family's origins in Calabria, it would be this pizza. It is like a love letter to all those who left everything in Italy to seek a better life in America. If you were a first-generation Italian American kid, you can probably remember your family returning from trips to the motherland smuggling things in their suitcases like a wheel of cheese, containers of preserved mushrooms and olives, and sticks of soppressata and other salumi. There was a cousin in our family who once got stopped at airport customs with a suitcase full of this kind of stuff, and when the officer was about to confiscate everything, he asked the officer if he could eat the soppressata instead of throwing it out. The officer shrugged his shoulders and allowed it. My cousin then proceeded to eat an entire soppressata in front of hundreds of people waiting to get through customs. When he finished the whole thing, he turned to the officer and said, "Can I pass now?" and the officer signaled him through.

One 290-gram ball Italian Artisan dough (page 58)

⅓ cup (80 ml) Rustic Hand-Crushed Sauce (page 79)

3 ounces (90 g) fior di latte mozzarella cheese, julienned ¼ inch (6 mm) thick (see page 48)

2 ounces (60 g) spicy soppressata, thinly sliced

¼ small red onion, thinly sliced (about ¼ cup [25 g])

¼ cup (35 g) oil-cured black olives, pitted

1 tablespoon grated Parmesan cheese, preferably Parmigiano-Reggiano

Remove the dough from the refrigerator and place it on the counter to proof until the dough temperature reads 55 to 60°F (13 to 16°C) using an instant-read thermometer, typically about 2 hours, or until dough has doubled in size.

One hour before baking the pizza, slide one rack into the lowest position of the oven and a second rack into the middle of the oven, leaving 6 to 8 inches (15 to 20 cm) between the racks. Place a pizza stone or steel on each rack and preheat the oven to 500°F (260°C) or the highest setting.

When ready to bake, using the method on page 42, lightly dust a pizza peel with flour and set to the side. Gently remove the dough ball from its container, dredge it in flour, place it on a well-floured work surface, and stretch it into a 12-inch (30 cm) round. Transfer the stretched dough to the peel.

Using a ladle, top the dough with the sauce, spreading it evenly over the surface and leaving a 1-inch (2.5 cm) border around the edges. Scatter the mozzarella evenly over the sauce. Lay the soppressata slices between the mozzarella strips and repeat with the onion slices and olives. Dust evenly with the Parmesan.

Slide the pizza off the peel onto the stone or steel on the lowest oven rack and bake the pizza for 5 to 6 minutes, or until the crust is golden brown.

Using the peel, remove the pizza from the oven and transfer to a cooling rack. After a few minutes, transfer to a clean cutting board to cut and serve.

TARTUFATO

Truffles are one of those ingredients that you either love or hate. I have been fortunate to have been exposed to some of the best truffles in the world and love them when used appropriately. Truffles come in two varieties, white and black. The white truffle is the rarer of the two and therefore the more expensive. Second, once truffles are harvested, they have a very short shelf life. They literally begin deteriorating as soon as they are retrieved from the ground by a specially trained pig or dog. (Pigs are rarely used anymore because dogs are gentler once they've located a truffle and begin to dig.) The relationship between truffle hunters and their dogs is magical.

If you can get your hands on a fresh truffle, shave it onto your pizza after it comes out of the oven. This recipe calls for truffle oil. Invest in the tiniest bottle of good truffle oil. The real stuff is expensive, but it's also like rattlesnake venom: a little goes a long way.

One 290-gram ball Italian Artisan dough (page 58)

2 ounces (60 g) fontina cheese, shredded

2 ounces (60 g) fior di latte mozzarella cheese, julienned ¼ inch (6 mm) thick (see page 48)

1 roasted garlic clove, sliced (see Garlic Oil, page 227)

½ cup (45 g) Sautéed Mushrooms (page 223)

Leaves from 2 fresh thyme sprigs

Extra-virgin olive oil for drizzling

¼ cup (30 g) Parmesan cheese, preferably Parmigiano-Reggiano, shaved with a vegetable peeler

Truffle oil of choice for drizzling

Remove the dough from the refrigerator and place it on the counter to proof until the dough temperature reads 55 to 60°F (13 to 16°F) using an instant-read thermometer, typically about 2 hours, or until dough has doubled in size.

One hour before baking the pizza, slide one rack into the lowest position of the oven and a second rack into the middle of the oven, leaving 6 to 8 inches (15 to 20 cm) between the racks. Place a pizza stone or steel on each rack and preheat the oven to 500°F (260°C) or the highest setting.

When ready to bake, using the method on page 42, lightly dust a pizza peel with flour and set to the side. Gently remove the dough ball from its container, dredge it in flour, place it on a well-floured work surface, and stretch it into a 12-inch (30 cm) round. Transfer the stretched dough to the peel.

Spread the fontina and then the mozzarella evenly over the surface of the dough, leaving a 1-inch (2.5 cm) border around the edges. Scatter the garlic, mushrooms, and thyme evenly over the cheeses. Drizzle with a little olive oil.

Slide the pizza off the peel onto the stone or steel on the lowest oven rack and bake the pizza for 5 to 6 minutes, or until the crust is golden brown.

Using the peel, remove the pizza from the oven and transfer to a cooling rack. After a few minutes, transfer to a clean cutting board, sprinkle with Parmesan, and finish with a drizzle of truffle oil. Cut and serve.

CASARECCIA

My mom has a way of being able to whip something up to eat whenever the doorbell rings and it's unannounced "company." My grandma was the same. How do you feed a dozen people without any planning and using only what you have in the house? This pizza is a perfect example. *Casareccia* means "homemade," or, in this case, "homestyle." The simplicity of this pizza has a powerful impact because it is the sum of all its parts. Each ingredient could easily shine on its own, but together they create something incredible.

One 290-gram ball Italian Artisan dough (page 58)

1 cup (200 g) canned Italian cherry tomatoes (*ciliegini*) in puree (about 7 ounces)

½ cup (30 g) yellow onion, thinly sliced (1 ounce)

¼ cup (30 g) oil-cured black olives, pitted (1 ounce)

1 teaspoon dried oregano

1 teaspoon coarse-ground black pepper

Extra-virgin olive oil for drizzling

1 tablespoon grated pecorino romano cheese, preferably Locatelli

Remove the dough from the refrigerator and place it on the counter to proof until the dough temperature reads 55 to 60°F (13 to 16°C) using an instant-read thermometer, typically about 2 hours, or until dough has doubled in size.

One hour before baking the pizza, slide one rack into the lowest position of the oven and a second rack into the middle of the oven, leaving 6 to 8 inches (15 to 20 cm) between the racks. Place a pizza stone or steel on each rack and preheat the oven to 500°F (260°C) or the highest setting

When ready to bake, using the method on page 42, lightly dust a pizza peel with flour and set to the side. Gently remove the dough ball from its container, dredge it in flour, place it on a well-floured work surface, and stretch it into a 12-inch (30 cm) round. Transfer the stretched dough to the peel.

Spread the cherry tomatoes and their puree evenly over the surface of the dough, leaving a 1-inch (2.5 cm) border around the edges. Scatter the onion and then the olives evenly over the tomatoes. Sprinkle evenly with the oregano and pepper and drizzle with a little oil.

Slide the pizza off the peel onto the stone or steel on the lowest oven rack and bake the pizza for 5 to 6 minutes, or until the crust is golden brown.

Using the peel, remove the pizza from the oven and transfer to a cooling rack. After a few minutes, transfer to a clean cutting board and sprinkle with the grated cheese. Cut and serve.

PANCETTA E PATATE

I've eaten this pizza throughout Italy. It's usually served for *merenda*, a midafternoon snack. The thinly sliced pancetta, which is salt cured, cooks in the heat of the oven, rendering its fat onto the dough to give it both a wonderful aroma and a flaky texture. It is paired with crispy roasted potatoes and fresh rosemary, often making me wish I could have this pizza for breakfast with a fried egg on top.

One 290-gram ball Italian Artisan dough (page 58)

4 ounces (115 g) fior di latte mozzarella cheese, julienned ¼ inch (6 mm) thick (see page 48)

1 garlic clove, chopped

⅓ cup (50 g) Roasted Potatoes (page 224)

1 ounce (30 g) pancetta, thinly sliced

Leaves from 1 fresh rosemary sprig

Extra-virgin olive oil for drizzling

Remove the dough from the refrigerator and place it on the counter to proof until the dough temperature reads 55 to 60°F (13 to 16°C) using an instant-read thermometer, typically about 2 hours, or until dough has doubled in size.

One hour before baking the pizza, slide one rack into the lowest position of the oven and a second rack into the middle of the oven, leaving 6 to 8 inches (15 to 20 cm) between the racks. Place a pizza stone or steel on each rack and preheat the oven to 500°F (260°C) or the highest setting.

When ready to bake, using the method on page 42, lightly dust a pizza peel with flour and set to the side. Gently remove the dough ball from its container, dredge it in flour, place it on a well-floured work surface, and stretch it into a 12-inch (30 cm) round. Transfer the stretched dough to the peel.

Scatter the mozzarella evenly over the dough, leaving a 1-inch (2.5 cm) border around the edges. Scatter the garlic and potatoes evenly over the mozzarella, then lay the pancetta slices evenly on top. Sprinkle the rosemary over the pancetta and drizzle with a little oil.

Slide the pizza off the peel onto the stone or steel on the lowest oven rack and bake the pizza for 5 to 6 minutes, or until the crust is golden brown.

Using the peel, remove the pizza from the oven and transfer to a cooling rack. After a few minutes, transfer to a clean cutting board to cut and serve.

PARMIGIANA

The best part of this pizza is the crispy fried eggplant and how it pairs perfectly with the salty bite of the Parmigiano-Reggiano. *Parmigiana di melanzane* inspired this pizza, which uses the same main ingredients in a light, tasty twist on that southern Italian classic.

One 290-gram ball Italian Artisan dough (page 58)

⅓ cup (80 ml) Classic Italian Sauce (page 76)

3 ounces (90 g) fior di latte mozzarella cheese, julienned ¼ inch (6 mm) thick (see page 48)

½ cup (40 g) Fried Eggplant, diced (page 224)

2 fresh basil leaves, torn, plus 2 leaves cut into chiffonade for finishing

7 cherry tomatoes, halved (see page 48)

¼ cup (30 g) grated Parmesan cheese, preferably Parmigiano-Reggiano, plus more for finishing

Extra-virgin olive oil for drizzling

Remove the dough from the refrigerator and place it on the counter to proof until the dough temperature reads 55 to 60°F (13 to 16°C) using an instant-read thermometer, typically about 2 hours, or until dough has doubled in size.

One hour before baking the pizza, slide one rack into the lowest position of the oven and a second rack into the middle of the oven, leaving 6 to 8 inches (15 to 20 cm) between the racks. Place a pizza stone or steel on each rack and preheat the oven to 500°F (260°C) or the highest setting.

When ready to bake, using the method on page 42, lightly dust a pizza peel with flour and set to the side. Using the method on page 42, gently remove the dough ball from its container, dredge it in flour, place it on a well-floured work surface, and stretch it into a 12-inch (30 cm) round. Transfer the stretched dough to the peel.

Using a ladle, top the dough with the sauce, spreading it evenly over the surface and leaving a 1-inch (2.5 cm) border around the edges. Scatter the mozzarella and then the eggplant, torn basil, tomatoes, and Parmesan evenly over the sauce. Drizzle with a little olive oil.

Slide the pizza off the peel onto the stone or steel on the lowest oven rack and bake the pizza for 5 to 6 minutes, or until the crust is golden brown.

Using the peel, remove the pizza from the oven and transfer to a cooling rack. After a few minutes, transfer to a clean cutting board, drizzle with a little more oil and add a sprinkle of basil chiffonade and Parmesan. Cut and serve.

Spizzirri

ROMAN PAN PIZZAS

The successful execution of a Roman-style pizza takes practice. The better you are at handling this dough, the lighter and airier the pizza will be. The direct-method dough (Traditional Roman Pan on page 59) works great, but if you opt for using the preferment (Contemporary Roman Pan with Biga on page 61), it will take your Roman pizza to another level. The goal is to capture the gases given off during fermentation and lock them into the dough as you're stretching it. If you push all the gases out of the dough, your crust may end up flat. Will it still eat like a pizza? Yes! Will it eat like a true Roman pizza? Probably not.

Don't give up if your first pizzas are flat. Just keep trying, because once you master dimpling the dough and laying it into the pan, you'll have unlocked the secrets to making incredible Roman *pizza in teglia*, *pizza alla pala*, and even ciabatta.

Each recipe in this chapter can be made using a par-baked dough (see page 47 for instructions). Your baking time will be shorter compared to starting with raw dough, which can really come in handy if you are making multiple pizzas. If using par-baked dough that has been refrigerated or frozen, be sure to bring it to room temperature before you begin topping it.

PATATE

I will never forget the first time I had potatoes on pizza. I thought it was such an unusual topping. I had no idea how much potatoes are utilized as a traditional pizza ingredient throughout Italy. I fell in love with this pizza when I dove into Roman pizzas and spent a ton of time tramping around Rome, eating everything in sight. On one trip, I ended up at the famous Bonci Pizzarium and had this pizza for the first time. The potatoes with their crispy edges, the sweetness of the white onion, and the bold punch of the black pepper make this pizza extraordinary.

One 627-gram ball Roman pan dough, traditional (page 59) or contemporary with biga (page 61), raw or par-baked crust

6 ounces (170 g) fior di latte mozzarella cheese, julienned ¼ inch (6 mm) thick (see page 48)

1 cup (100 g) white onion, thinly sliced

1 whole medium russet potato, peeled, sliced thin on a mandolin lengthwise, then soaked in water for 2 hours to overnight

1 tablespoon freshly cracked black pepper

1 teaspoon flake sea salt, preferably Maldon

¼ cup (60 ml) extra-virgin olive oil

Leaves from 1 fresh rosemary sprig

If using raw dough, remove it from the refrigerator and place it on the counter to proof until the dough temperature reads 55 to 60°F (13 to 16°C) using an instant-read thermometer, typically about 2 hours, or until dough has doubled in size. If using a par-baked crust, prepare as directed on page 47.

One hour before baking the pizza, slide one rack into the lowest position of the oven and a second rack into the middle of the oven, leaving 6 to 8 inches (15 to 20 cm) between the racks. Place a pizza stone or steel on each rack and preheat the oven to 500°F (260°C) or the highest setting.

When ready to bake, if using raw dough, use the panning method on page 45. Liberally sprinkle your work surface with flour, dust the dough ball with more flour, and gently lift it from its container and place it on the well-floured surface. Dimple and stretch the dough as directed and then lay it in a 12-by-16-inch (30 to 40 cm) pan. If using a par-baked crust, lay it in a 12-by-16-inch (30 to 40 cm) pan.

Distribute the mozzarella uniformly across the dough, leaving a 1-inch (2.5 cm) border around the edges. Spread the onion slices evenly on top of the mozzarella. Pat the potato slices dry, then lay them in a single layer on top of the mozzarella and onion. Sprinkle with the pepper and salt and drizzle with the oil.

Transfer the pan to the stone or steel on the lowest oven rack and bake the pizza for 13 to 15 minutes if using raw dough or 8 to 10 minutes if using a par-baked crust, or until the crust is golden brown.

Remove the pan from the oven. Using an offset spatula, lift the pizza out of the pan and transfer it to a cooling rack. After a few minutes, transfer to a clean cutting board. Using scissors, cut into squares. Sprinkle with rosemary and serve.

MARGHERITA

Traditionally, *pizza bianca* and *pizza rossa* are treated as types of focaccia that are eaten as bread or can be finished with additional toppings. *Pizza bianca* (white pizza) is typically topped with just olive oil and salt, while *pizza rossa* (red pizza) is spread with tomato sauce. Here, *pizza rossa* is given a Margherita topping of mozzarella and basil.

One 627-gram ball Roman pan dough, traditional (page 59) or contemporary with biga (page 61), raw or par-baked crust

¾ cup (180 ml) Classic Italian Sauce (page 76)

5 fresh basil leaves, torn

8 ounces (225 g) fior di latte mozzarella cheese, julienned ¼ inch (6 mm) thick (see page 48)

1 tablespoon grated Parmesan cheese, preferably Parmigiano-Reggiano

¼ cup (60 ml) extra-virgin olive oil

If using raw dough, remove it from the refrigerator and place it on the counter to proof until the dough temperature reads 55 to 60°F (13 to 16°C) using an instant-read thermometer, typically about 2 hours, or until dough has doubled in size. If using a par-baked crust, prepare as directed on page 47.

One hour before baking the pizza, slide one rack into the lowest position of the oven and a second rack into the middle of the oven, leaving 6 to 8 inches (15 to 20 cm) between the racks. Place a pizza stone or steel on each rack and preheat the oven to 500°F (260°C) or the highest setting.

When ready to bake, if using raw dough, use the panning method on page 45. Liberally sprinkle your work surface with flour, dust the dough ball with more flour, and gently lift it from its container and place it on the well-floured surface. Dimple and stretch the dough as directed and then lay it in a 12-by-16-inch (30 by 40 cm) pan. If using a par-baked crust, lay it in a 12-by-16-inch (30 by 40 cm) pan.

Using a ladle, add the sauce to the pizza base and spread it over the surface, leaving a 1-inch (2.5 cm) border around the edges. Using your fingers as described on page 47, continue to spread the sauce until it fills any little hollows and the base is evenly covered. Scatter the basil evenly over the sauce. Distribute the mozzarella uniformly across the dough, then dust with the Parmesan and drizzle evenly with the oil.

Transfer the pan to the stone or steel on the lowest oven rack and bake the pizza for 13 to 15 minutes if using raw dough or 8 to 10 minutes if using a par-baked crust, or until the crust is golden brown.

Remove the pan from the oven. Using an offset spatula, lift it out of the pan and transfer it to a cooling rack. After a few minutes, transfer to a clean cutting board. Using scissors, cut into squares and serve.

POLLO

On a trip to Calabria to celebrate Ferragosto, the August 15 national holiday that marks the height of summer and sends the entire country to the beach, my layover in Rome turned into a long day trip—and a great meal. One of the best things I can suggest you try the next time you're in Rome is a dish served almost at room temperature called _pollo alla romana_ (chicken Roman-style). Grab some good bread and a cold bottle of Frascati to accompany it, and you will soon understand where this pizza got its start.

One 627-gram ball Roman pan dough, traditional (page 59) or contemporary with biga (page 61), raw or par-baked crust

¾ cup (180 ml) Rustic Hand-Crushed Sauce (page 79)

6 ounces (170 g) fior di latte mozzarella cheese, julienned ¼ inch (6 mm) thick (see page 48)

½ cup (85 g) shredded roasted chicken (store-bought rotisserie or home-cooked will do)

¼ cup (45 g) drained Marinated Artichoke Hearts (page 227)

¼ cup (35 g) thinly sliced red bell pepper

¼ cup (35 g) thinly sliced yellow bell pepper

¼ cup (25 g) thinly sliced yellow onion

1 teaspoon dried oregano

1 tablespoon chopped fresh flat-leaf parsley

¼ cup (60 ml) extra-virgin olive oil

1 teaspoon flake sea salt, preferably Maldon

If using raw dough, remove it from the refrigerator and place it on the counter to proof until the dough temperature reads 55 to 60°F (13 to 16°C) using an instant-read thermometer, typically about 2 hours, or until dough has doubled in size. If using a par-baked crust, prepare as directed on page 47.

One hour before baking the pizza, slide one rack into the lowest position of the oven and a second rack into the middle of the oven, leaving 6 to 8 inches (15 to 20 cm) between the racks. Place a pizza stone or steel on each rack and preheat the oven to 500°F (260°C) or the highest setting.

When ready to bake, if using raw dough, use the panning method on page 45. Liberally sprinkle your work surface with flour, dust the dough ball with more flour, and gently lift it from its container and place it on the well-floured surface. Dimple and stretch the dough as directed and then lay it in a 12- by 16-inch (30 by 40 cm) pan. If using a par-baked crust, lay it in a 12-by-16-inch (30 to 40 cm) pan.

Using a ladle, add the sauce to the pizza base and spread it over the surface, leaving a 1-inch (2.5 cm) border around the edges. Using your fingers as described on page 47, continue to spread the sauce until it fills any little hollows and the base is evenly covered. Distribute the mozzarella uniformly across the dough. Scatter the chicken and then the artichokes evenly over the mozzarella. In a small bowl, toss together the bell peppers and onion, then scatter evenly on top followed by the oregano.

Transfer the pan to the stone or steel on the lowest oven rack and bake the pizza for 13 to 15 minutes if using raw dough or 8 to 10 minutes if using a par-baked crust, or until the crust is golden brown.

Remove the pan from oven. Using an offset spatula, lift the pizza out of the pan and transfer it to a cooling rack. After a few minutes, transfer to a clean cutting board. Using scissors, cut into squares. Then, sprinkle with parsley, drizzle evenly with oil, and finish with the sea salt. Serve.

AUTUNNO

When Italians think of the flavors of fall, their thoughts are very different from people in the United States who tend to anxiously await the start of pumpkin spice season. This pizza gathers pears at the end of their season, around October, and partners them with the radicchio that is just beginning its harvest. Add some funky Gorgonzola, toasted walnuts, and a bit of honey, and you'll have fall on a plate.

One 627-gram ball Roman pan dough, traditional (page 59) or contemporary with biga (page 61), raw or par-baked crust

1½ cups (70 g) radicchio, cored and leaves cut into 1-inch-wide (2.5 cm) strips

6 ounces (170 g) fior di latte mozzarella cheese, julienned ¼ inch (6 mm) thick (see page 48)

½ cup (60 g) crumbled Gorgonzola cheese (2 ounces)

One Bosc pear, halved, cored, and sliced lengthwise ¼ inch (6 mm) thick with a mandoline or sharp knife

1 tablespoon freshly cracked black pepper

2 tablespoons extra-virgin olive oil

Wildflower honey, for drizzling

¼ cup (30 g) toasted walnuts, chopped

1 teaspoon flake sea salt, preferably Maldon

If using raw dough, remove it from the refrigerator and place it on the counter to proof until the dough temperature reads 55 to 60°F (13 to 16°F) using an instant-read thermometer, typically about 2 hours, or until dough has doubled in size. If using a par-baked crust, prepare as directed on page 47.

One hour before baking the pizza, slide one rack into the lowest position of the oven and a second rack into the middle of the oven, leaving 6 to 8 inches (15 to 20 cm) between the racks. Place a pizza stone or steel on each rack and preheat the oven to 500°F (260°C) or the highest setting.

When ready to bake, if using raw dough, use the panning method on page 45. Liberally sprinkle your work surface with flour, dust the dough ball with more flour, and gently lift it from its container and place it on the well-floured surface. Dimple and stretch the dough as directed and then lay it in a 12-by-16-inch (30 by 40 cm) pan. If using a par-baked crust, lay it in a 12-by-16-inch (30 by 40 cm) pan.

Distribute the radicchio uniformly across the dough, leaving a 1-inch (2.5 cm) border around the edges. Scatter the mozzarella evenly over the radicchio, followed by the Gorgonzola. Arrange the pear slices over the cheeses in a single layer and dust with the pepper.

Transfer the pan to the stone or steel on the lowest oven rack and bake the pizza for 13 to 15 minutes if using raw dough or 8 to 10 minutes if using a par-baked crust, or until the crust is golden brown.

Remove the pizza from the oven. Using an offset spatula, lift the pizza out of the pan and transfer it to a cooling rack. After a few minutes, transfer to a clean cutting board. Using scissors, cut into squares. Drizzle evenly with the oil and wildflower honey. Top with the walnuts, sprinkle with the salt, and serve.

AMATRICIANA

The region of Lazio has four historic pastas that have been revered over time: *cacio e pepe*, carbonara, *gricia*, and *amatriciana*. *Pasta all'amatriciana* originated in the town of Amatrice and was allegedly created in the early 1600s following the arrival of tomatoes in Italy about fifty years earlier. While there are variations of this dish that include onions and other ingredients, the traditional version calls for guanciale (cured pork cheek), olive oil, white wine, tomato sauce, black pepper, and a touch of chile. Here, I've taken what's traditional in the pasta sauce and put it on a pizza, then added some mozzarella. Don't forget to save the guanciale pan juices for drizzling on the pizza before baking.

One 627-gram ball Roman pan dough, traditional (page 59) or contemporary with biga (page 61), raw or par-baked crust

¾ cup (180 ml) Rustic Hand-Crushed Sauce (page 79)

6 ounces (170 g) fior di latte mozzarella cheese, julienned ¼ inch (6 mm) thick (see page 48)

4 ounces (115 g) guanciale, cut into ½-inch (1 cm) cubes, rendered, and drained with pan juices reserved (directions on following page)

1 teaspoon red pepper flakes

¼ cup (60 ml) extra-virgin olive oil

¼ cup (30 g) grated pecorino romano cheese, preferably Locatelli

If using raw dough, remove it from the refrigerator and place it on the counter to proof until the dough temperature reads 55 to 60°F (13 to 16°C) using an instant-read thermometer, typically about 2 hours, or until dough has doubled in size. If using a par-baked crust, prepare as directed on page 47.

One hour before baking the pizza, slide one rack into the lowest position of the oven and a second rack into the middle of the oven, leaving 6 to 8 inches (15 to 20 cm) between the racks. Place a pizza stone or steel on each rack and preheat the oven to 500°F (260°C) or the highest setting.

When ready to bake, if using raw dough, use the panning method on page 45. Liberally sprinkle your work surface with flour, dust the dough ball with more flour, and gently lift it from its container and place it on the well-floured surface. Dimple and stretch the dough as directed and then lay it in a 12-by-16-inch (30 by 40 cm) pan. If using a par-baked crust, lay it in a 12-by-16-inch (30 by 40 cm) pan.

Using a ladle, add the sauce to the pizza base and spread it over the surface, leaving a 1-inch (2.5 cm) border around the edges. Using your fingers as described on page 47, continue to spread the sauce until it fills any little hollows and the base is evenly covered. Distribute the mozzarella, then the cooked guanciale and red pepper flakes.

Transfer the pan to the stone or steel on the lowest oven rack and bake the pizza for 13 to 15 minutes if using raw dough or 8 to 10 minutes if using a par-baked crust, or until the crust is golden brown.

Remove the pan from the oven. Using an offset spatula, lift the pizza out of the pan and transfer it to a cooling rack. After a few minutes, transfer to a clean cutting board. Using scissors, cut into squares. Then, drizzle with the olive oil, dust with the pecorino romano, and serve.

CONTINUED

FOR THE RENDERED GUANCIALE

6 ounces (170 g) guanciale, cut into ½-inch (1½ cm) cubes

1 tablespoon extra-virgin olive oil

1 teaspoon ground black pepper

¼ cup (60 ml) dry white wine

In a medium sauté pan over medium-high heat, combine the guanciale, oil, and pepper and heat together, stirring continuously with a wooden spoon.

When the guanciale starts to bubble and foam, turn down the heat to medium and continue stirring, watching the guanciale closely to make sure it is not cooking too fast or it will burn.

Once the guanciale starts to brown, add the wine and deglaze the pan, stirring to scrape up any browned bits from the pan bottom. Keep stirring for 5 minutes, or until the liquid is reduced by half.

Remove the pan from the heat. Place a fine-mesh sieve over a small heatproof bowl and pour the contents of the pan into the sieve. Transfer the guanciale to paper towels to drain. Set aside the pan juices in the bowl and the guanciale at room temperature until ready to use.

PROSCIUTTO E FICHI

If you've never had prosciutto and figs together, stop what you're doing and go grab some now. I love to make this pizza during the summer months when fresh figs are in season and serve it either hot as a first course or at room temperature in small squares on a grazing table or charcuterie board. If you can't find fresh figs because they are not in season or just aren't available where you live, go ahead and use dried figs. Make sure to sort through them and find the ones that are soft to the touch and pliable.

One 627-gram ball Roman pan dough, traditional (page 59) or contemporary with biga (page 61), raw or par-baked crust

6 ounces (170 g) fior di latte mozzarella cheese, julienned ¼ inch (6 mm) thick (see page 48)

2 ounces (60 g) fresh goat cheese, crumbled

Extra-virgin olive oil for drizzling

2 cups (40 g) loosely packed arugula

8 thin slices prosciutto crudo, preferably prosciutto di Parma

8 fresh figs, sliced partially in half and spread open

Balsamic Reduction (page 227) for drizzling

If using raw dough, remove it from the refrigerator and place it on the counter to proof until the dough temperature reads 55 to 60°F (13 to 16°C) using an instant-read thermometer, typically about 2 hours, or until dough has doubled in size. If using a par-baked crust, prepare as directed on page 47.

One hour before baking the pizza, slide one rack into the lowest position of the oven and a second rack into the middle of the oven, leaving 6 to 8 inches (15 to 20 cm) between the racks. Place a pizza stone or steel on each rack and preheat the oven to 500°F (260°C) or the highest setting.

When ready to bake, if using raw dough, use the panning method on page 45. Liberally sprinkle your work surface with flour, dust the dough ball with more flour, and gently lift it from its container and place it on the well-floured surface. Dimple and stretch the dough as directed and then lay it in a 12-by-16-inch (30 to 40 cm) pan. If using a par-baked crust, lay it in a 12-by-16-inch (30 to 40 cm) pan.

Distribute the mozzarella uniformly across the dough, leaving a 1-inch (2.5 cm) border around the edges. Top evenly with the goat cheese, then drizzle with the oil.

Transfer the pan to the stone or steel on the lowest oven rack and bake the pizza for 13 to 15 minutes if using raw dough or 8 to 10 minutes if using a par-baked crust, or until the crust is golden brown.

Remove the pizza from the oven. Using an offset spatula, lift the pizza out of the pan and transfer it to a cooling rack. After a few minutes, transfer to a clean cutting board. Using scissors, cut into squares. Scatter the arugula evenly over the top. Arrange the prosciutto slices on the pizza, spacing them evenly apart. Then set a fig on each pizza slice, pulling each fig open slightly as you position it. Finish with a drizzle of oil followed by a drizzle of balsamic reduction. Serve.

FIORI DI ZUCCA

During the summer months, squash blossoms can be found in every open market in Italy. I like them stuffed, then battered and fried. I also like them on top of a pizza. The combination of Taleggio, a soft, creamy washed-rind cheese, and salty, savory pancetta pairs beautifully with the sweet, fragrant flavor of squash blossoms. The window for finding the blossoms is small, so if you miss the harvest, crimp the corner of this page and set a reminder on your calendar to make this recipe next summer!

One 627-gram ball Roman pan dough, traditional (page 59) or contemporary with biga (page 61), raw or par-baked crust

3 ounces (90 g) Taleggio cheese, thinly sliced

6 ounces (170 g) fior di latte mozzarella cheese, julienned ¼ inch (6mm) thick (see page 48)

12 squash blossoms

4 ounces (115 g) pancetta, thinly sliced (about 8 slices)

2 tablespoons pine nuts, toasted

1 teaspoon red pepper flakes

1 tablespoon chopped fresh chives

¼ cup (60 ml) extra virgin olive oil

If using raw dough, remove it from the refrigerator and place it on the counter to proof until the dough temperature reads 55 to 60°F (13 to 16°C) using an instant-read thermometer, typically about 2 hours, or until dough has doubled in size. If using a par-baked crust, prepare as directed on page 47.

One hour before baking the pizza, slide one rack into the lowest position of the oven and a second rack into the middle of the oven, leaving 6 to 8 inches (15 to 20 cm) between the racks. Place a pizza stone or steel on each rack and preheat the oven to 500°F (260°C) or the highest setting.

When ready to bake, if using raw dough, use the panning method on page 45. Liberally sprinkle your work surface with flour, dust the dough ball with more flour, and gently lift it from its container and place it on the well-floured surface. Dimple and stretch the dough as directed and then lay it in a 12-by-16-inch (30 by 40 cm) pan. If using a par-baked crust, lay it in a 12-by-16-inch (30 by 40 cm) pan.

Lay the Taleggio slices evenly over the dough, leaving a 1-inch (2.5 cm) border around the edges. Distribute the mozzarella uniformly across the Taleggio. Arrange the squash blossoms in a uniform staggered pattern over the cheese and then layer the pancetta slices over.

Sprinkle the pine nuts and then the red pepper flakes evenly over the top.

Transfer the pan to the stone or steel on the lowest oven rack and bake the pizza for 13 to 15 minutes if using raw dough or 8 to 10 minutes if using a par-baked crust, or until the crust is golden brown.

Remove the pan from the oven. Using an offset spatula, lift the pizza out of the pan and transfer it to a cooling rack. After a few minutes, transfer to a clean cutting board. Using scissors, cut into squares. Sprinkle with the chives, drizzle with the oil, and serve.

TAVERN-STYLE PIZZAS

I'm a native of Chicago, so you might think that's why I love this pizza. However, as I travel around the country opening restaurants and demonstrating how to make traditional tavern-style pizza, I've learned that everyone loves this style and why. It's thin and crispy, with an almost cracker-like bite. It's a great base for whatever you want to put on top. The dough is super simple to make and doesn't require any fancy ingredients. Plus, it can be baked directly on any pizza stone or steel at temperatures under 500°F (260°C), which makes it one of the easiest pizzas for home bakers to master.

Just do me a favor. Don't cut this pizza into triangular slices. In Chicago, we cut our pizza into squares—because we don't cut corners!

BUTCHER BOY

Here's my take on the classic meat lover's pizza. This might be surprising: I didn't always aspire to be a pizzaiolo. For a long time, I wanted to be a professional butcher! If you ever get the chance to look at the ink on my body, you'll see that there is a constant nod to my love of sharp knives and butchery. I even had two nicknames, one that stuck and one that faded away: "Butcher Boy" and "Leo Pizza." Any guesses which is which?

One 290-gram ball Chicago Tavern dough (page 66)

¾ cup (180 ml) All-American Sauce (page 80)

6 ounces (170 g) whole-milk mozzarella cheese, shredded

3 ounces (90 g) Italian sausage, bulk or casing removed

2 slices applewood-smoked bacon, cut into 1-inch (2.5 cm) pieces

2 ounces (60 g) sliced pepperoni

1 ounce (30 g) Canadian Bacon, sliced ¼ inch (6 mm) thick, then quartered

Scant ¼ cup (35 g) drained, sliced pepperoncini in brine

1 teaspoon dried oregano

1 tablespoon grated Parmesan cheese, preferably Parmigiano-Reggiano

Remove the dough from the refrigerator and place it on the counter to proof until the dough temperature reads 55 to 60°F (13 to 16°C) using an instant-read thermometer, typically about 2 hours, or until dough has doubled in size.

One hour before baking the pizza, slide one rack into the lowest position of the oven and a second rack into the middle of the oven, leaving 6 to 8 inches (15 to 20 cm) between the racks. Place a pizza stone or steel on each rack and preheat the oven to 500°F (260°C) or the highest setting.

When ready to bake, lightly dust a pizza peel with coarse cornmeal and set to the side. Place the dough ball on a lightly floured work surface. Using your hand, flatten the dough ball into a thick disk. Then, using a rolling pin, roll it out from side to side in an even layer, avoiding any thick or thin spots. For a thicker crust, make a 12-inch (30 cm) round, or for a thinner crust, make a 14-inch (35 cm) round. Transfer the stretched dough to the peel.

Using a ladle, top the dough with the sauce, spreading it evenly over the surface and leaving a 1-inch (2.5 cm) border around the edges. Spread the mozzarella evenly on top of the sauce. Pinch the sausage into quarter-size chunks, press each one flat, and distribute them evenly over the cheese. Layer the applewood-smoked bacon, pepperoni, Canadian bacon, and finally the pepperoncini on top. Sprinkle evenly with the oregano followed by the Parmesan.

Slide the pizza off the peel onto the stone or steel (see page 42) on the lowest oven rack and bake for 12 to 15 minutes, or until the crust is golden brown, the cheese is spotted, and the applewood-smoked bacon and sausage are cooked through.

Using the peel, remove the pizza from the oven and transfer to a cooling rack. After a few minutes, transfer to a clean cutting board, and using a pizza cutter, cut into squares and serve.

CHICAGO
S.M.O.G

This pizza gets its name not because Chicago is covered in smog but because it's one of the most popular topping combinations: sausage, mushroom, onion, and green pepper. It is a timeless mix, and I can remember eating this pizza on pizza night at home back when I could barely see over the kitchen table.

One 290-gram ball Chicago Tavern dough (page 66)

¾ cup (180 ml) All-American Sauce (page 80)

6 ounces (170 g) whole-milk mozzarella cheese, shredded

¼ cup (25 g) Spanish onion, thinly sliced

¼ cup (35 g) green bell pepper, thinly sliced

¼ cup (25 g) Sautéed Mushrooms (page 223)

3 ounces (90 g) Italian sausage, bulk or casing removed

1 teaspoon dried oregano

1 teaspoon grated Parmesan cheese, preferably Parmigiano-Reggiano

Remove the dough from the refrigerator and place it on the counter to proof until the dough temperature reads 55 to 60°F (13 to 16°C) using an instant-read thermometer, typically about 2 hours, or until dough has doubled in size.

One hour before baking the pizza, slide one rack into the lowest position of the oven and a second rack into the middle of the oven, leaving 6 to 8 inches (15 to 20 cm) between the racks. Place a pizza stone or steel on each rack and preheat the oven to 500°F (260°C) or the highest setting.

When ready to bake, lightly dust a pizza peel with coarse cornmeal and set to the side. Place the dough ball on a lightly floured work surface. Using your hand, flatten the dough ball into a thick disk. Then, using a rolling pin, roll it out from side to side in an even layer, avoiding any thick or thin spots. For a thicker crust, make a 12-inch (30 cm) round, or for a thinner crust, make a 14-inch (35 cm) round. Transfer the stretched dough to the peel.

Using a ladle, top the dough with the sauce, spreading it evenly over the surface and leaving a 1-inch (2.5 cm) border around the edges. Spread the mozzarella evenly on top of the sauce, then layer the onion, green pepper, and mushrooms over the cheese. Pinch the sausage into quarter-size chunks, press each one flat, and distribute them evenly across the pizza. Sprinkle evenly with the oregano followed by the Parmesan.

Slide the pizza off the peel onto the stone or steel (see page 42) on the lowest oven rack and bake for 8 to 10 minutes, or until the crust is golden brown, the cheese is spotted, and the sausage is cooked through.

Using the peel, remove the pizza from the oven and transfer to a cooling rack. After a few minutes, transfer to a clean cutting board. Using a pizza cutter, cut into squares and serve.

LEO SPECIAL

My students and social media followers are always asking me what my favorite pizza combination is. It's actually very simple, and I can use these toppings on every style of pizza no matter where I am in the world. So here it is, step by step, exactly the way I order it when I'm out and in the mood for a pizza. My favorite part of this combo is that because there is double the amount of both tomato sauce and sausage and no mozzarella, the tomatoes become more concentrated and sweeter as the pizza bakes. If your oven is hot enough, you may get some charring around the edges, which I love. I also love the way the pork fat from the sausage renders on top of the pizza and almost dissolves into the sauce. Add a little garlic and some dried oregano—crumbling it directly from the dried branches if possible—and you'll understand why I love this pizza so much.

One 290-gram ball Chicago Tavern dough (page 66)

1 cup (240 ml) All-American Sauce (page 80)

10 ounces (285 g) Italian sausage, bulk or casing removed

2 garlic cloves, finely chopped

1 tablespoon dried oregano

Extra-virgin olive oil for drizzling

Remove the dough from the refrigerator and place it on the counter to proof until the dough temperature reads 55 to 60°F (13 to 16°C) using an instant-read thermometer, typically about 2 hours, or until dough has doubled in size.

One hour before baking the pizza, slide one rack into the lowest position of the oven and a second rack into the middle of the oven, leaving 6 to 8 inches (20 to 25 cm) between the racks. Place a pizza stone or steel on each rack and preheat the oven to 500°F (260°C) or the highest setting.

When ready to bake, lightly dust a pizza peel with coarse cornmeal and set to the side. Place the dough ball on a lightly floured work surface. Using your hand, flatten the dough ball into a thick disk and then, using a rolling pin, roll it out from side to side in an even layer, avoiding any thick or thin spots. For a thicker crust, make a 12-inch (30 cm) round, or for a thinner crust, make a 14-inch (35 cm) round. Transfer the stretched dough to the peel.

Using a ladle, top the dough with the sauce, spreading it evenly over the surface and leaving a 1-inch (2.5 cm) border around the edges. Pinch the sausage into quarter-size chunks, press each one flat, and distribute them evenly over the sauce. Scatter the garlic evenly on top, then sprinkle with the oregano and finish with a good drizzle of oil.

Slide the pizza off the peel onto the stone or steel (see page 42, beginning with step 4) on the lowest oven rack and bake for 12 to 14 minutes, or until the crust is golden brown and the sausage is cooked through.

Using the peel, remove the pizza from the oven and transfer to a cooling rack. After a few minutes, transfer to a clean cutting board. Using a pizza cutter, cut into squares and serve.

CHICKEN CLUB

This pizza goes by various names around the country, and its topping of roasted chicken and creamy white sauce is a favorite of many. Although it can be great anytime, it has been a particularly popular addition to my Mother's Day brunch menus over the years. Throw a couple of poached eggs on top for a new spin on your favorite breakfast pizza.

One 290-gram ball Chicago Tavern dough (page 66)

½ cup (120 ml) Creamy White Sauce (page 81)

6 ounces (170 g) whole-milk mozzarella cheese, shredded

2 roasted garlic cloves, chopped (see Garlic Oil, page 227)

¼ cup (45 g) shredded roasted chicken (store-bought rotisserie or leftovers will do)

2 slices applewood-smoked bacon, cut into 1-inch (2.5 cm) pieces

¼ cup (60 g) Whipped Ricotta (page 229)

¼ cup (30 g) grated Parmesan cheese, preferably Parmigiano-Reggiano

1 tablespoon chopped fresh flat-leaf parsley

Remove the dough from the refrigerator and place it on the counter to proof until the dough temperature reads 55 to 60°F (13 to 16°C) using an instant-read thermometer, typically about 2 hours, or until dough has doubled in size.

One hour before baking the pizza, slide one rack into the lowest position of the oven and a second rack into the middle of the oven, leaving 6 to 8 inches (15 to 20 cm) between the racks. Place a pizza stone or steel on each rack and preheat the oven to 500°F (260°C) or the highest setting.

When ready to bake, lightly dust a pizza peel with coarse cornmeal and set to the side. Place the dough ball on a lightly floured work surface. Using your hand, flatten the dough ball into a thick disk and then, using a rolling pin, roll it out from side to side in an even layer, avoiding any thick or thin spots. For a thicker crust, make a 12-inch (30 cm) round, or for a thinner crust, make a 14-inch (35 cm) round. Transfer the stretched dough to the peel.

Using a ladle, top the dough with the sauce, spreading it evenly over the surface and leaving a 1-inch (2.5 cm) border around the edges. Spread the mozzarella evenly on top of the sauce, then layer the garlic, chicken, and bacon over the cheese. Add dollops (about ½ tablespoon each) of the ricotta evenly over the top, then sprinkle with the Parmesan.

Slide the pizza off the peel onto the stone or steel (see page 42) on the lowest oven rack and bake for 12 to 14 minutes, for until the crust is golden brown and the bacon is cooked through.

Using the peel, remove the pizza from the oven, transfer to a cooling rack After a few minutes, transfer to a clean cutting board and sprinkle with the parsley. Using a pizza cutter, cut into squares and serve.

CHICAGO
BEEF

We have our own style of beef sandwich in Chicago. If you're from the East Coast, you may say our beef sandwich is unusual because it's served hot rather than cold like the typical deli beef sandwich. Ours begins with Italian-style slow-roasted beef, which is thinly sliced, simmered briefly in the beef juice (au jus) left over from cooking the meat, piled on French bread, and almost always topped with sweet roasted green peppers or hot giardiniera. Then, just before your first bite, you "baptize" the sandwich by dunking the whole thing in the hot beef juice. You can use store-bought giardiniera for this pizza, but if you have the time, make a batch of my giardiniera for better, fresher flavors.

One 290-gram ball Chicago Tavern dough (page 66)

¾ cup (180 ml) All-American Sauce (page 80)

6 ounces (170 g) whole-milk mozzarella cheese, shredded

6 ounces (170 g) Italian-style roast beef or deli roast beef, thinly sliced

⅓ cup (50 g) drained Homemade Giardiniera (page 220) or store-bought

1 teaspoon dried oregano

1 tablespoon grated Parmesan cheese, preferably Parmigiano-Reggiano

Remove the dough from the refrigerator and place it on the counter to proof until the dough temperature reads 55 to 60°F (13 to 16°C) using an instant-read thermometer, typically about 2 hours, or until dough has doubled in size.

One hour before baking the pizza, slide one rack into the lowest position of the oven and a second rack into the middle of the oven, leaving 6 to 8 inches (20 to 25 cm) between the racks. Place a pizza stone or steel on each rack and preheat the oven to 500°F (260°C) or the highest setting.

When ready to bake, lightly dust a pizza peel with coarse cornmeal and set to the side. Place the dough ball on a lightly floured work surface. Using your hand, flatten the dough ball into a thick disk and then, using a rolling pin, roll it out from side to side in an even layer, avoiding any thick or thin spots. For a thicker crust, make a 12-inch (30 cm) round, or for a thinner crust, make a 14-inch (35 cm) round. Transfer the stretched dough to the peel.

Using a ladle, top the dough with the sauce, spreading it evenly over the surface and leaving a 1-inch (2.5 cm) border around the edges. Spread the mozzarella evenly on top of the sauce. Place small mounds of the beef evenly around the pizza and then scatter the giardiniera over the top. Sprinkle evenly with the oregano followed by the Parmesan.

Slide the pizza off the peel onto the stone or steel (see page 42) on the lowest oven rack and bake for 10 to 12 minutes, or until the crust is golden brown and the cheese is spotted.

Using the peel, remove the pizza from the oven and transfer to a cooling rack. After a few minutes, transfer to a clean cutting board. Using a pizza cutter, cut into squares and serve.

THE UNCLE TONY

Growing up, there was no greater influence on this chubby Italian kid than my uncle Tony. He was that cool uncle that introduced me to rock 'n' roll. He pretty much gave me the tools to grow up in America that my Italian immigrant parents weren't giving me. He has always been my biggest fan and cheerleader throughout my journey as a pizza maker. This is his most requested pizza from me.

One 290-gram ball Chicago Tavern dough (page 66)

¾ cup (180 ml) All-American Sauce (page 80)

6 ounces (170 g) whole-milk mozzarella cheese, shredded

6 to 8 Homemade Meatballs (page 223), halved and tossed in All-American Sauce

¼ cup (60 g) Whipped Ricotta (page 229)

1 tablespoon dried oregano

1 tablespoon grated pecorino romano cheese, preferably Locatelli

3 fresh basil leaves, cut into chiffonade

Garlic Oil for drizzling (page 227)

Remove the dough from the refrigerator and place it on the counter to proof until the dough temperature reads 55 to 60°F (13 to 16°C) using an instant-read thermometer, typically about 2 hours, or until dough has doubled in size.

One hour before baking the pizza, slide one rack into the lowest position of the oven and a second rack into the middle of the oven, leaving 6 to 8 inches (15 to 20 cm) between the racks. Place a pizza stone or steel on each rack and preheat the oven to 500°F (260°C) or the highest setting.

When ready to bake, lightly dust a pizza peel with coarse cornmeal and set to the side. Place the dough ball on a lightly floured work surface. Using your hand, flatten the dough ball into a thick disk and then, using a rolling pin, roll it out from side to side in an even layer, avoiding any thick or thin spots. For a thicker crust, make a 12-inch (30 cm) round, or for a thinner crust, make a 14-inch (35 cm) round. Transfer the stretched dough to the peel.

Using a ladle, top the dough with the sauce, spreading it evenly over the surface and leaving a 1-inch (2.5 cm) border around the edges. Spread the mozzarella evenly on top of the sauce, then layer the meatballs over the cheese. Add dollops of the ricotta evenly over the top. Sprinkle with the oregano followed by the pecorino romano.

Slide the pizza off the peel onto the stone or steel (see page 42) on the lowest oven rack and bake for 12 to 14 minutes, or until the crust is golden brown and the sauce on the meatballs has slightly concentrated (thickened).

Using the peel, remove the pizza from the oven and transfer to a cooling rack. After a few minutes, transfer to a clean cutting board. Then, sprinkle with the basil and drizzle with a little oil. Using a pizza cutter, cut into squares and serve.

THE GOODFELLA

Sausage, peppers, and onions can be found in grocery stores in any Italian neighborhood in the country. This pizza takes me back to trips to Taylor Street in Chicago's Little Italy as a kid. That's a place that's no stranger to sausage and peppers or to Cadillacs being better than Lincolns . . . fugetaboutit!

One 290-gram ball Chicago Tavern dough (page 66)

¾ cup (180 ml) All-American Sauce (page 80)

6 ounces (170 g) whole-milk mozzarella cheese, shredded

3 ounces (90 g) Italian sausage, bulk or casing removed

¼ cup (45 g) Marinated Roasted Red Peppers (page 219), cut into strips

¼ small red onion, thinly sliced (about ¼ cup [25 g])

1 tablespoon dried oregano

1 tablespoon grated pecorino romano cheese, preferably Locatelli

Remove the dough from the refrigerator and place it on the counter to proof until the dough temperature reads 55 to 60°F (13 to 16°C) using an instant-read thermometer, typically about 2 hours, or until dough has doubled in size.

One hour before baking the pizza, slide one rack into the lowest position of the oven and a second rack into the middle of the oven, leaving 6 to 8 inches (15 to 20 cm) between the racks. Place a pizza stone or steel on each rack and preheat the oven to 500°F (260°C) or the highest setting.

When ready to bake, lightly dust a pizza peel with coarse cornmeal and set to the side. Place the dough ball on a lightly floured work surface. Using your hand, flatten the dough ball into a thick disk and then, using a rolling pin, roll it out from side to side in an even layer, avoiding any thick or thin spots. For a thicker crust, make a 12-inch (30 cm) round, or for a thinner crust, make a 14-inch (35 cm) round. Transfer the stretched dough to the peel.

Using a ladle, top the dough with the sauce, spreading it evenly over the surface and leaving a 1-inch (2.5 cm) border around the edges. Spread the mozzarella evenly on top of the sauce. Pinch the sausage into quarter-size chunks, press each one flat, and distribute them evenly over the mozzarella. Layer the roasted peppers and onion on top, then sprinkle evenly with the oregano followed by the Parmesan.

Slide the pizza off the peel onto the stone or steel (see page 42) on the lowest oven rack and bake for 12 to 14 minutes, or until the crust is golden brown, the cheese is spotted, and the sausage is cooked through.

Using the peel, remove the pizza from the oven and transfer to a cooling rack. After a few minutes, transfer to a clean cutting board. Using a pizza cutter, cut into squares and serve.

NEW YORK–STYLE CLASSIC PIZZAS

When the first pizzas left Italy and arrived in New York, they became a product of their new environment. Everything from ingredients to ovens was different, and to make pizzas in America, the pizza once again needed to evolve. With a few small changes to the dough and process, you can make a very different pizza. Italian Artisan Pizza (page 101) was transformed into New York pizza. I love that you can make the pizzas in this chapter successfully in a home oven. Just remember to set your oven as high as it will go and use the double-pizza-stone method that I describe in this chapter's recipes for optimal results.

Practice your technique for stretching dough with this pizza style. It is a great one for getting your reps in. Keep on eye on how thin you stretch the middle of the crust. You don't want a giant *cornicione* and a paper-thin middle.

THE UPSIDE-DOWN

"Upside-down" refers to the build of toppings on this pizza. The mozzarella, rather than the sauce, is added to the dough base first, which is how this pizza gets its name. I first saw it a long time ago in New York and then found it in other cities on the East Coast. The mozzarella on an upside-down pizza is typically sliced, but I've seen shredded mozzarella as well, especially when baking in a coal-fired oven. I love the way the sauce cooks on top. It develops a more concentrated, sweeter flavor and melts deliciously into the cheese.

One 270-gram ball Classic New York dough (page 68)

4 ounces (115 g) whole-milk mozzarella cheese, sliced ¼ inch thick (6 mm), then slices halved

¾ cup (180 ml) All-American Sauce (page 80)

Extra-virgin olive oil for drizzling

3 fresh basil leaves, cut into chiffonade

1 tablespoon grated Parmesan cheese, preferably Parmigiano-Reggiano

Remove the dough from the refrigerator and place it on the counter to proof until the dough temperature reads 55 to 60°F (13 to 16°C) using an instant-read thermometer, typically about 2 hours, or until dough has doubled in size.

One hour before baking the pizza, slide one rack into the lowest position of the oven and a second rack into the middle of the oven, leaving 6 to 8 inches (15 to 20 cm) between the racks. Place a pizza stone or steel on each rack and preheat the oven to 500°F (260°C) or the highest setting.

When ready to bake, lightly dust a pizza peel with fine cornmeal and set to the side. Using the method on page 42, gently remove the dough ball from its container, dredge it in a mixture of 00 flour and fine semolina flour, place it on a well-floured work surface, and stretch it into a 12-inch (30 cm) round. Transfer the stretched dough to the peel.

Spread the mozzarella evenly on top of the dough, leaving a 1-inch (2.5 cm) border around the edges. Using a ladle, spread the sauce evenly on top of the cheese. Alternatively, add the sauce in dollops, spacing them evenly around the pizza. Drizzle with a little oil.

Slide the pizza off the peel onto the stone or steel (see page 42) on the lowest oven rack and bake for 13 to 15 minutes, or until the crust is golden brown and the cheese is lightly spotted.

Using the peel, remove the pizza from the oven and transfer to a cooling rack. After a few minutes, transfer to a clean cutting board. Sprinkle with the basil and Parmesan. Cut and serve.

HELL'S KITCHEN

My love for cherry peppers began when I first discovered them on a pizza in New York City's once-gritty Hell's Kitchen neighborhood. I love the vinegary bite that these peppers add to this pizza, which contrasts beautifully with the richness of the mozzarella. I always keep jars of cherry peppers around, and I especially like the kick of the hot ones!

One 270-gram ball Classic New York dough (page 68)

⅓ cup (80 ml) All-American Sauce (page 80)

4 ounces (115 g) whole-milk mozzarella cheese, cut into ½-inch (1 cm) cubes

¼ cup (35 g) cherry peppers, drained and sliced

¼ cup (25 g) thinly sliced red onion

4 ounces (115 g) Italian sausage, uncooked or roasted and cut into ¼-inch-thick (6 mm thick) coins

2 tablespoons grated Parmesan cheese, preferably Parmigiano-Reggiano, divided

1 teaspoon dried oregano

Extra-virgin olive oil for drizzling

Remove the dough from the refrigerator and place it on the counter to proof until the dough temperature reads 55 to 60°F (13 to 16°C) using an instant-read thermometer, typically about 2 hours, or until dough has doubled in size.

One hour before baking the pizza, slide one rack into the lowest position of the oven and a second rack into the middle of the oven, leaving 6 to 8 inches (15 to 20 cm) between the racks. Place a pizza stone or steel on each rack and preheat the oven to 500°F (260°C) or the highest setting.

When ready to bake, lightly dust a pizza peel with fine semolina flour and set to the side. Using the method on page 42, gently remove the dough ball from its container, dredge it in a mixture of 00 flour and fine semolina flour, place it on to well-floured work surface, and stretch it into a 12-inch (30 cm) round. Transfer the stretched dough to the peel.

Using a ladle, top the dough with the sauce, spreading it evenly over the surface and leaving a 1-inch (2.5 cm) border around the edges. Spread the mozzarella in a single layer uniformly across the pizza. Scatter the cherry peppers and then the red onion on top. If using uncooked sausage, remove from the casing, pinch into quarter-size chunks, press each one flat, and distribute them evenly across the pizza. If using roasted sausage, scatter the slices evenly over the pizza. Sprinkle with 1 tablespoon of the Parmesan and the oregano and drizzle with a little oil.

Slide the pizza off the peel onto the stone or steel (see page 42) on the lowest oven rack and bake for 10 to 12 minutes, or until the crust is golden brown, the cheese is lightly spotted, and the raw sausage, if using, is cooked through.

Using the peel, remove the pizza from the oven and transfer to a cooling rack. After a few minutes, transfer to a clean cutting board. Sprinkle with the remaining 1 tablespoon Parmesan. Cut and serve.

THE WHITE PIE

No matter what slice counter you visit in New York, there's bound to be a white pie on display. This is New York pizza with a little surprise of fresh garlic. My version uses creamy white sauce as the base, which takes each bite over the top. If you love a good cheese pizza, this one is for you!

One 270-gram ball Classic New York dough (page 68)

½ cup (120 ml) Creamy White Sauce (page 81)

2 ounces (60 g) fior di latte mozzarella cheese, julienned ¼ inch thick (6 mm thick; page 48)

2 ounces (60 g) whole-milk mozzarella cheese, shredded

¼ cup (60 g) Whipped Ricotta (page 229)

1 garlic clove, chopped

1 tablespoon chopped fresh flat-leaf parsley

Garlic Oil (page 227) for drizzling

Remove the dough from the refrigerator and place it on the counter to proof until the dough temperature reads 55 to 60°F (13 to 16°C) using an instant-read thermometer, typically about 2 hours, or until dough has doubled in size.

One hour before baking the pizza, slide one rack into the lowest position of the oven and a second rack into the middle of the oven, leaving 6 to 8 inches (15 to 20 cm) between the racks. Place a pizza stone or steel on each rack and preheat the oven to 500°F (260°C) or the highest setting.

When ready to bake, lightly dust a pizza peel with fine semolina flour and set to the side. Using the method on page 42, gently remove the dough ball from its container, dredge it in a mixture of 00 flour and fine semolina flour, place it on a well-floured work surface, and stretch it into a 12-inch (30 cm) round. Transfer the stretched dough to the peel.

Using a ladle, top the dough with the sauce, spreading it evenly over the surface and leaving a 1-inch (2.5 cm) border around the edges. Spread both mozzarellas uniformly across the pizza and then add dollops (about ½ tablespoon each) of the ricotta evenly on top. Scatter the garlic evenly over the cheeses.

Slide the pizza off the peel onto the stone or steel (see page 42) on the lowest oven rack and bake for 10 to 12 minutes, or until the crust is golden brown and the cheese is lightly spotted.

Using the peel, remove the pizza from the oven and transfer to a cooling rack. After a few minutes, transfer to a clean cutting board. Sprinkle with the parsley and drizzle with a little oil. Cut and serve.

CLAMS CASINO

While Clams Casino originated in Rhode Island, the rest of the East Coast is no stranger to clams on top of a pizza. Use fresh littleneck clams for this pizza, and it will be great. If the thought of clam shells on top of your pizza freaks you out, spread the clams in a single layer on a sheet pan and slide the pan into a preheated 350°F (180°C) oven for 6 to 7 minutes, or until the clams start to open and you can pick them out of their shells. As the bacon cooks on top of the pizza, it renders its fat into the sauce, creating a great smoky flavor that marries with the clams.

One 270-gram ball Classic New York dough (page 68)

⅓ cup (80 ml) Creamy Lemon Sauce (page 229)

3 ounces (90 g) whole-milk mozzarella cheese, shredded

12 littleneck clams, scrubbed, then immersed in 3 cups (700 ml) water mixed with ½ cup (100 g) fine sea salt for 2 hours

2 slices applewood-smoked bacon, cut into 1-inch (2.5 cm) pieces

¼ cup (35 g) red bell pepper, cut into ¼-inch (6 mm) dice

1 garlic clove, chopped

½ cup (50 g) Toasted Breadcrumbs (page 219)

1 tablespoon chopped fresh flat-leaf parsley

Garlic oil (page 227) for drizzling

Remove the dough from the refrigerator and place it on the counter to proof until the dough temperature reads 55 to 60°F (13 to 16°C) using an instant-read thermometer, typically about 2 hours, or until dough has doubled in size.

One hour before baking the pizza, slide one rack into the lowest position of the oven and a second rack into the middle of the oven, leaving 6 to 8 inches (15 to 20 cm) between the racks. Place a pizza stone or steel on each rack and preheat the oven to 500°F (260°C) or the highest setting.

When ready to bake, lightly dust a pizza peel with fine semolina flour and set to the side. Using the method on page 42, gently remove the dough ball from its container, dredge it in a mixture of 00 flour and fine semolina flour, place it on a well-floured work surface, and stretch it into a 12-inch (30 cm) round. Transfer the stretched dough to the peel.

Using a ladle, top the dough with the sauce, spreading it evenly over the surface and leaving a 1-inch (2.5 cm) border around the edges. Spread the mozzarella uniformly across the pizza. Drain the clams and pat dry, discarding any that fail to close to the touch. Arrange the clams, hinge side down, atop the cheese, spacing them evenly. Scatter the bacon, red pepper, and garlic evenly on top.

Slide the pizza off the peel onto the stone or steel (see page 42) on the lowest oven rack and bake for 13 to 15 minutes, or until the crust is golden brown, all the clams have opened, and the cheese is lightly spotted. (Discard any clams that failed to open.)

Using the peel, remove the pizza from the oven and transfer to a cooling rack. After a few minutes, transfer to a clean cutting board. Sprinkle with the breadcrumbs and parsley, then drizzle with a little oil. Cut and serve.

CHICKEN AND BROWN SAUCE

Who doesn't love a chicken cutlet? I mean, growing up, I was that kid with the greasy brown-paper bag in the lunchroom. To say that a pizza topped with chicken cutlets will be good is one thing, but then to throw a base of killer Marsala-laced sauce on it blows the roof off the whole thing. When you make the sauce, grab a bottle of good Marsala from a wine store, not the sodium-laced stuff in the grocery-store aisle. You'll thank me later!

One 270-gram ball Classic New York dough (page 68)

½ cup (120 ml) Brown Sauce (page 228)

3 ounces (90 g) whole-milk mozzarella cheese, cut into ½-inch (1 cm) cubes

1 Chicken Cutlet (page 220), cut into cubes

¼ cup (70 g) Sautéed Mushrooms (page 223)

1 tablespoon chopped fresh flat-leaf parsley

1 tablespoon grated Parmesan cheese, preferably Parmigiano-Reggiano

Remove the dough from the refrigerator and place it on the counter to proof until the dough temperature reads 55 to 60°F (13 to 16°C) using an instant-read thermometer, typically about 2 hours, or until dough has doubled in size.

One hour before baking the pizza, slide one rack into the lowest position of the oven and a second rack into the middle of the oven, leaving 6 to 8 inches (15 to 20 cm) between the racks. Place a pizza stone or steel on each rack and preheat the oven to 500°F (260°C) or the highest setting.

When ready to bake, lightly dust a pizza peel with fine semolina flour and set to the side. Using the method on page 42, gently remove the dough ball from its container, dredge it in a mixture of 00 flour and fine semolina flour, place it on a well-floured work surface, and stretch it into a 12-inch (30 cm) round. Transfer the stretched dough to the peel.

Using a ladle, top the dough with the sauce, spreading it evenly over the surface and leaving a 1-inch border around the edges. Spread the mozzarella in a single layer uniformly across the pizza. Scatter the chicken evenly over the cheese followed by the mushrooms.

Slide the pizza off the peel onto the stone or steel (see page 42) on the lowest oven rack and bake for 12 to 14 minutes, or until the crust is golden brown and cheese is lightly spotted.

Using the peel, remove the pizza from the oven and transfer to a cooling rack. After a few minutes, transfer to a clean cutting board. Sprinkle with the parsley and Parmesan. Cut and serve.

ARTICHOKE PIE

The details are blurry, but let's just say I stumbled onto Artichoke Basille's in New York City around one a.m. I can vividly remember the smell of pizza throughout the entire neighborhood as I waited in the long line. Once I finally got inside the door, I could see the counter display of all the pizzas. There was one pizza, however, that never made it to the counter. The staff was pretty much serving it right out of the oven. It was the pizzeria's signature artichoke pie, and this is my tribute to that New York classic. Many people have said that I liked the pizza so much because I had been out running amok all night. But I've been back many times since (and at lunchtime!), and it really is great. The base sauce is similar to spinach artichoke dip but without the spinach and with tons of artichokes. The slice is usually dripping the sauce over the sides and down your arm. Oh man, I wish I were there right now!

One 270-gram ball Classic New York dough (page 68)

½ cup (120 ml) Creamy Artichoke Sauce (page 228)

3 ounces (90 g) whole-milk mozzarella cheese, cut into ½-inch (1 cm) cubes

3 fresh basil leaves, torn, plus 3 leaves cut into chiffonade, for finishing

¼ cup (45 g) Marinated Artichoke Hearts (page 227)

Grated zest of ½ lemon

¼ cup (30 g) grated Parmesan cheese, preferably Parmigiano-Reggiano

Remove the dough from the refrigerator and place it on the counter to proof until the dough temperature reads 55 to 60°F (13 to 16°C) using an instant-read thermometer, typically about 2 hours, or until dough has doubled in size.

One hour before baking the pizza, slide one rack into the lowest position of the oven and a second rack into the middle of the oven, leaving 6 to 8 inches (15 to 20 cm) between the racks. Place a pizza stone or steel on each rack and preheat the oven to 500°F (260°C) or the highest setting.

When ready to bake, lightly dust a pizza peel with fine semolina flour and set to the side. Using the method on page 42, gently remove the dough ball from its container, dredge it in a mixture of 00 flour and fine semolina flour, place it on a well-floured work surface, and stretch it into a 12-inch (30 cm) round. Transfer the stretched dough to the peel.

Using a ladle, top the dough with the sauce, spreading it evenly over the surface and leaving a 1-inch (2.5 cm) border around the edges. Spread the mozzarella in a single layer uniformly across the pizza, then scatter the torn basil on top followed by the artichoke hearts.

Slide the pizza off the peel onto the stone or steel (see page 42) on the lowest oven rack and bake for 12 to 14 minutes, or until the crust is golden brown and the cheese is lightly spotted.

Using the peel, remove the pizza from the oven and transfer to a cooling rack. After a few minutes, transfer to a clean cutting board. Sprinkle with the lemon zest, Parmesan, and basil chiffonade. Cut and serve.

THE MEATBALL PIE

The first time I had a meatball pie was at Lombardi's, a place known for having one of the oldest coal-fired pizza ovens in New York. It reminded me so much of Sunday dinner with my family at my grandmother's house, where meatballs were always on the table. Lombardi's has since lost its coal-fired oven, but my version of its famous meatball pie will have you re-creating the original in your home kitchen. This pie is especially delicious made with my meatballs.

One 270-gram ball Classic New York dough (page 68)

½ cup (120 ml) All-American Sauce (page 80)

4 ounces (120 g) whole-milk mozzarella cheese, cut into ½-inch (1 cm) cubes

6 to 8 Homemade Meatballs (page 223), quartered and tossed in All-American Sauce

¼ cup (40 g) roasted red pepper strips (see Marinated Roasted Red Peppers, page 219, omitting the marinade)

2 tablespoons grated pecorino romano cheese, preferably Locatelli, divided

3 fresh basil leaves, cut into chiffonade

Remove the dough from the refrigerator and place it on the counter to proof until the dough temperature reads 55 to 60°F (13 to 16°C) using an instant-read thermometer, typically about 2 hours, or until dough has doubled in size.

One hour before baking the pizza, slide one rack into the lowest position of the oven and a second rack into the middle of the oven, leaving 6 to 8 inches (15 to 20 cm) between the racks. Place a pizza stone or steel on each rack and preheat the oven to 500°F (260°C) or the highest setting.

When ready to bake, lightly dust a pizza peel with fine semolina flour and set to the side. Using the method on page 42, gently remove the dough ball from its container, dredge it in a mixture of 00 flour and fine semolina flour, place it on a well-floured work surface, and stretch it into a 12-inch (30 cm) round. Transfer the stretched dough to the peel.

Using a ladle, top the dough with the sauce, spreading it evenly over the surface and leaving a 1-inch (2.5 cm) border around the edges. Spread the mozzarella in a single layer uniformly across the pizza, then place the meatball halves evenly over the cheese. Scatter the roasted peppers on top and finish with 1 tablespoon of the pecorino.

Slide the pizza off the peel onto the stone or steel (see page 42) on the lowest oven rack and bake for 10 to 12 minutes, or until the crust is golden brown and the cheese is lightly spotted.

Using the peel, remove the pizza from the oven and transfer to a cooling rack. After a few minutes, transfer to a clean cutting board. Sprinkle with the basil and the remaining 1 tablespoon of pecorino. Cut and serve.

PEPPERONI AND MUSHROOM

Pepperoni and mushroom pizza is as much a classic as a peanut butter and jelly sandwich. Here, I add shredded fontina to the cheese mix, which helps round out the flavor. I like to bake this pizza, let it cool without cutting it, and then I slice it and pop the slices onto a hot pizza stone for a couple of minutes for the ultimate New York slice at home.

One 270-gram ball Classic New York dough (page 68)

½ cup (120 ml) All-American Sauce (page 80)

¼ cup (30 g) shredded fontina cheese

2 ounces (60 g) whole-milk mozzarella cheese, cut into ½-inch (1 cm) cubes

2 ounces (60 g) sliced pepperoni

¼ cup (25 g) Sautéed Mushrooms (page 223)

1 tablespoon grated Parmesan cheese, preferably Parmigiano-Reggiano

Remove the dough from the refrigerator and place it on the counter to proof until the dough temperature reads 55 to 60°F (13 to 16°C) using an instant-read thermometer, typically about 2 hours, or until dough has doubled in size.

One hour before baking the pizza, slide one rack into the lowest position of the oven and a second rack into the middle of the oven, leaving 6 to 8 inches (15 to 20 cm) between the racks. Place a pizza stone or steel on each rack and preheat the oven to 500°F (260°C) or the highest setting.

When ready to bake, lightly dust a pizza peel with fine semolina flour and set to the side. Using the method on page 42, gently remove the dough ball from its container, dredge it in a mixture of 00 flour and fine semolina flour, place it on a well-floured work surface, and stretch it into a 12-inch (30 cm) round. Transfer the stretched dough to the peel.

Using a ladle, top the dough with the sauce, spreading it evenly over the surface and leaving a 1-inch (2.5 cm) border around the edges. Spread the fontina and mozzarella uniformly across the pizza, then top evenly with the pepperoni and mushrooms. Sprinkle with the Parmesan.

Slide the pizza off the peel onto the stone or steel (see page 42) on the lowest oven rack and bake for 10 to 12 minutes, or until the crust is golden brown and cheese is lightly spotted.

Using the peel, remove the pizza from the oven and transfer to a cooling rack. After a few minutes, transfer to a clean cutting board. Cut and serve.

NEW YORK–STYLE PAN PIZZAS

Pan pizzas are always great because once you get the dough pressed into the pan, a good proof is all you need to get a great result. I prefer to bake New York pan pizzas all the way through with the ingredients on top, rather than using a par-baked crust. Yes, you can use a par-baked crust, and that option is in the recipes that follow. But if you want that classic bite of a New York square, you need to let the pizza crust bake from start to finish so the dough has a chance to fry slowly in the oil used to grease the pan. The crunchy bottom bite and light and airy crumb of the slowly fried crust are what everybody loves and what set the New York pan pizza apart from other pan pizzas.

Each recipe in this chapter can be made using a par-baked dough (see page 47 for instructions). Your baking time will be shorter compared to starting with raw dough, which can really come in handy if you are making multiple pizzas. If using par-baked dough that has been refrigerated or frozen, be sure to bring it to room temperature before you begin topping it.

THE CAPO

One year, as part of the Fancy Food Show in New York, I was invited to make pizzas at the Javits Center for a VIP dinner hosted by Lidia Bastianich (a hero of mine and one of the most celebrated Italian chefs in America). During the show, I had the honor of meeting acclaimed New York baker Jim Lahey of Sullivan Street Bakery. Jim was incredible, and his knowledge of artisan bread made me feel like I'd never even touched flour in my life. After chatting for a while, he invited me to the bakery to check out his operation and his amazing *pizza bianca* (which took two of us to hold up because it was so long). He then showed me a pizza that was insane: a *pizza in teglia* (pan pizza) with capocollo (pork salume; also known as coppa and capicola, depending on region) and house-made lacto-fermented chiles. After I left, I couldn't get that pizza out of my mind. This pizza is a tribute to Jim and everything he has done as a baker and as an inspiration to the next generation of great bakers.

One 770-gram ball New York Pan dough (page 69), raw or par-baked crust

1¼ cups (300 ml) Rustic Hand-Crushed Sauce (page 79)

10 ounces (285 g) whole-milk mozzarella cheese, cut into ½-inch (1 cm) cubes

12 thin slices capocollo

3 ounces (90 g) fennel bulb (½ small bulb), thinly sliced lengthwise on a mandoline or with a sharp knife

¼ cup (60 g) jarred whole Calabrian chiles in oil, sliced, with oil reserved

If using raw dough, remove it from the refrigerator and place it on the counter to proof until the dough temperature reads 55 to 60°F (13 to 16°C) using an instant-read thermometer, typically about 2 hours, or until dough has doubled in size. If using a par-baked crust, prepare as directed on page 47.

One hour before baking the pizza, slide one rack into the lowest position of the oven and a second rack into the middle of the oven, leaving 6 to 8 inches (15 to 20 cm) between the racks. Place a pizza stone or steel on each rack and preheat the oven to 500°F (260°C) or the highest setting.

When ready to bake, stretch the dough into a 12-by-16-inch (30 by 40 cm) pan as described on page 46. If using a par-baked crust, lay it in a 12-by-16-inch (30 by 40 cm) pan.

Using a ladle, add the sauce to the pizza base and spread it over the surface, leaving a 1-inch (2.5 cm) border around the edges. Using your fingers as described on page 47, continue to spread the sauce until it fills any little hollows and the base is evenly covered. Spread the mozzarella in a single layer over the sauce, then lay the capocollo slices on the mozzarella, arranging them in three lengthwise rows of four slices each. Scatter the fennel followed by the chiles and their oil evenly over the top.

Transfer the pan to the stone or steel on the lowest oven rack and bake the pizza for 13 to 15 minutes if using raw dough or 7 to 9 minutes if using a par-baked crust, or until the cheese is spotted and the crust is oily and crispy.

Remove the pan from the oven and, using an offset spatula, lift the pizza out of the pan and transfer it to a cooling rack. After a few minutes, transfer to a clean cutting board. Cut into squares and serve.

CLASSIC
PEPPERONI

Pepperoni is the number-one pizza topping in America, so it's no surprise if some of you are looking for a killer pepperoni pizza in this book. I've never made a trip to New York without eating at least one slice of pepperoni. This is my take on the classic. I use cup and char pepperoni, which is made with natural casings that shrink in the heat of the oven, causing the slices to curl up and char around the edges. All the pepperoni juice is captured in these little "cups," so there's a little surprise burst of pepperoni flavor in every bite.

One 770-gram ball New York Pan dough (page 69), raw or par-baked crust

1¼ cups (350 ml) Rustic Hand-Crushed Sauce (page 79)

8 ounces (225 g) whole-milk mozzarella cheese, shredded

5 ounces (140 g) sliced cup and char pepperoni

3 fresh basil leaves, cut into chiffonade

¼ cup (30 g) grated Parmesan cheese, preferably Parmigiano-Reggiano

If using raw dough, remove it from the refrigerator and place it on the counter to proof until the dough temperature reads 55 to 60°F (13 to 16°C) using an instant-read thermometer, typically about 2 hours, or until dough has doubled in size. If using a par-baked crust, prepare as directed on page 47.

One hour before baking the pizza, slide one rack into the lowest position of the oven and a second rack into the middle of the oven, leaving 6 to 8 inches (15 to 20 cm) between the racks. Place a pizza stone or steel on each rack and preheat the oven to 500°F (260°C) or the highest setting.

When ready to bake, stretch the dough into a 12-by-16-inch (30 by 40 cm) pan as described on page 42. If using a par-baked crust, lay it in a 12-by-16-inch (30 by 40 cm) pan.

Using a ladle, top the dough with the sauce, spreading it evenly over the surface and leaving a 1-inch (2.5 cm) border around the edges. Spread the mozzarella evenly on top of the sauce, then arrange the pepperoni in a single layer on top of the mozzarella.

Transfer the pan to the stone or steel on the lowest oven rack and bake the pizza for 13 to 15 minutes if using raw dough or 7 to 9 minutes if using a par-baked crust, or until the crust is oily and crispy, the cheese is spotted, and the pepperoni slices are "cupped."

Remove the pan from the oven. Using an offset spatula, lift the pizza out of the pan and transfer it to a cooling rack. After a few minutes, transfer to a clean cutting board. Sprinkle evenly with the basil and Parmesan. Cut into squares and serve.

SFINCIONE

You can't have a chapter that covers New York pan pizza without including its inspiration, the Sicilian pan pizza known as *sfincione*. This is the traditional version from Palermo, which includes a sauce that cooks down and thickens during the bake, lots of caramelized onions, and a ton of toasty-brown breadcrumbs. The star of this recipe is the caciocavallo cheese, a stretched-curd cheese made from cow's or sheep's milk. It has a nutty, rich flavor that contrasts nicely with the rest of the ingredients. If you can't find caciocavallo, substitute aged provolone.

One 770-gram ball New York Pan dough (page 69), raw or par-baked crust

1¼ cups (300 ml) Rustic Hand-Crushed Sauce (page 79)

4 ounces (115 g) caciocavallo or aged provolone cheese, grated

2 cups (200 g) Caramelized Onions (page 223)

¾ cup (75 g) Toasted Breadcrumbs (page 219)

½ cup (120 ml) extra-virgin olive oil

If using raw dough, remove it from the refrigerator and place it on the counter to proof until the dough temperature reads 55 to 60°F (13 to 16°C) using an instant-read thermometer, typically about 2 hours, or until dough has doubled in size. If using a par-baked crust, prepare as directed on page 47.

One hour before baking the pizza, slide one rack into the lowest position of the oven and a second rack into the middle of the oven, leaving 6 to 8 inches (15 to 20 cm) between the racks. Place a pizza stone or steel on each rack and preheat the oven to 500°F (260°C) or the highest setting.

When ready to bake, stretch the dough into a 12-by-16-inch (30 by 40 cm) pan as described on page 42. If using a par-baked crust, lay it in a 12-by-16-inch (30 by 40 cm) pan.

Using a ladle, add the sauce to the pizza base and spread it over the surface, leaving a 1-inch (2.5 cm) border around the edges. Using your fingers as described on page 47, continue to spread the sauce until it fills any little hollows and the base is evenly covered. Distribute the caciocavallo evenly on top of the sauce, then top with the onions followed by the breadcrumbs. Drizzle the oil evenly over the breadcrumbs.

Transfer the pan to the stone or steel on the lowest oven rack and bake the pizza for 13 to 15 minutes if using raw dough or 7 to 9 minutes if using a par-baked crust, or until the cheese is spotted and the crust is oily and crispy.

Remove the pan from the oven and, using an offset spatula, lift the pizza out of the pan and transfer it to a cooling rack. After a few minutes, transfer to a clean cutting board. Cut into squares and serve.

LOADED CHICKEN

The toppings on this pizza may sound too heavy, but because of the thickness of the crust, the pizza is actually well balanced. The potatoes get super crispy and almost fry in the rendered fat from the bacon. If you've never had potatoes on a pizza, this is a great introduction.

One 770-gram New York Pan dough (page 69), raw or par-baked crust

1 cup (240 ml) Creamy White Sauce (page 81)

12 ounces (340 g) whole-milk mozzarella cheese, cut into ½-inch (1 cm) cubes

½ cup (85 g) shredded roasted chicken (store-bought rotisserie or leftovers will do)

10 ounces (285 g) Yukon Gold potatoes (about 2 medium), boiled until fork-tender, then gently smashed

3 slices applewood-smoked bacon, cut into 1-inch (2.5 cm) pieces

¼ cup (30 g) grated Parmesan cheese, preferably Parmigiano-Reggiano

Leaves from 1 fresh rosemary sprig

If using raw dough, remove it from the refrigerator and place it on the counter to proof until the dough temperature reads 55 to 60°F (13 to 16°C) using an instant-read thermometer, typically about 2 hours, or until dough has doubled in size. If using a par-baked crust, prepare as directed on page 47.

One hour before baking the pizza, slide one rack into the lowest position of the oven and a second rack into the middle of the oven, leaving 6 to 8 inches (15 to 20 cm) between the racks. Place a pizza stone or steel on each rack and preheat the oven to 500°F (260°C) or the highest setting.

When ready to bake, stretch the dough into a 12-by-16-inch (30 by 40 cm) pan as described on page 42. If using a par-baked crust, lay it in a 12-by-16-inch (30 by 40 cm) pan.

Using a ladle, add the sauce to the pizza base and spread it over the surface, leaving a 1-inch (2.5 cm) border around the edges. Using your fingers as described on page 47, continue to spread the sauce until it fills any little hollows and the base is evenly covered. Spread the mozzarella in a single layer on top of the sauce and top evenly with the chicken. Spoon the potatoes evenly across the top, then top with the bacon. Sprinkle evenly with the Parmesan and rosemary.

Transfer the pan to the stone or steel on the lowest oven rack and bake the pizza for 13 to 15 minutes if using raw dough or 7 to 9 minutes if using a par-baked crust, or until the cheese is spotted, the bacon is cooked, the potatoes are crispy, and crust is oily and crispy.

Remove the pan from the oven and, using an offset spatula, lift the pizza out of the pan and transfer it to a cooling rack. After a few minutes, transfer to a clean cutting board. Cut into squares and serve.

VECCHIA SCUOLA

This pizza reminds me of being a kid. Maybe it's an Italian thing more than an East Coast or Midwest thing, but combining sausage, peppers, and onions is an old-school (*vecchia scuola*) staple. I can't remember a time in my life when a family get-together didn't have sausage and peppers on the menu.

One 770-gram ball New York Pan dough (page 69), raw or par-baked crust

1¼ cups (350 ml) Rustic Hand-Crushed Sauce (page 79)

8 ounces (225 g) whole-milk mozzarella cheese, cut into ½-inch (1 cm) cubes

6 ounces (170 g) Italian sausage, bulk or casing removed

½ cup (85 g) roasted red pepper strips (see Marinated Roasted Red Peppers, page 219, omitting the marinade)

½ cup (50 g) thinly sliced red onion

1 tablespoon dried oregano

3 fresh basil leaves, cut into chiffonade

¼ cup (30 g) grated Parmesan cheese, preferably Parmigiano-Reggiano

If using raw dough, remove it from the refrigerator and place it on the counter to proof until the dough temperature reads 55 to 60°F (13 to 16°C) using an instant-read thermometer, typically about 2 hours, or until dough has doubled in size. If using a par-baked crust, prepare as directed on page 47.

One hour before baking the pizza, slide one rack into the lowest position of the oven and a second rack into the middle of the oven, leaving 6 to 8 inches (15 to 20 cm) between the racks. Place a pizza stone or steel on each rack and preheat the oven to 500°F (260°C) or the highest setting.

When ready to bake, stretch the dough into a 12-by-16-inch (30 by 40 cm) pan as described on page 42. If using a par-baked crust, lay it in a 12-by-16-inch (30 by 40 cm) pan.

Using a ladle, top the dough with the sauce, spreading it evenly over the surface and leaving a 1-inch (2.5 cm) border around the edges. Spread the mozzarella in a single layer across the pizza. Pinch the sausage into quarter-size chunks, press each one flat, and distribute them evenly over the cheese. Spread the red peppers and onion uniformly across the pizza, then sprinkle with the oregano.

Transfer the pan to the stone or steel on the lowest oven rack and bake the pizza for 13 to 15 minutes if using raw dough or 7 to 9 minutes if using a par-baked crust, or until the cheese is spotted and the crust is oily and crispy.

Remove the pizza from the oven. Using an offset spatula, lift the pizza out of the pan and transfer it to a cooling rack. After a few minutes, transfer to a clean cutting board. Sprinkle evenly with the basil and Parmesan. Cut into squares and serve.

FRESH
CAPRESE

I wait until summer when tomato season is in full swing to make this pizza. Sure, you can find tomatoes all year long, but everyone knows when the best ones are harvested. If you want to make this in the middle of winter, look for some good tomatoes on the vine, such as Campari, or even cherry tomatoes. The whole idea here is for the marinated tomatoes to end up being the sauce for the pizza, so the juicier the tomato, the better the pizza.

One 770-gram ball New York Pan dough (page 69), raw or par-baked crust

1 pound (450 g) ripe, juicy tomatoes, cut into 1-inch (2.5 cm) dice

½ cup (120 ml) extra-virgin olive oil, divided

2 garlic cloves, chopped

1 teaspoon dried oregano

1 teaspoon kosher salt

Pinch ground black pepper

6 ounces (170 g) fior di latte mozzarella cheese, sliced ¼ inch (6 mm) thick

¼ cup (30 g) Parmesan cheese, preferably Parmigiano-Reggiano, shaved with a vegetable peeler

3 fresh basil leaves, cut into chiffonade

If using raw dough, remove it from the refrigerator and place it on the counter to proof until the dough temperature reads 55 to 60°F (13 to 16°C) using an instant-read thermometer, typically about 2 hours, or until dough has doubled in size. If using a par-baked crust, prepare as directed on page 47.

In a medium bowl, combine the tomatoes, ¼ cup (60 ml) of the oil, the garlic, oregano, salt, and pepper and toss to combine. Cover and marinate in the refrigerator for 1 hour.

One hour before baking the pizza, slide one rack into the lowest position of the oven and a second rack into the middle of the oven, leaving 6 to 8 inches (15 to 20 cm) between the racks. Place a pizza stone or steel on each rack and preheat the oven to 500°F (260°C) or the highest setting.

When ready to bake, stretch the dough into a 12-by-16-inch (30 by 40 cm) pan as described on page 42. If using a par-baked crust, lay it in a 12-by-16-inch (30 by 40 cm) pan.

Spoon the tomatoes in a single layer evenly across the dough, leaving a 1-inch (2.5 cm) border around the edges. Drizzle the tomato juices remaining in the bowl over the entire base.

Transfer the pan to the stone or steel on the lowest oven rack and bake the pizza for 5 to 7 minutes if using raw dough or 3 to 4 minutes if using a par-baked crust, or until the tomatoes caramelize and start to turn blistered and the crust starts to brown on top.

Remove the pan from the oven and lay the fresh mozzarella slices in uniform rows on top of the tomatoes. Return the pan to the oven and continue to bake for 8 to 10 minutes, or until the cheese is spotted and the crust is oily and crispy.

Remove the pan from the oven. Using an offset spatula, lift the pizza out of the pan and transfer it to a cooling rack. After a few minutes, transfer to a clean cutting board. Top with Parmesan, a sprinkle of basil, and drizzle with the remaining ¼ cup (60 ml) oil. Cut into squares and serve.

THE L&B

I've been a huge fan of L&B Spumoni Gardens since the first time I tried it. It's a bit of a hike to get to the original location in Bensonhurst (there's now one in Dumbo too) but definitely worth the trip. What I fell in love with about this square is that the sliced mozzarella goes on the base of the pizza and the tomato sauce is spread on top, exposing it during the bake. As the mozzarella melts, some of the sauce seeps into the nooks and crannies of the cheese and what remains on top gets pasty and sweet. This results in both an amazing look and a wonderfully balanced bite— neither too heavy nor too light, just perfection in a simple slice.

One 770-gram ball New York Pan dough (page 69), raw or par-baked crust

12 ounces (340 g) whole-milk mozzarella cheese, sliced ¼ inch (6 mm) thick, then slices cut in half

1¼ cups (300 ml) All-American Sauce (page 80)

¼ cup (30 g) grated pecorino romano cheese, preferably Locatelli

If using raw dough, remove it from the refrigerator and place it on the counter to proof until the dough temperature reads 55 to 60°F (13 to 16°C) using an instant-read thermometer, typically about 2 hours, or until dough has doubled in size. If using a par-baked crust, prepare as directed on page 47.

One hour before baking the pizza, slide one rack into the lowest position of the oven and a second rack into the middle of the oven, leaving 6 to 8 inches (15 to 20 cm) between the racks. Place a pizza stone or steel on each rack and preheat the oven to 500°F (260°C) or the highest setting.

When ready to bake, stretch the dough into a 12-by-16-inch (30 by 40 cm) pan as described on page 42. If using a par-baked crust, lay it in a 12-by-16-inch (30 by 40 cm) pan.

Lay the mozzarella slices in a single layer on top of the pizza base, leaving a 1-inch (2.5 cm) border around the edges. Using a ladle, top the mozzarella with the sauce, spreading it evenly. Sprinkle the pecorino evenly over the sauce.

Transfer the pan to the stone or steel on the lowest oven rack and bake the pizza for 12 to 15 minutes if using raw dough or 8 to 10 minutes if using a par-baked crust, or until the crust is oily and crispy.

Remove the pan from the oven and, using an offset spatula, lift the pizza out of the pan and transfer it to a cooling rack. After a few minutes, transfer to a clean cutting board. Cut into squares and serve.

SICILIAN STYLE WITH
VODKA SAUCE

There are many arguments over who makes the best vodka sauce in New York. The one thing that's for sure is that it belongs on a pizza! I love the tanginess that the crushed tomatoes add to the creamy white sauce and the sweetness of the cooked-down vodka. It is perfect for balancing the bread-to-topping ratio of thick-crust pizzas. For me, nothing says New York pizza more than a corner square of a vodka Sicilian.

One 770-gram ball New York Pan dough (page 69), raw or par-baked crust

12 ounces (340 g) whole-milk mozzarella cheese, sliced ¼ inch (6 mm) thick, then slices halved

1½ cups (350 ml) Creamy Vodka Sauce (page 228)

5 ounces (140 g) fior di latte mozzarella cheese, sliced ¼ inch (6 mm) thick

¼ cup (30 g) grated pecorino romano cheese, preferably Locatelli

5 fresh basil leaves, cut into chiffonade

If using raw dough, remove it from the refrigerator and place it on the counter to proof until the dough temperature reads 55 to 60°F (13 to 16°C) using an instant-read thermometer, typically about 2 hours, or until dough has doubled in size. If using a par-baked crust, prepared as directed on page 47.

One hour before baking the pizza, slide one rack into the lowest position of the oven and a second rack into the middle of the oven, leaving 6 to 8 inches (15 and 20 cm) between the racks. Place a pizza stone or steel on each rack and preheat the oven to 500°F (260°C) or the highest setting.

When ready to bake, stretch the dough into a 12-by-16-inch (30 to 40 cm) pan as described on page 42. If using a par-baked crust, lay it in a 12-by-16-inch (30 by 40 cm) pan.

Lay the whole-milk mozzarella slices in three evenly spaced rows on top of the dough. Using a ladle, spread the sauce in three lengthwise strips in the spaces between the mozzarella.

Transfer the pan to the stone or steel on the lowest oven rack and bake the pizza for 5 to 7 minutes if using raw dough or 3 to 4 minutes if using a par-baked crust, or until the cheese has started to melt (I usually wait until the mozzarella rows melt to touch each other, almost forming a solid sheet of coverage).

Remove the pan from the oven and lay the fresh mozzarella slices on top of the sauce strips in uniform rows. Return the pan to the oven and continue to bake for 8 to 10 minutes, or until the cheese is spotted and the crust is oily and crispy.

Remove the pan from the oven. Using an offset spatula, lift the pizza out of the pan and transfer it to a cooling rack. After a few minutes, transfer to a clean cutting board. Sprinkle evenly with the pecorino and basil. Cut into squares and serve.

DETROIT PAN PIZZAS

In the Master Doughs section, I included two recipes for Detroit pan pizza dough. The Traditional Detroit Pan (page 71) is the one most commonly used in the city. The second recipe, Contemporary Detroit Pan with Poolish (page 70), is my personal formula and process and makes what I consider an amazing Detroit pizza. You'll need to make the poolish the night before you plan to make the final dough, but the payoff in flavor, in the texture of the crumb, and the exterior color is well worth the extra step.

Whether I use the traditional dough or the poolish dough, I par-bake the pizza base before baking the final pizza. This double baking delivers a ridiculously crispy bottom that everyone loves. What's really great about this recipe is that you can par-bake a couple of crusts ahead of time, let them cool, double wrap them in plastic wrap, and put them in the freezer for up to a month. Then if on a whim you decide you want a Detroit pan pizza, all you have to do is bring the par-baked dough to room temperature, gather some topping ingredients, preheat the oven, pop the crust into the pan, top it, and finish baking the pizza. You can literally have pizza night any night of the week!

MOTOR CITY

I discovered this pizza on a trip to Detroit before I even knew what a "Detroit pizza" was. My first stop was the iconic Buddy's (see headnote, page 70), which I soon found out was the birthplace of Detroit pan pizza. This combination of toppings with some minor variations can be found throughout the Midwest. In many places, such as Chicago, Italian sausage is traditional, but Buddy's uses pepperoni. It not only works but it's great!

One 700-gram ball Detroit pan dough, traditional (page 71) or contemporary with poolish (page 70), par-baked (see page 47)

10 slices white cheddar cheese, sliced ¼ inch (6 mm) thick, then halved into 2-by-4-inch (5 by 10 cm) pieces

5 ounces (140 g) brick cheese or other semihard white melting cheese, shredded

5 ounces (140 g) whole-milk mozzarella cheese, shredded

¼ cup (35 g) green bell pepper, cut into strips ¼ inch (6 mm) wide

¼ cup (25 g) thinly sliced red onion

¼ cup (25 g) Sautéed Mushrooms (page 223)

2 ounces (60 g) sliced pepperoni

¾ cup (180 ml) All-American Sauce (page 80), warmed

2 tablespoons grated Parmesan cheese, preferably Parmigiano-Reggiano

Pinch dried oregano

One hour before baking the pizza, slide one rack into the lowest position of the oven and a second rack into the middle of the oven, leaving 6 to 8 inches (15 to 20 cm) between the racks. Place a pizza stone or steel on each rack and preheat the oven to 475°F (245°C).

Generously grease the bottom and sides of a 10-by-14-inch (25 by 35 cm) Detroit pizza pan with solid vegetable shortening.

Arrange the cheddar slices evenly against the side walls of the pan, pressing gently so the slices adhere to the shortening. The cheese will not completely cover the side walls. Gaps are okay. Lay the par-baked crust in the pan, nestling the cheddar between the crust and the pan walls. Spread the brick and mozzarella cheeses evenly across the crust, leaving a 1-inch (2.5 cm) border around the edges. Layer the bell pepper, onion, mushrooms, and pepperoni evenly over the cheeses.

Transfer the pan to the stone or steel on the lowest oven rack and bake the pizza for 12 to 14 minutes, or until the crust is oily and crispy and the cheese is melted and spotted brown.

Remove the pan from the oven and, using an offset spatula, lift the pizza out of the pan and place on a cooling rack. After a few minutes, transfer to a clean cutting board.

Using a ladle, spread the sauce on the pizza, arranging it in two wide lengthwise lines down the center and leaving a 2-inch (5 cm) gap between the lines. Sprinkle the pizza evenly with the Parmesan and oregano.

Using a rocking pizza cutter or a long, sharp knife, cut into squares and serve.

THE G.O.A.T.

I'm dedicating this pizza to one of my mentors, Tony Gemignani, who has guided me and helped pave the way for me to be where I am today professionally. I've watched Tony make this pizza many times, and I never tire of seeing the intensity in his face as he executes every step, from dolloping the ricotta to getting the perfect amount of basil on top to finish. He's clearly the GOAT, and the pizza renaissance might never have happened if it wasn't for Tony pioneering the way for the rest of us.

One 700-gram ball Detroit pan dough, traditional (page 71) or contemporary with poolish (page 70), par-baked (see page 47)

10 slices white cheddar cheese, sliced ¼ inch (6 mm) thick, then halved into 2-by-4-inch (5 by 10 cm) pieces

5 ounces (140 g) brick cheese or other semihard white melting cheese, shredded

5 ounces (140 g) whole-milk mozzarella cheese, shredded

6 ounces (170 g) sliced cup and char pepperoni

¾ cup (180 ml) All-American Sauce (page 80), warmed

½ cup (115 g) Whipped Ricotta (page 229), dollops from a piping bag fitted with a star tip

5 fresh basil leaves, cut into chiffonade

Garlic Oil (page 227) for drizzling

¼ cup (30 g) grated Parmesan cheese, preferably Parmigiano-Reggiano

One hour before baking the pizza, slide one rack into the lowest position of the oven and a second rack into the middle of the oven, leaving 6 to 8 inches (15 to 20 cm) between the racks. Place a pizza stone or steel on each rack and preheat the oven to 475°F (245°C).

Generously grease the bottom and sides of a 10-by-14-inch (25 by 35 cm) Detroit pizza pan with solid vegetable shortening.

Arrange the cheddar slices evenly against the side walls of the pan, pressing gently so the slices adhere to the shortening. The cheese will not completely cover the side walls. Gaps are okay. Lay the par-baked crust in the pan, nestling the cheddar between the crust and the pan walls. Spread the brick and mozzarella cheeses evenly across the crust, leaving a 1-inch (2.5 cm) border around the edges. Arrange the pepperoni in a single layer over the cheeses.

Transfer the pan to the stone or steel on the lowest oven rack and bake the pizza for 10 to 12 minutes, or until the pepperoni is slightly cupped, and the cheese is melted and spotted brown.

Remove the pan from the oven and, using an offset spatula, lift the pizza out of the pan and place on a cooling rack. After a few minutes, transfer to a clean cutting board.

Using a ladle, spread the sauce on the pizza, arranging it in two wide lengthwise lines down the center and leaving a 2-inch (5 cm) gap between the lines. Alongside the sauce lines, pipe dollops of the ricotta in four uniform rows. Scatter the basil over the pizza, drizzle with a little oil, and sprinkle evenly with the Parmesan.

Using a rocking pizza cutter or a long, sharp knife, cut into squares and serve.

FOUR CHEESE

Who doesn't love a good cheese pizza? I mean, there's not a pizza joint in the world that doesn't offer a cheese pizza. When it comes to Detroit style, consider this recipe your cheese pizza primer. The cheese blend is important, and when the Detroit style started, the traditional cheese of choice was not everyone's go-to mozzarella. Instead, it was a white, semihard melting cheese from the Midwest called brick cheese. The combination of cheeses I use here hits the mark on tradition and flavor and can be the basis for creating lots of other pizzas, all with the cheese pizza as the base. Learn how to make this Detroit pan pizza correctly first and you'll be rewarded for a lifetime.

One 700-gram ball Detroit pan dough, traditional (page 71) or contemporary with poolish (page 70), par-baked (page 47)

10 slices white cheddar cheese, sliced ¼ inch (6 mm) thick, then halved into 2-by-4-inch (5 by 10 cm) pieces

2 ounces (60 g) provolone cheese, shredded

4 ounces (115 g) brick cheese or other semihard white melting cheese, shredded

4 ounces (115 g) whole-milk mozzarella cheese, shredded

¼ cup (30 g) plus 2 tablespoons grated Parmesan cheese, preferably Parmigiano-Reggiano, divided

1¼ cups (300 ml) All-American Sauce (page 80), warmed

One hour before baking the pizza, slide one rack into the lowest position of the oven and a second rack into the middle of the oven, leaving 6 to 8 inches (15 to 20 cm) between the racks. Place a pizza stone or steel on each rack and preheat the oven to 475°F (245°C).

Generously grease the bottom and sides of a 10-by-14-inch (25 by 35 cm) Detroit pizza pan with solid vegetable shortening.

Arrange the cheddar slices evenly against the side walls of the pan, pressing gently so the slices adhere to the shortening. The cheese will not completely cover the side walls. Gaps are okay. Lay the par-baked crust in the pan, nestling the cheddar between the crust and the pan walls. Spread the provolone, brick, and mozzarella cheeses and ¼ cup (30 g) of the Parmesan evenly across the crust, leaving a 1-inch (2.5 cm) border around the edges.

Transfer the pan to the stone or steel on the lowest oven rack and bake the pizza for 8 to 10 minutes, or until the crust is oily and crispy and the cheese is melted and spotted brown.

Remove the pan from the oven and, using an offset spatula, lift the pizza out of the pan and transfer to a cooling rack. After a few minutes, transfer to a clean cutting board.

Using a ladle, spread the sauce on the pizza, arranging it in two wide lengthwise lines down the center and leaving a 2-inch (5 cm) gap between the lines. Sprinkle the pizza evenly with the remaining 2 tablespoons Parmesan.

Using a rocking pizza cutter or a long, sharp knife, cut into squares and serve.

TRIPLE PEPPERONI

The most ordered topping in any pizzeria is pepperoni, and this pizza uses it in three different preparations, delivering an amazing variety of textures with every bite. This is the ultimate pepperoni pizza for true pepperoni lovers.

One 700-gram ball Detroit pan dough, traditional (page 71) or contemporary with poolish (page 70), par-baked (see page 47)

10 slices white cheddar cheese, sliced ¼ inch (6 mm) thick, then halved into 2-by-4-inch (5 by 10 cm) pieces

5 ounces (140 g) brick cheese or other semihard white melting cheese, shredded

5 ounces (140 g) whole-milk mozzarella cheese, shredded

2 ounces (60 g) sliced pepperoni

2 ounces (60 g) sliced pepperoni, diced

¾ cup (180 ml) All-American Sauce (page 80), warmed

2 ounces (60 g) sliced pepperoni, cooked in a skillet on the stovetop until crisp

¼ cup (30 g) Parmesan cheese, preferably Parmigiano-Reggiano, shaved with a vegetable peeler

One hour before baking the pizza, slide one rack into the lowest position of the oven and a second rack into the middle of the oven, leaving 6 to 8 inches (15 to 20 cm) between the racks. Place a pizza stone or steel on each rack and preheat the oven to 475°F (245°C).

Generously grease the bottom and sides of a 10-by-14-inch (25 by 35 cm) Detroit pizza pan with solid vegetable shortening.

Arrange the cheddar slices evenly against the side walls of the pan, pressing gently so the slices adhere to the shortening. The cheese will not completely cover the side walls. Gaps are okay. Lay the par-baked crust in the pan, nestling the cheddar between the crust and the pan walls. Spread the brick and mozzarella cheeses evenly across the crust, leaving a 1-inch (2.5 cm) border around the edges. Layer the uncooked pepperoni slices and diced pepperoni evenly over the cheeses.

Transfer the pan to the stone or steel on the lowest oven rack and bake the pizza for 10 to 12 minutes, or until the crust is oily and crispy and the cheese is melted and spotted brown.

Remove the pan from the oven and, using an offset spatula, lift the pizza out of the pan and place on a cooling rack. After a few minutes, transfer to a clean cutting board.

Using a ladle, spread the sauce on the pizza, arranging it in two wide lengthwise lines down the center and leaving a 2-inch (5 cm) gap between the lines. Spread the crisp pepperoni slices evenly across the pizza and finish with the Parmesan.

Using a rocking pizza cutter or a long, sharp knife, cut into squares and serve.

BBQ CHICKEN

I have always loved this combination of smoked Gouda and red onion with chicken, but I often feel like the barbecue sauce can overpower the whole thing. My version allows all the toppings to play supporting roles to one another, and then I finish it with just a drizzle of barbecue sauce. You'll notice at first bite how balanced this pizza is.

One 700-gram ball Detroit pan dough, traditional (page 71) or contemporary with poolish (page 70), par-baked (see page 47)

10 slices white cheddar cheese, sliced ¼ inch (6 mm) thick, then halved into 2-by-4-inch (5 by 10 cm) pieces

5 ounces (140 g) brick cheese or other semihard white melting cheese, shredded

5 ounces (140 g) whole-milk mozzarella cheese, shredded

2 ounces (60 g) smoked Gouda cheese, shredded

¼ cup (45 g) shredded roasted chicken (store-bought rotisserie or leftovers will do)

¼ cup (25 g) thinly sliced red onion

1 tablespoon plus a pinch grated Parmesan cheese, preferably Parmigiano-Reggiano, divided

Barbecue sauce of choice for drizzling

1 tablespoon chopped fresh cilantro

One hour before baking the pizza, slide one rack into the lowest position of the oven and a second rack into the middle of the oven, leaving 6 to 8 inches (15 to 20 cm) between the racks. Place a pizza stone or steel on each rack and preheat the oven to 475°F (245°C).

Generously grease the bottom and sides of a 10-by-14-inch (25 by 35 cm) Detroit pizza pan with solid vegetable shortening.

Arrange the cheddar slices evenly against the side walls of the pan, pressing gently so the slices adhere to the shortening. The cheese will not completely cover the side walls. Gaps are okay. Lay the par-baked crust in the pan, nestling the cheddar between the crust and the pan walls. Spread the brick, mozzarella, and Gouda cheeses evenly across the crust, leaving a 1-inch (2.5 cm) border around the edges. Layer the chicken and red onion evenly over the cheeses, then sprinkle with 1 tablespoon of the Parmesan.

Transfer the pan to the stone or steel on the lowest oven rack and bake the pizza for 10 to 12 minutes, or until the crust is oily and crispy and the cheese is melted and spotted brown.

Remove the pan from the oven and, using an offset spatula, lift the pizza out of the pan and place on a cooling rack. After a few minutes, transfer to a clean cutting board. Drizzle with the sauce and sprinkle with the cilantro and the remaining pinch of Parmesan.

Using a rocking pizza cutter or a long, sharp knife, cut into squares and serve.

THE BIG THREE

As you make your way through all the classic Detroit pizza spots, you'll find that Detroiters love their pizzas with meat on top. If you fall into that category, you'll love this pizza as much as they do. My version has a surprise kick at the end that takes the flavor profile to another level.

One 700-gram ball Detroit pan dough, traditional (page 71) or contemporary with poolish (page 70), par-baked (see page 47)

10 slices white cheddar cheese, sliced ¼ inch (6 mm) thick, then halved into 2-by-4-inch (5 by 10 cm) pieces

5 ounces (140 g) brick cheese or other semihard white melting cheese, shredded

5 ounces (140 g) whole-milk mozzarella cheese, shredded

3 ounces (90 g) Italian sausage, bulk or casing removed

2 ounces (60 g) pepperoni

2 slices applewood-smoked bacon, cut into 1-inch (2.5 cm) pieces

¼ cup (40 g) hot cherry peppers, drained and sliced

¾ cup (180 ml) All-American Sauce (page 80), warmed

1 tablespoon grated Parmesan cheese, preferably Parmigiano-Reggiano

One hour before baking the pizza, slide one rack into the lowest position of the oven and a second rack into the middle of the oven, leaving 6 to 8 inches between the racks. Place a pizza stone or steel on each rack and preheat the oven to 475°F (245°C).

Generously grease the bottom and sides of a 10-by-14-inch (25 by 35 cm) Detroit pizza pan with solid vegetable shortening.

Arrange the cheddar slices evenly against the side walls of the pan, pressing gently so the slices adhere to the shortening. The cheese will not completely cover the side walls. Gaps are okay. Lay the par-baked crust in the pan, nestling the cheddar between the crust and the pan walls. Spread the brick and mozzarella cheeses evenly across the crust, leaving a 1-inch (2.5 cm) border around the edges. Pinch the sausage into quarter-size chunks, press each one flat, and distribute them evenly over the cheeses. Layer the pepperoni and bacon across the pizza, then spread the cherry peppers on top.

Transfer the pan to the stone or steel on the lowest oven rack and bake the pizza for 10 to 12 minutes, or until the crust is oily and crispy and the cheese is melted and spotted brown.

Remove the pan from the oven and, using an offset spatula, lift the pizza out of the pan and place on a cooling rack. After a few minutes, transfer to a clean cutting board.

Using a ladle, spread the sauce on the pizza, arranging it in two wide lengthwise lines down the center and leaving a 2-inch (5 cm) gap between the lines. Sprinkle the pizza evenly with the Parmesan.

Using a rocking pizza cutter or a long, sharp knife, cut into squares and serve.

THE BLT

I love this method for a BLT pizza. Cooking the bacon from raw on top of the pizza just makes sense. The bacon gets super crispy, while the rendered fat helps brown the pizza and gives it a great smoky flavor. I like to use the best fresh tomatoes and greens available. If tomatoes aren't in season, grab some tomatoes on the vine or even cherry tomatoes at the grocery store. A drizzle of Spicy White Sauce is the perfect finish—it beats mayo any day.

One 700-gram ball Detroit pan dough, traditional (page 71) or contemporary with poolish (page 70), par-baked (see page 47)

10 slices white cheddar cheese, sliced ¼ inch (6 mm) thick, then halved into 2-by-4-inch (5 by 10 cm) pieces

5 ounces (140 g) brick cheese or other semihard white melting cheese, shredded

5 ounces (140 g) whole-milk mozzarella cheese, shredded

5 slices applewood-smoked bacon

8 thin tomato slices, preferably heirloom

4 cups (120 g) loosely packed mixed salad greens

Spicy White Sauce (page 82) for drizzling

One hour before baking the pizza, slide one rack into the lowest position of the oven and a second rack into the middle of the oven, leaving 6 to 8 inches (15 to 20 cm) between the racks. Place a pizza stone or steel on each rack and preheat the oven to 475°F (245°C).

Generously grease the bottom and sides of a 10-by-14-inch (25 by 35 cm) Detroit pizza pan with solid vegetable shortening.

Arrange the cheddar slices evenly against the side walls of the pan, pressing gently so the slices adhere to the shortening. The cheese will not completely cover the side walls. Gaps are okay. Lay the par-baked crust in the pan, nestling the cheddar between the crust and the pan walls. Spread the brick and mozzarella cheeses evenly across the crust, leaving a 1-inch (2.5 cm) border around the edges. Lay the bacon slices lengthwise over the cheeses, stretching them to cover.

Transfer the pan to the stone or steel on the lowest oven rack and bake the pizza for 12 to 14 minutes, or until the crust is oily and crispy, the bacon is crispy, and the cheese is melted and spotted brown.

Remove the pan from the oven and, using an offset spatula, lift the pizza out of the pan and place on a cooling rack. After a few minutes, transfer to a clean cutting board.

Arrange the tomato slices in two rows of four slices. Top with the salad greens. Drizzle with the sauce.

Using a rocking pizza cutter or a long, sharp knife, cut into squares so each square has a tomato slice topped with greens. Drizzle with more sauce, if needed, and serve.

GREEK STYLE

This Mediterranean-inspired pizza can be found all over Detroit. I love how the vinegary flavor of the pepperoncini cuts through all the other ingredients. It might seem like this pizza is weighted down with too many toppings, but when it comes out of the oven, you'll be delighted with how light it is.

One 700-gram ball Detroit pan dough, traditional (page 71) or contemporary with poolish (page 70), par-baked (see page 47)

10 slices white cheddar cheese, sliced ¼ inch (6 mm) thick, then halved into 2-by-4-inch (5 by 10 cm) pieces

5 ounces (140 g) brick cheese or other semihard white melting cheese, shredded

2 ounces (60 g) baby spinach, chopped

¼ cup (30 g) plus 1 tablespoon grated Parmesan cheese, preferably Parmigiano-Reggiano, divided

5 ounces (140 g) whole-milk mozzarella cheese, shredded

12 cherry tomatoes (about 3 ounces [90 g]), halved (see page 48)

¼ cup (45 g) shredded roasted chicken (store-bought rotisserie or leftovers will do)

¼ cup (40 g) kalamata olives, pitted

2 tablespoons feta, crumbled

Scant ¼ cup (50 g) pepperoncini, sliced

Extra-virgin olive oil for drizzling

Pinch dried oregano

One hour before baking the pizza, slide one rack into the lowest position of the oven and a second rack into the middle of the oven, leaving 6 to 8 inches (15 to 20 cm) between the racks. Place a pizza stone or steel on each rack and preheat the oven to 475°F (245°C).

Generously grease the bottom and sides of a 10-by-14-inch (25 by 35 cm) Detroit pizza pan with vegetable shortening.

Arrange the cheddar slices evenly against the side walls of the pan, pressing gently so the slices adhere to the shortening. The cheese will not completely cover the side walls. Gaps are okay. Lay the par-baked crust in the pan, nestling the cheddar between the crust and the pan walls. Spread the brick cheese evenly across the crust, leaving a 1-inch (2.5 cm) border around the edges. Layer the spinach, ¼ cup (30 g) of the Parmesan, and the mozzarella evenly on top. Scatter the tomatoes, chicken, and olives over the mozzarella, then sprinkle evenly with the feta and pepperoncini.

Transfer the pan to the stone or steel on the lowest oven rack and bake the pizza for 12 to 14 minutes, or until the crust is oily and crispy, and the cheese is melted and spotted brown.

Remove the pan from the oven and, using an offset spatula, lift the pizza out of the pan and place on a cooling rack. After a few minutes, transfer to a clean cutting board. Drizzle with a little oil, then sprinkle with the oregano and the remaining 1 tablespoon Parmesan.

Using a rocking pizza cutter or a long, sharp knife, cut into squares and serve.

CHICAGO PAN PIZZAS

While many people think that Chicago deep dish is the only pan pizza Chicago has, the reality is we have two: the deep dish and the stuffed. I would be doing you a disservice if I did not teach you how to make both. You can find the dough formula for the deep dish on page 64. For the stuffed, you'll need the Chicago Tavern dough on page 66. The deep dish is more about the thick, airy dough, while the stuffed pizza is all about how much mozzarella and other fillings you can put inside of it. I admit that a stuffed pizza is my guilty pleasure.

No matter which Chicago pan pizza you decide to make, both will come out great in your home oven because the oven temperature for baking one never exceeds 500°F (260°C). The only question you will ask yourself as you sit at the dinner table with one these Chicago classics will be, "Should I go for a second (or third) slice?"

THE SPINACH PIE

The stuffed pizza is a timeless classic in Chicago that's actually eaten by locals even when nobody is visiting from out of town. The combination of fresh spinach, a hint of nutmeg, and layers of mozzarella will make you think that you're eating a pizza that's healthy—at least that's what I tell myself!

Three 290-gram balls Chicago Tavern dough (page 66)

6 ounces (180 g) baby spinach, coarsely chopped

Pinch ground nutmeg

½ cup (60 g) grated Parmesan cheese, preferably Parmigiano-Reggiano, divided

1 pound (450 g) whole-milk mozzarella cheese, shredded

1½ cups (350) Rustic Hand-Crushed Sauce (page 79), plus more if needed

Remove the dough from the refrigerator and place it on the counter to proof until the dough temperature reads 55 to 60°F (13 to 16°C) using an instant-read thermometer, typically about 2 hours, or until the dough has doubled in size.

One hour before baking the pizza, slide one rack into the lowest position of the oven and a second rack into the middle of the oven, leaving 6 to 8 inches (15 to 20 cm) between the racks. Place a pizza stone or steel on each rack and preheat the oven to 475°F (245°C).

Following the directions for panning Chicago stuffed pizza on page 45, grease a 12-inch (30 cm) pizza pan with 2-inch (5 cm) sides with solid vegetable shortening. Press two dough balls together and roll out ¼ inch (6 mm) thick, then lay the dough in the prepared pan as directed.

In a medium bowl, combine the spinach, nutmeg, and ¼ cup (30 g) of the Parmesan and toss to mix well.

Add half of the mozzarella in an even layer to the dough-lined pan. Top with all the spinach mixture, then layer the remaining mozzarella on top.

Roll out the remaining dough for the top crust and gently lay it over the pan, ensuring it covers the filling and extends onto the bottom layer's overhang. Press the top and bottom layers together firmly along the side walls to seal securely, then pinch five or six small holes in the center to allow steam to escape.

Holding a sharp knife at an angle, trim the excess dough by sliding the blade along the pan rim to create a clean, even edge. Discard the scraps.

Using a ladle, add the sauce to the center and shake the pan until it fully covers the dough's surface. Add more by the tablespoon if needed. Finish by sprinkling the remaining Parmesan on top.

Transfer the pan to the stone or steel on the lowest oven rack and bake the pizza for 20 to 22 minutes, or until the crust is golden brown.

Remove the pizza from the oven and use an offset spatula to lift it directly onto a cooling rack. After a few minutes, transfer to a cutting board, slice with a rocking pizza cutter or sharp knife, and serve.

CHICAGO
SPECIAL

In Chicago, if you see a pizza on the menu called the Special, it's probably going to have this combination of toppings and maybe a few extras. This stuffed pizza is a favorite of many Chicagoans and these topings are a staple at every Chicago pizzeria.

Three 290-gram balls Chicago Tavern dough (page 66)

10 ounces (285 g) Italian sausage, bulk or casing removed

1 pound (450 g) whole-milk mozzarella cheese, shredded

½ medium green bell pepper, thinly sliced

½ small Spanish or yellow onion, thinly sliced

¼ cup (25 g) Sautéed Mushrooms (page 223)

1½ cups (350 ml) Rustic Hand-Crushed Pizza Sauce (page 79), plus more if needed

¼ cup (30 g) grated Parmesan cheese, preferably Parmigiano-Reggiano

Remove the dough from the refrigerator and place it on the counter to proof until the dough temperature reads 55 to 60°F (13 to 16°C) using an instant-read thermometer, typically about 2 hours, or until dough has doubled in size.

One hour before baking the pizza, slide one rack into the lowest position of the oven and a second rack into the middle of the oven, leaving 6 to 8 inches (15 to 20 cm) between the racks. Place a pizza stone or steel on each rack and preheat the oven to 475°F (245°C).

Following the directions for panning Chicago stuffed pizza on page 45, grease a 12-inch (30 cm) pizza pan with 2-inch (5 cm) sides with solid vegetable shortening. Press two dough balls together and roll out ¼ inch (6 mm) thick, then lay the dough in the prepared pan as directed.

Pinch the sausage into quarter-size chunks, press each one flat, and distribute them evenly across the dough-lined pan. Spread the mozzarella evenly on top of the sausage and then shake the pan gently so the cheese fills any gaps. Layer the bell pepper, onion, and mushrooms on top of the mozzarella in an even layer.

Roll out the remaining dough and gently lay it on top, extending it onto the bottom layer's overhang. Press the top layer against the bottom along the side walls to seal securely. Finally, pinch five or six small holes in the center to vent steam during baking.

Holding a sharp knife at an angle, trim the excess dough with a smooth slide along the pan rim to create a clean, even edge. Discard the scraps.

Ladle the sauce onto the center of the dough, shaking the pan until it flows uniformly to the edges. Add more sauce by the tablespoon if needed, ensuring no white dough is visible.

Sprinkle the Parmesan over the sauce, then transfer the pan to the stone or steel on the lowest rack. Bake for 20 to 22 minutes, or until the crust is golden brown.

Remove the pan from the oven and, using an offset spatula, lift the pizza out of the pan and place on a cooling rack.

After a few minutes, transfer the pizza to a cutting board. Using a rocking pizza cutter or a long, sharp knife, cut into slices and serve.

PIZZA
RUSTICA

This southern Italian Easter pie made its way to the United States and eventually evolved into the first stuffed pizza. This pizza has no sauce on top, and the flaky exterior is the perfect vessel for the creamy egg-and-ricotta filling dotted with chunks of salumi (cured meats) and smoked scamorza cheese. It calls for the Chicago Pan dough, which you will need to form into a 400-gram ball and a 300-gram ball especially for this recipe.

One 400-gram ball Chicago Pan dough (page 64) for the bottom layer

One 300-gram ball Chicago Pan ball (page 64) for the top layer

1 pound 6 ounces (625 g) assorted salumi, such as soppressata, salami, and prosciutto cotto, cut into ¼-inch (6 mm) cubes

10 ounces (285 g) smoked scamorza or smoked mozzarella cheese, cut into ¼-inch (6 mm) cubes

6 ounces (170 g) whole-milk mozzarella cheese, cut into ¼-inch (6 mm) cubes

1 pound (450 g) whole-milk ricotta cheese

5 large eggs, beaten with a pinch of red pepper flakes

1 egg, beaten with 1 tablespoon water for egg wash

Remove the dough from the refrigerator and place it on the counter to proof until the dough temperature reads 55 to 60°F (13 to 16°C) using an instant-read thermometer, typically about 2 hours, or until dough has doubled in size.

One hour before baking the pizza, slide one rack into the lowest position of the oven and a second rack into the middle of the oven, leaving 6 to 8 inches (15 to 20 cm) between the racks. Place a pizza stone or steel on each rack and preheat the oven to 400°F (200°C).

Following the directions for panning Chicago stuffed pizza on page 45, grease a 12-inch (30 cm) pizza pan with 2-inch (5 cm) sides with solid vegetable shortening. Roll out the dough for the bottom layer to ¼ inch (6 mm) thick, then lay the dough in the prepared pan as directed, ensuring that the bottom dough hangs over the edges of the pan.

In a large bowl, combine the salumi, scamorza, mozzarella, ricotta, and eggs and stir until well mixed.

Pour the egg mixture into the dough-lined pan and, using a rubber spatula, press against the surface to remove any air pockets.

Roll out the dough for the top layer to ¼ inch (6 mm) thick, then gently lay the dough on top of the pan. Using your fingers, pull the edges of the bottom dough layer over the top layer, then pinch the two layers to seal, forming a crimped edge similar to a rustic pie crust. Using a fork, poke the top dough layer in the center and the four corners to allow excess moisture to escape. Using a pastry brush, brush the entire top dough with egg wash.

Transfer the pan to the stone or steel on the lowest oven rack and bake the pizza for about 1 hour, or until the crust has browned and the interior registers 145°F (63°C) when tested with an instant-read thermometer.

Remove the pizza from the oven and place on a cooling rack to cool for 1 hour. Once near room temperature, transfer to a clean cutting board to cut and serve.

THE HEARTSTOPPER

Here is the king of Chiago pizzas for meat lovers! The only person who will love this pizza more is your cardiologist.

Three 290-gram balls Chicago Tavern dough (page 66)

8 ounces (225 g) Italian sausage, bulk or casing removed

4 ounces (115 g) Canadian bacon, sliced ¼ inch (6 mm) thick, then slices halved

1 pound (450 g) whole-milk mozzarella cheese, shredded

1½ cups (350 ml) Rustic Hand-Crushed Sauce (page 79), plus more if needed

3 slices applewood-smoked bacon, cut into 1-inch (2.5 cm) pieces

2 ounces (60 g) sliced pepperoni

¼ cup (30 g) grated Parmesan cheese, preferably Parmigiano-Reggiano

Remove the dough from the refrigerator and place it on the counter to proof until the dough temperature reads 55 to 60°F (13 to 16°C) using an instant-read thermometer, typically about 2 hours, or until dough has doubled in size.

One hour before baking the pizza, slide one rack into the lowest position of the oven and a second rack into the middle of the oven, leaving 6 to 8 inches (15 to 20 cm) between the racks. Place a pizza stone or steel on each rack and preheat the oven to 475°F (245°C).

Following the directions for panning Chicago stuffed pizza on page 45, grease a 12-inch (30 cm) pizza pan with 2-inch (5 cm) sides with solid vegetable shortening. Press two dough balls together and roll out ¼ inch (6 mm) thick, then lay the dough in the prepared pan as directed.

Pinch the sausage into quarter-size chunks, press each one flat, and distribute them evenly across the dough-lined pan. Layer the Canadian bacon on top. Spread the mozzarella evenly on top of the meats and then shake the pan gently so the cheese fills any gaps.

Roll out the remaining dough and gently lay it on top, extending it onto the bottom layer's overhang. Press the top layer against the bottom along the side walls to seal securely. Finally, pinch five or six small holes in the center to vent steam during baking.

Using a sharp knife held at an angle, trim the excess dough cleanly along the pan rim and discard the scraps.

Ladle the sauce onto the dough's center, shaking the pan until it flows uniformly to the edges. Add more sauce by the tablespoon if needed, ensuring no white dough is visible.

Layer the applewood-smoked bacon and then the pepperoni evenly on top of the sauce, then sprinkle with the Parmesan.

Transfer the pan to the stone or steel on the lowest oven rack and bake the pizza for 20 to 22 minutes, or until the crust is golden brown.

Remove the pan from the oven and, using an offset spatula, lift the pizza out of the pan and place on a cooling rack.

After a few minutes, transfer the pizza to a cutting board. Using a rocking pizza cutter or a long, sharp knife, cut into slices and serve.

THE BIG MEATY

This deep-dish pizza is a tribute to the famous Lou Malnati's Pizzeria. The Malnati family helped shape the pizza scene in Chicago, and their pizzas are now enjoyed all around the country. This sausage pizza is the stuff of legends, with a large slab of sausage covering the entire pizza. If you love Italian sausage, you have to try this one.

One 530-gram ball Chicago Pan dough (page 64)

10 ounces (285 g) whole-milk mozzarella cheese, sliced ¼ inch (6 mm) thick, then slices halved

1 pound (450 g) Italian sausage, bulk or casing removed

1½ cups (350 ml) Rustic Hand-Crushed Sauce (page 79), plus more if needed

¼ cup (30 g) grated Parmesan cheese, preferably Parmigiano-Reggiano

Remove the dough from the refrigerator and place it on the counter to proof until the dough temperature reads 55 to 60°F (13 to 16°C) using an instant-read thermometer, typically about 2 hours, or until dough has doubled in size.

One hour before baking the pizza, slide one rack into the lowest position of the oven and a second rack into the middle of the oven, leaving 6 to 8 inches (15 to 20 cm) between the racks. Place a pizza stone or steel on each rack and preheat the oven to 475°F (245°C).

Following the directions for panning deep-dish pizza on page 45, grease a 12-inch (30 cm) pizza pan with 2-inch (5 cm) sides with solid vegetable shortening. Press the dough onto the bottom and up the sides of the prepared pan, making the dough an even ¼ inch (6 mm) thick.

Starting at the outer edge of the pan, lay the mozzarella slices along the sides and across the base of the dough as directed.

Line the bottom of a 12-inch (30 cm) round pizza pan with plastic wrap, then, using your fingers, grease the plastic wrap with a little olive oil. Put the sausage on top of the plastic wrap and, using your fingers, gently press the sausage into a uniform 12-inch (30 cm) disk.

Flip the pan with the sausage disk upside down on top of the pan with the mozzarella and dough. Gently pull down on the edge of the plastic wrap; it should release along with the sausage directly on top of the mozzarella. Lift off the pan and then peel away the plastic wrap from the sausage. Adjust the edges of the sausage disk as needed for the disk to be evenly seated inside the dough on top of the mozzarella.

Using a ladle, add the sauce to the center of the pizza and then spread it evenly to the edges. If the pizza is not evenly covered with sauce, add a couple tablespoons at a time until no bare spots remain. Sprinkle evenly with the Parmesan.

Transfer the pan to the stone on the lowest oven rack and bake the pizza for 20 to 22 minutes, or until the crust is golden brown.

Remove the pan from the oven and, using an offset spatula, lift the pizza out of the pan and place on a cooling rack. After a few minutes, transfer the pizza to a cutting board. Using a rocking pizza cutter or a long, sharp knife, cut into slices and serve.

THE COMBO

Combo is the name of a famous Chicago sandwich that features Italian sausage and Italian beef. This deep-dish pizza is a tribute to that sandwich. Of course, no combo would be complete without some spicy giardiniera on top.

One 530-gram ball Chicago Pan dough (page 64)

10 ounces (285 g) whole-milk mozzarella cheese, sliced ¼ inch (6 mm) thick, then slices halved

6 ounces (170 g) Italian sausage, bulk or casing removed

4 ounces (115 g) Italian-style roast beef or deli roast beef, thinly sliced

1½ cups (350 ml) Rustic Hand-Crushed Sauce (page 79), plus more if needed

½ cup (75 g) Homemade Giardiniera (page 220), drained, chopped, with oil reserved for drizzling

¼ cup (30 g) grated Parmesan cheese, preferably Parmigiano-Reggiano

Remove the dough from the refrigerator and place it on the counter to proof until the dough temperature reads 55 to 60°F (13 to 16°C) using an instant-read thermometer, typically about 2 hours, or until dough has doubled in size.

One hour before baking the pizza, slide one rack into the lowest position of the oven and a second rack into the middle of the oven, leaving 6 to 8 inches (15 to 20 cm) between the racks. Place a pizza stone or steel on each rack and preheat the oven to 475°F (245°C).

Following the directions for panning deep-dish pizza on page 45, grease a 12-inch (30 cm) pizza pan with 2-inch (5 cm) sides with solid vegetable shortening. Press the dough onto the bottom and up the sides of the prepared pan, making the dough an even ¼ inch (6 mm) thick.

Starting at the outer edge of the pan, lay the mozzarella slices along the sides and across the base of the dough as directed. Next, pinch the sausage into quarter-size chunks, press each one flat, and distribute them evenly over the mozzarella. Layer the beef over the sausage.

Using a ladle, add the sauce to the center of the pizza and then spread it evenly to the edges. If the pizza is not evenly covered with sauce, add a couple tablespoons at a time until no bare spots remain. Spread the giardiniera evenly on top of the sauce, followed by the Parmesan.

Transfer the pan to the stone or steel on the lowest oven rack and bake the pizza for 20 to 22 minutes, or until the crust is golden brown.

Remove the pan from the oven and, using an offset spatula, lift the pizza out of the pan and place on a cooling rack.

After a few minutes, transfer the pizza to a cutting board. Using a rocking pizza cutter or a long, sharp knife, cut into slices and serve.

Spizzirri

PIZZA
ALFREDO

Years ago, a pizza maker named Al worked for me, and he wanted to be Italian so badly that I decided to tease him by nicknaming him Alfredo. I called him Alfredo so much that the name stuck, and everyone began calling him Alfredo. In time, he passed away following a terminal illness, and a benefit was held in his honor to help his family recover from the financial burden his treatments had put on their household. This is the pizza I created for that occasion. People went nuts for it, and soon it was popping up on menus all over the city. Like Oscar Wilde said, "Imitation is the sincerest form of flattery."

One 530-gram ball Chicago Pan dough (page 64)

10 ounces (285 g) whole-milk mozzarella cheese, sliced ¼ inch (6 mm) thick, then slices halved

¾ cups (180 ml) Creamy White Sauce (page 81)

3 fresh basil leaves, torn

½ cup (60 g) grated Parmesan cheese, preferably Parmigiano-Reggiano

½ cup (85 g) shredded roasted chicken (store-bought rotisserie or leftovers will do)

½ cup (90 g) drained Marinated Artichoke Hearts (page 227)

¼ cup (35 g) roasted red pepper strips (see Marinated Roasted Red Peppers, page 219, omitting the marinade)

¼ cup (35 g) feta crumbles

Extra-virgin olive oil for drizzling

Remove the dough from the refrigerator and place it on the counter to proof until the dough temperature reads 55 to 60°F (13 to 16°C) using an instant-read thermometer, typically about 2 hours, or until dough has doubled in size.

One hour before baking the pizza, slide one rack into the lowest position of the oven and a second rack into the middle of the oven, leaving 6 to 8 inches (15 to 20 cm) between the racks. Place a pizza stone or steel on each rack and preheat the oven to 475°F (245°C).

Following the directions for panning deep-dish pizza on page 45, grease a 12-inch (30 cm) pizza pan with 2-inch (5 cm) sides with solid vegetable shortening. Press the dough onto the bottom and up the sides of the prepared pan, making the dough an even ¼ inch (6 mm) thick.

Starting at the outer edge of the pan, lay the mozzarella slices along the sides and across the base of the dough as directed.

Using a ladle, spread the sauce evenly over the mozzarella. Scatter the basil over the sauce followed by the Parmesan. Then distribute the chicken evenly across the pizza followed by the artichoke hearts and then the red peppers. Finally, sprinkle with the feta and finish with a drizzle of oil.

Transfer the pan to the stone or steel on the lowest oven rack and bake for 18 to 20 minutes, or until the crust is golden brown.

Remove the pan from the oven and, using an offset spatula, lift the pizza out of the pan and place on a cooling rack.

After a few minutes, transfer the pizza to a cutting board. Using a rocking pizza cutter or a long, sharp knife, cut into slices and serve.

CALZONE, STROMBOLI, AND FOCACCIA

Now that you've gotten this far into your pizza-making voyage, why not learn some of the other essentials of any great pizzeria. Here are some of the most requested recipes from my students that aren't a traditional pizza but are nice to have in your back pocket for a rainy day. These can even be made a day ahead and stored in the refrigerator, then rewarmed for a quick snack or a fun appetizer for your next dinner party. Just place them on a baking sheet and pop them into a 425°F (220°C) oven for 10 to 15 minutes, to get the cheese centers remelted or the outsides crispy again.

STROMBOLI

This recipe is the classic formula, but once you learn how to assemble a stromboli, the sky's the limit when it comes to the ingredients you can bake inside. I love to make stromboli by the dozen ahead of time, so when I'm having people over, I just pop them into the oven for 5 minutes to rewarm and then cut them up for appetizers just before the doorbell rings.

One 270-gram ball Classic New York dough (page 68)

2 ounces (60 g) provolone cheese, sliced (2 slices)

¼ cup (35 g) roasted red pepper strips (see Marinated Roasted Red Peppers, page 219, omitting the marinade)

1 ounce (30 g) Genoa salami, sliced (6 slices)

4 thin slices oven-roasted turkey breast

3 thin slices Black Forest ham

2 thin slices whole-milk mozzarella cheese

1 large egg beaten with 1 teaspoon water for egg wash

Sesame seeds for finishing (optional)

Remove the dough from the refrigerator and place it on the counter to proof until the dough temperature reads 55 to 60°F (13 to 16°C) using an instant-read thermometer, typically about 2 hours, or until dough has doubled in size.

One hour before baking the stromboli, slide one rack into the lowest position of the oven and a second rack into the middle of the oven, leaving 6 to 8 inches (15 to 20 cm) between the racks. Place a pizza stone or steel on each rack and preheat the oven to 500°F (260°C) or the highest setting.

When ready to bake, using the method on page 42, gently remove the dough ball from its container, dredge it in a mixture of flour and fine semolina flour, place it on a well-floured work surface, and stretch it to about 12 inches (30 cm), creating a uniform thickness, then square off the edges to make a rectangle.

Layer the provolone, roasted peppers, salami, turkey, and ham in a lengthwise strip along the center of the rectangle. Top evenly with the mozzarella. Make sure to keep the ingredients in the center, using the bottom layer of provolone as your guide.

Pull the edge of the dough closest to you over the filling. Now turn the stromboli over so it rests on the uncovered dough farthest from you. This gives the stromboli its classic shape.

Line a sheet pan and transfer the stromboli. Use scissors to trim the excess dough from the long sides, exposing the filling. Slice three deep, evenly spaced slits into the top crust with a serrated knife to allow moisture to escape. Brush with the egg wash and sprinkle with sesame seeds, if using.

Transfer the pan to the stone or steel on the lowest oven rack and bake the stromboli for 12 to 14 minutes, or until the crust is golden brown.

Remove the stromboli from the oven and transfer it to a cooling rack using an offset spatula. For easier slicing into pieces, wait about 5 minutes before moving it to a cutting board and cutting it with a serrated knife.

TRADITIONAL
ITALIAN CALZONE: RIPIENO

This is my take on the classic *ripieno* from Napoli. Once you learn the principles of stretching the dough into a thin, even layer and then closing the edge properly, you can fill it with any combination of ingredients you like.

One 290-gram ball Neapolitan dough (page 55)

½ cup (115 g) whole-milk ricotta cheese

1 ounce (30 g) fior di latte mozzarella cheese, cubed (1 heaping tablespoon; see page 48)

1 ounce (30 g) Neapolitan salami, julienned (scant ¼ cup)

¼ cup (30 g) grated Parmesan cheese, preferably Parmigiano-Reggiano

4 fresh basil leaves, torn in half

½ teaspoon freshly cracked black pepper

¼ cup (60 ml) Neapolitan Sauce (page 75)

Remove the dough from the refrigerator and place it on the counter to proof until the dough temperature reads 55 to 60°F (13 to 16°C) using an instant-read thermometer, typically about 2 hours, or until dough has doubled in size.

One hour before baking the ripieno, position a rack in the middle of the oven (8 to 10 inches [20 to 25 cm] from the heat source), place a pizza stone or steel on the rack, and preheat the oven to 500°F (260°C) or the highest setting.

When ready to bake, lightly dust a pizza peel with all-purpose flour or fine semolina and set to the side. Using the method on page 42, gently remove the dough ball from its container, dredge it in flour, place it on a well-floured work surface, and stretch it into a 12-inch (30 cm) round, pressing the dough to the edges to make a flat, uniform surface. Transfer the stretched dough to the peel.

Working quickly on the half of the dough closest to you, spread the ricotta evenly over the surface, leaving a 1-inch (2.5 cm) border. Layer the mozzarella and salami evenly on top, then sprinkle with the Parmesan, basil, and pepper.

Carefully lift the dough's far edge and pull it over the fillings, matching it to the near edge to form a half-moon. Do not overstretch or the dough will burn. Starting from one side, press the edges with your fingertips to seal them securely, lightly pressing the middle to release any trapped air. Avoid pressing filling into the edges. Trim the excess dough neatly with a pizza cutter.

Once the edges are sealed, gently press lengthwise along the middle of the *ripieno* to create a shallow pocket, then spoon the sauce into the pocket, taking care not to drip it down the sides.

Slide the ripieno off the peel onto the stone or steel (see page 42) and bake for 10 to 12 minutes, or until the crust is blistered and the sauce is charred on the edges.

Use the peel to remove the *ripieno* and place it on a cooling rack. For easier slicing, let it cool for about 5 minutes before transferring it to a cutting board and serving.

TRADITIONAL
NEW YORK CALZONE

Although the calzone has its roots in Italy, once it hit the United States, it never looked back. The classic calzone is stuffed with ricotta, and my version is built from that tradition.

One 270-gram ball Classic New York dough (page 68)

2 ounces (60 g) whole-milk mozzarella cheese, shredded

1 cup (225 g) Whipped Ricotta (page 229)

2 tablespoons All-American Sauce (page 80)

2 ounces (60 g) Italian sausage, bulk or casing removed

1 teaspoon grated pecorino romano cheese, preferably Locatelli

1 large egg beaten with 1 teaspoon water for egg wash

Sesame seeds for finishing (optional)

Remove the dough from the refrigerator and place it on the counter to proof until the dough temperature reads 55 to 60°F (13 to 16°C) using an instant-read thermometer, typically about 2 hours, or until dough has doubled in size.

One hour before baking the calzone, slide one rack into the lowest position of the oven and a second rack into the middle of the oven, leaving 6 to 8 inches (15 to 20 cm) between the racks. Place a pizza stone or steel on each rack and preheat the oven to 500°F (260°C) or the highest setting.

When ready to bake, using the method on page 42, gently remove the dough ball from its container, dredge it in a mixture of flour and fine semolina flour, place it on a well-floured work surface, and stretch it into a 12-inch (30 cm) round, creating a uniform surface.

Working on the half of the dough closest to you, lay down the mozzarella slices, leaving a 1-inch (2.5 cm) border. Spread the ricotta evenly over the mozzarella, then spoon the sauce lengthwise down the center. Pinch the sausage into quarter-size chunks, flatten them, and distribute evenly. Sprinkle with the pecorino. Keep all fillings off the 1-inch border.

Lift the far edge and fold it over the fillings, matching the near edge to form a half-moon; avoid stretching the dough too thin. Press the edges firmly with your fingertips to seal, working around the dough while gently pressing the middle to release trapped air. (Avoid forcing filling into the edges.) Trim the excess dough neatly with a pizza cutter.

Line a sheet pan, transfer the calzone, and brush it with the egg wash before sprinkling with sesame seeds (if using). Use scissors to snip three evenly spaced holes into the top to allow moisture to escape during baking.

Transfer the pan to the stone or steel on the lowest oven rack and bake the calzone for 10 to 12 minutes, or until crust is golden brown.

Remove the pan from the oven and, using an offset spatula, transfer the calzone to a cooling rack. When ready to cut, transfer to a clean cutting board, cut and serve. If cutting more than just in half, it's easier to cut into slices after baking for about 5 minutes on the cooling rack using a serrated knife.

TOMATO FOCACCIA

This tomato focaccia is my personal go-to when I need a great starter or accompaniment for a dinner party or a good addition to a grazing table. I look for the best fresh tomatoes and prefer cherry tomatoes on the vine when available. By starting with very ripe tomatoes and then cutting and marinating them, the juice that's released and sitting in the bottom of the bowl creates a slightly sweet and charred top once the focaccia is baked. I use the juice as the last topping on the focaccia before it goes into the oven, so don't throw any of it out. This focaccia is light and spongy in the middle and crispy on the bottom and top. It's what everyone knows and loves when they hear the word *focaccia*.

One 700-gram ball Detroit pan dough, traditional (page 71) or contemperay with poolish (page 70)

About 15 cherry tomatoes, halved (see page 48)

½ cup (120 ml) extra-virgin olive oil, plus more for drizzling

1 teaspoon dried oregano

1 tablespoon kosher salt

Garlic Oil (page 227) for drizzling

¼ cup (30 g) grated Parmesan cheese

Remove the dough from the refrigerator and place it on the counter to proof until the dough temperature reads 55 to 60°F (13 to 16°C) using an instant-read thermometer, typically about 2 hours, or until dough has doubled in size.

One hour before baking the focaccia, slide one rack into the lowest position of the oven and a second rack into the middle of the oven, leaving 6 to 8 inches between the racks. Place a pizza stone or steel on each rack and preheat the oven to 475°F (245°C).

In a small bowl, combine the tomatoes, olive oil, oregano, and salt and stir to mix. Set aside to marinate.

Grease the bottom and sides of a 10-by-14-inch (25 by 35 cm) pan with solid vegetable shortening.

Using a bench scraper, transfer the dough ball to a lightly oiled work surface. Using the pads of your fingertips, gently dimple the dough, stretching it as you work, until it is about the same dimensions as the pan.

Slide the backs of both hands under the dough and, using caution not to overstretch the middle, lift the dough off the work surface and carefully lay it onto the center of the pan in a uniform layer. Press the dough as needed so it reaches the sides and into the corners of the pan. Cover the pan with plastic wrap and let the dough proof in a warm area of your kitchen for up to 1 hour, or until the dough has risen halfway up the sides of the pan.

CONTINUED

Uncover the pan and scatter the marinated tomatoes evenly across the dough. Then gently push the tomatoes into the dough. Drizzle any liquid remaining in the bowl evenly over the top of the focaccia, then drizzle with a little olive oil. The top of the dough should appear slightly damp and the excess tomato juices and oil should pool in the dimples created by your fingers. Cover the pan with plastic wrap and proof the dough in a warm area of your kitchen for 30 minutes.

Uncover the pan, transfer it to the stone or steel on the lowest oven rack, and bake the focaccia for 15 to 18 minutes, or until the crust is golden brown and the tomatoes are slightly charred.

Remove the pan from the oven and, using an offset spatula, lift the focaccia out of the pan and transfer to a cooling rack. Drizzle the focaccia with Garlic Oil and sprinkle with the Parmesan. The residual heat of the focaccia will melt the cheese a bit.

When ready to cut, transfer the focaccia to cutting board. Using a serrated knife, cut into squares and serve.

FOCACCIA
RIPIENA

This is literally the most insane sandwich you'll ever eat. I saw it the first time while I was in Rome and went to bed that night and dreamed about it. This classic is stuffed with mortadella and burrata cheese. It is all about the bread, and I love to use the Roman pan dough with biga for it.

Two 627-gram balls Roman pan dough, traditional (page 59) or contemporary with biga (page 61)

¾ cup (180 ml) extra-virgin olive oil, preferably Partanna from Sicily, divided

10 ounces (285 g) mortadella with pistachios, thinly sliced (24 slices)

1 pound (450 g) burrata cheese

4 cups (60 g) loosely packed arugula

2 tablespoons pistachio nuts, chopped

2 tablespoons grated Parmesan cheese, preferably Parmigiano-Reggiano

Remove the dough from the refrigerator and place it on the counter to proof until the dough temperature reads 55 to 60°F (13 to 16°C) using an instant-read thermometer, typically about 2 hours, or until dough has doubled in size.

One hour before baking the focaccia, slide one rack into the lowest position of the oven and a second rack into the middle of the oven, leaving 6 to 8 inches between the racks. Place a pizza stone or steel on each rack and preheat the oven to 500°F (260°C) or the highest setting.

When ready to bake, using the Roman panning method on page 46, dimple and stretch each dough ball separately and then lay one stretched dough in a 12-by-16-inch (30 by 40 cm) pan.

Drizzle the dough in the pan with ½ cup of the oil, then carefully place the second stretched dough on top, covering the bottom dough completely. Using your fingers, dimple the two doughs together. Drizzle the top dough with more olive oil.

Transfer the pan to the stone or steel on the lowest oven rack and bake the focaccia for 10 to 12 minutes, or until the crust is golden brown.

Remove the pan from the oven and, using an offset spatula, lift the focaccia out of the pan and place on a cooling rack. Carefully pull the top crust off the bottom crust. Use caution, as the steam released from between the layers is very hot.

Arrange the mortadella slices lengthwise on the bottom crust in four rows of six slices each, covering as much of the crust as possible. Break up the burrata into pieces and dollop the filling across the mortadella, slipping the curds into any gaps. Scatter the arugula evenly on top, then drizzle with the remaining oil and sprinkle with the pistachios and Parmesan.

Using the spatula, carefully transfer the loaded bottom crust to a cutting board. Close with the top crust and, using a serrated knife, cut into 6 to 8 pieces, and serve.

ROMANA ROSSA

This red-top focaccia can be used as a bread on its own or as the base for a pizza. As the tomato sauce cooks during the bake, it becomes concentrated and more robust. The balance between bread and sauce makes this a great favorite.

One 627-gram ball Roman pan dough, traditional (page 59) or contemporary with biga (page 61)

1 cup (240 ml) Rustic Hand-Crushed Sauce (page 79)

1 tablespoon dried oregano

1 tablespoon flake sea salt, preferably Maldon

½ cup (120 ml) extra-virgin olive oil, preferably Partanna from Sicily

Remove the dough from the refrigerator and place it on the counter to proof until the dough temperature reads 55 to 60°F (13 to 16°C) using an instant-read thermometer, typically about 2 hours, or until dough has doubled in size.

One hour before baking the focaccia, slide one rack into the lowest position of the oven and a second rack into the middle of the oven, leaving 6 to 8 inches (15 to 20 cm) between the racks. Place a pizza stone or steel on each rack and preheat the oven to 500°F (260°C) or the highest setting.

When ready to bake, using the Roman panning method on page 46, dimple and stretch the dough and then lay it in a 12-by-16-inch (30 by 40 cm) pan.

Using a ladle, top the dough with the sauce, spreading it evenly over the surface. Using your fingers as described on page 47, continue to spread the sauce until it fills any little hollows and the dough is evenly covered. Sprinkle with oregano and salt, then drizzle evenly with the oil.

Transfer the pan to the stone or steel on the lowest oven rack and bake the focaccia for 12 to 14 minutes, or until the edges are golden brown and the sauce is concentrated.

Remove the pan from the oven and, using an offset spatula, lift the focaccia out of the pan and place on a cooling rack. When ready to cut, transfer to a clean cutting board, cut, and serve.

ROMANA BIANCA

This versatile focaccia can be used as a side dish on its own or as the base for a pizza. It's also amazing split open horizontally and used as the bread for your favorite sandwich. The best part is that even when it's a day old and starting to go stale, it can be cut up, toasted, and used for breadcrumbs or croutons.

One 627-gram ball Roman pan dough, traditional (page 59) or contemporary with biga (page 61)

½ cup (120 ml) extra-virgin olive oil, preferably Partanna from Sicily

Leaves from 1 fresh rosemary sprig

1 tablespoon flake sea salt, preferably Maldon

Remove the dough from the refrigerator and place it on the counter to proof until the dough temperature reads 55 to 60°F (13 to 16°C) using an instant-read thermometer, typically about 2 hours, or until dough has doubled in size.

One hour before baking the focaccia, slide one rack into the lowest position of the oven and a second rack into the middle of the oven, leaving 6 to 8 inches (15 to 20 cm) between the racks. Place a pizza stone or steel on each rack and preheat the oven to 500°F (260°C) or the highest setting.

When ready to bake, using the Roman panning method on page 46, dimple and stretch the dough and then lay it in a 12-by-16-inch (30 to 40 cm) pan.

Drizzle the dough with the oil, then sprinkle with the rosemary and salt.

Transfer the pan to the stone or steel on the lowest oven rack and bake the focaccia for 12 to 14 minutes, or until golden brown.

Remove the pan from the oven and, using an offset spatula, lift the focaccia out the pan and place onto a cooling rack. When ready to cut, transfer to a clean cutting board, cut, and serve.

Spizzirri

ESSENTIAL STASH

How could I give you a book full of my favorite pizzas without my arsenal of essential secret-stash recipes as well? From my must-have chicken cutlets to my grandmother's meatballs, this section will take your pizza game to another level! These are all simple enough to follow, and the ingredients can be found in most grocery stores. You'll be amazed at how easy they are to make, and the flavors and quality will be much better than what you will find premade.

TOASTED BREADCRUMBS

YIELD: ABOUT 1 CUP (100 G)

TIME: ABOUT 25 MINUTES

4 tablespoons unsalted butter

1 oil-packed anchovy fillet, drained

2 tablespoons minced shallot

1 cup (100 g) panko breadcrumbs

1 garlic clove, minced

Grated zest of 1 lemon

1 tablespoon fresh lemon juice

2 tablespoons bottled clam juice

2 tablespoons grated pecorino romano cheese, preferable Locatelli

1 tablespoon finely chopped fresh flat-leaf parsley

Pinch ground black pepper

Pinch red pepper flakes

In a medium sauté pan over medium-high heat, combine the butter, anchovy fillet, and shallot. As the butter melts and then begins to bubble, stir with a wooden spoon until the anchovy breaks up and melts into the butter. Continue stirring for about 3 to 4 minutes, or until the shallot is translucent.

Add the breadcrumbs and stir constantly for about 3 to 4 minutes, or until they are browned and crispy.

Remove the pan from the heat and stir in the garlic, lemon zest and juice, clam juice, pecorino, parsley, black pepper, and pepper flakes. Continue to stir until the liquids are absorbed and then return the pan to medium-high heat and heat, stirring constantly, for about 1 minute to finish toasting.

Remove the pan from the heat and let the breadcrumbs cool completely. Store in an airtight container in the refrigerator for up to 7 days.

MARINATED TOMATOES

YIELD: ABOUT 2 CUPS (500 G)
TIME: ABOUT 10 MINUTES

1 pound (450 g) Roma or plum tomatoes, cut into ½-inch (1 cm) dice

¼ cup (60 ml) extra-virgin olive oil

1 tablespoon balsamic vinegar

1 tablespoon dried oregano

1 garlic clove, chopped

½ teaspoon sea salt

In a medium bowl, combine the tomatoes, oil, vinegar, oregano, garlic, and salt. Using a rubber spatula, gently stir from the bottom of the bowl over the top of the tomatoes so as not to break up the tomato pieces too much.

Store in an airtight container in the refrigerator for up to 48 hours.

MARINATED ROASTED RED PEPPERS

YIELD: ABOUT 1 CUP (170 G)
TIME: ABOUT 50 MINUTES

3 large red bell peppers

1 teaspoon kosher salt

1 teaspoon dried oregano

1 tablespoon chopped fresh flat-leaf parsley

1 garlic clove, finely chopped

Pinch red pepper flakes (optional)

½ cup (120 ml) extra-virgin olive oil

Preheat the oven to 350°F (180°C). Line a sheet pan with aluminum foil.

Place the bell peppers on the center of the prepared pan, spacing them a few inches apart. Transfer to the oven and roast for about 25 minutes, or until the skins are charred and wrinkled and the peppers have collapsed.

Remove the pan from the oven, transfer the peppers to a large brown-paper bag, and roll the top of the bag closed to create a seal. The peppers will steam in the closed bag, making them easier to peel later. Put the paper bag on the sheet pan and leave the pan on the counter for 20 minutes.

Carefully open the bag and remove the peppers, which should now be cool enough to handle. Using your fingers, peel off and discard the charred skin from each pepper. Cut each pepper in half lengthwise and remove the stem, seeds, and white pithy ribs. Then cut lengthwise into ½-inch-long (1 cm long) strips.

CONTINUED

Transfer the strips to a medium bowl. Add the salt, oregano, parsley, garlic, red pepper flakes (if using), and oil and toss to coat evenly.

Store the peppers in an airtight container in the refrigerator for up to 1 week.

HOMEMADE GIARDINIERA

YIELD: ABOUT 4 CUPS (600 G)
TIME: ABOUT 3 HOURS (INCLUDES 2 HOURS STEEPING TIME)

5 carrots, peeled and cut into 1-inch (2.5 cm) dice

5 celery stalks, cut into 1-inch (2.5 cm) dice

1 head cauliflower, stemmed, cored, and cut into 1-inch (2.5 cm) dice

1 red bell pepper, cut into 1-inch (2.5 cm) dice

½ cup kosher salt

1½ cups (350 ml) distilled white vinegar

1½ cups (350 ml) white wine vinegar

2 tablespoons dried oregano

1 tablespoon red pepper flakes

1 teaspoon coarse-ground black pepper

2 serrano chiles, stemmed and chopped

3 jalapeño chiles, stemmed and chopped

½ habanero chile (optional)

2 cups (475 ml) extra-virgin olive oil

In a large heatproof bowl, combine the carrots, celery, cauliflower, and bell pepper.

In a medium saucepan over high heat, combine both vinegars, the oregano, red pepper flakes, black pepper, serrano and jalapeño chiles, and the habanero, if using, and bring to a boil. Remove from the heat.

Pour the hot vinegar mixture evenly over the vegetables and let steep for 2 hours at room temperature until cool.

Drain the vegetables into a fine-mesh sieve placed over a medium bowl. Discard the liquid.

Return the vegetables to the large bowl, add the oil, and toss and stir to coat evenly.

Store in an airtight container in the refrigerator for up to 5 days.

CHICKEN CUTLETS

YIELD: ABOUT 4 TO 5 CUTLETS
TIME: ABOUT 40 MINUTES

Olive oil for frying

1 cup (115 g) all-purpose flour

4 large eggs

Kosher salt and ground black pepper

2 cups (200 g) unseasoned dried breadcrumbs

2 tablespoons dried parsley

¼ cup (30 g) grated pecorino romano cheese, preferably Locatelli

4 to 5 boneless, skinless chicken breasts, sliced widthwise and pounded with a meat mallet

Pour oil to a depth of 1 inch (2.5 cm) into a medium sauté pan and heat over medium-high heat to 375°F (190°C) on a deep-frying thermometer. Line a sheet pan with paper towels and set it near the stove.

While the oil is heating, set up a breading station: Arrange three shallow medium bowls side by side. Put the flour into the bowl on the left. Crack the eggs into the middle bowl, beat until blended, and season with a pinch of salt. In the third bowl, add the breadcrumbs, parsley, pecorino cheese, 1 tablespoon salt, and 1 teaspoon pepper, and stir to mix well.

Sprinkle each chicken fillet with salt and pepper. Working with one fillet at a time, first dredge in the flour, tapping off the excess, and then coat both sides in the egg, allowing the excess to drip off. Finally, dredge the fillet in the breadcrumb mixture, coating on both sides and patting to adhere. Check to make sure the fillet is completely coated with the breadcrumbs and no eggy parts are visible. Set the breaded fillet aside on a sheet pan and repeat with the remaining fillets.

When the oil registers 375°F (190°C), add one breaded fillet to the pan and fry, turning once, for 3 to 4 minutes on each side, or until golden brown and cooked through. Using tongs, transfer to the towel-lined pan to drain. Repeat with the remaining breaded fillets, frying them one at a time and allowing the oil to return to 375°F (190°C) before each fillet is added.

Let the cutlets cool completely, then store in an airtight container in the refrigerator for up to 3 days.

HOMEMADE
MEATBALLS

YIELD: ABOUT 20 MEATBALLS
TIME: ABOUT 14 HOURS (INCLUDES 12 HOURS OVERNIGHT REST IN THE REFRIGERATOR)

1 pound (450 g) ground chuck

1 pound (450 g) Italian sausage, bulk or casing removed

1 pound (450 g) ground veal

4 ounces (115 g) day-old artisan bread, cut into ½-inch (1 cm) cubes

½ bunch fresh flat-leaf parsley, chopped

¾ cup (180 ml) whole milk

2 large eggs, beaten

1 garlic clove, minced

½ teaspoon ground black pepper

8 ounces (225 g) pecorino romano cheese, preferably Locatelli, grated

2 cups (475 g) Rustic Hand-Crushed Sauce (page 79)

In a large bowl, combine the ground chuck, sausage, and veal and mix well. Set aside.

In a medium bowl, combine the bread, parsley, milk, eggs, garlic, pepper, and cheese and stir until well blended. Let the bread soak for 30 minutes.

Fold the bread mixture into the meat mixture and mix until well blended. Cover the bowl with plastic wrap and refrigerate for 12 hours.

Preheat the oven to 400°F (200°C). Have ready a sheet pan.

To shape each meatball, scoop up about a golf ball size of the mixture and, using your hands, gently shape into a smooth ball. Set on the sheet pan. Repeat with the remaining meat mixture, arranging the balls in a single layer and spacing them about 1 inch (2.5 cm) apart. You should have about 20 meatballs.

Bake the meatballs for 30 to 40 minutes, or until an instant-read thermometer inserted into the center of a meatball registers 145°F (63°C).

Remove the pan from the oven and drain off any liquid.

If using that day, heat the sauce to warm and then place meatballs in sauce until ready to use. To store the meatballs for later use, let cool to room temperature on the pan, then transfer to an airtight container, add sauce and refrigerate for up to 5 days. To freeze the meatballs, line a clean sheet pan with parchment paper, arrange the cooled meatballs in a single layer on the parchment-lined pan, freeze until frozen solid, and then transfer to a ziplock bag and return to the freezer for up to two months.

CARAMELIZED
ONIONS

YIELD: ABOUT 2 CUPS (400 G)
TIME: ABOUT 25 MINUTES

¼ cup (60 ml) extra-virgin olive oil

1 garlic clove, chopped

1 oil-packed anchovy fillet, drained

2 large white onions (about 1 pound [450 g]), cut into ½-inch-thick (1 cm thick) slices

1 tablespoon kosher salt

In a medium sauté pan over medium-high heat, combine the oil, garlic, and anchovy fillet. Stir with a wooden spoon until the anchovy breaks up and melts into the oil.

Add the onions, stir to coat with the oil, and then sprinkle with the salt. Continue to cook over medium-high heat, stirring constantly, for about 10 to 12 minutes, or until the onions have turned a light brown color. Remove the pan from the heat and let the onions cool in the pan.

Use immediately, or transfer to an airtight container and store in refrigerator for up to 5 days.

SAUTÉED
MUSHROOMS

YIELD: ABOUT 3 CUPS (270 G)
TIME: 40 MINUTES, INCLUDING 10 MINUTES PREP TIME

8 ounces (225 g) cremini mushrooms, trimmed, then half quartered and half sliced

8 ounces (225 g) white button mushrooms, trimmed, then half quartered and half sliced

¼ cup (60 ml) water

CONTINUED

½ cup (120 ml) extra-virgin olive oil

2 garlic cloves, smashed

Leaves from 3 fresh thyme sprigs

Leaves from 1 fresh rosemary sprig

1 tablespoon kosher salt

1½ teaspoons freshly cracked black pepper

2 tablespoons chopped fresh flat-leaf parsley

1 teaspoon truffle oil, black or white is fine

Preheat a 12-inch (30 cm) skillet over high heat. Add all the mushrooms and the water and let the mushrooms cook undisturbed for about 5 minutes before stirring. This allows them to steam, causing them to heat up more quickly and release their moisture faster.

Start stirring while still over high heat. When you notice most of the water and mushroom moisture has evaporated, add the olive oil and garlic and stir to coat with the oil. Keep an eye on the garlic to make sure it doesn't burn.

Now add the thyme and rosemary while stirring continuously. As soon as the mushrooms start to brown, season with the salt and pepper. Then continue to cook, stirring, for about 3 to 4 minutes, or until the mushrooms are browned and tender.

Remove from the heat, add the parsley and truffle oil, and toss to coat the mushrooms evenly. Let cool completely in the pan, then store in an airtight container in the refrigerator for up to 3 days.

ROASTED
POTATOES

YIELD: ABOUT 2 CUPS (600 G)
TIME: 45 MINUTES

2 large russet potatoes, cut into ¼- to ½-inch (6 to 12 mm) cubes

1 teaspoon kosher salt

1 teaspoon coarse-ground black pepper

½ teaspoon smoked paprika

1 teaspoon dried oregano

¼ cup (60 ml) extra-virgin olive oil

Preheat the oven to 475°F (245°C). Line a sheet pan with a nonstick baking mat or parchment paper.

In a medium bowl, combine the potatoes, salt, pepper, paprika, oregano, and oil and toss to coat evenly. Pour the potatoes and any oil in the bottom of the bowl onto the prepared pan and spread in a single layer.

Bake the potatoes, rotating the pan 180 degrees halfway through baking, for 25 to 30 minutes, or until browned, crispy on the outside, and a fork inserted into a piece meets little resistance.

Remove from the oven and let cool completely on the pan. Store in an airtight container in the refrigerator for up to a week.

FRIED
EGGPLANT

YIELD: ABOUT 2 CUPS (450 G)
TIME: 1 HOUR (INCLUDES 30 MINUTES DEGORGING TIME)

1 large eggplant (about 1 pound [450 g]), stemmed and cut into 1-inch (2.5 cm) cubes

Kosher salt

1 teaspoon ground black pepper, divided

Vegetable oil for frying

Lay a large kitchen towel on a work surface. Spread the eggplant cubes in a single layer on the towel and sprinkle liberally with salt. Let sit for 30 minutes. Pat the eggplant cubes dry with a paper towel.

Pour oil to a depth of about 2 inches (5 cm) into a 12-inch (30 cm) sauté pan and heat over medium heat to 375°F (190°C) on a deep-frying thermometer. Line a sheet pan with paper towels and set it near the stove.

When the oil registers 375°F (190°C), add about half of the eggplant to the hot oil and fry for 4 to 5 minutes, or until the exterior is golden brown. Using a slotted spoon, transfer the eggplant to the towel-lined pan, season with 1½ teaspoons salt and ½ teaspoon of the pepper, and let cool.

Allow the oil to return to 375°F (190°C), then repeat with the remaining eggplant and season with 1½ teaspoons salt and the remaining ½ teaspoon pepper.

If not using immediately, store in an airtight container in the refrigerator for up to 1 week.

MARINATED ARTICHOKE HEARTS

YIELD: ABOUT 2 CUPS (45 G)
TIME: 15 MINUTES

One 14-ounce (397 g) can whole artichoke hearts in water, rinsed and quartered

Pinch crushed red pepper flakes

1 tablespoon dried oregano

1 tablespoon Italian parsley, chopped

1 teaspoon sea salt

1 clove garlic, roughly chopped

¼ cup (60 ml) extra-virgin olive oil

In a medium bowl, combine all ingredients except for the oil. Stir to coat.

Add the oil and stir until well combined.

Place the marinated artichoke hearts in a resealable container. They can be stored for up to 5 days in the refrigerator.

BALSAMIC REDUCTION

YIELD: ABOUT ½ CUP (120 ML)
TIME: 20 MINUTES

1 cup (240 ml) aged balsamic vinegar from Modena

2 tablespoons pure cane sugar or turbinado sugar

In a small saucepan over medium heat, combine the vinegar and sugar and bring just to a gentle boil, stirring to dissolve the sugar. Turn down the heat to a simmer and simmer gently for 10 to 15 minutes, or until reduced by almost half.

Remove from the heat and let cool to room temperature in the pan. Store in a tightly capped bottle or jar at room temperature for up to 1 month.

GARLIC OIL

YIELD: ABOUT 1 CUP (240 ML)
TIME: 20 MINUTES

12 to 16 garlic cloves, peeled and left whole

1 cup (240 ml) extra-virgin olive oil

In a small saucepan over medium heat, combine the garlic and oil and bring to a boil. Turn down the heat to a simmer and simmer gently for 15 to 20 minutes, or until the garlic is golden brown.

Remove the pan from the heat and let the oil and garlic cool to room temperature.

Strain the oil through a fine-mesh sieve placed over a small bowl. Transfer the roasted garlic cloves to an airtight container and store in the refrigerator for up to 1 week. Transfer the oil to a tightly capped bottle or jar and store at room temperature for up to 1 month.

TRUFFLE MUSHROOM SAUCE

YIELD: ABOUT 1 CUP (240 ML)
TIME: ABOUT 15 MINUTES

1 cup Creamy White Sauce (page 81)

1 tablespoon truffle sauce or paté

¼ cup (25 g) Sautéed Mushrooms (page 223), chopped

In a medium sauté pan over medium-high heat, combine the white sauce, truffle sauce, and mushrooms and bring to a simmer, stirring often.

Remove from the heat and let the sauce cool completely in the pan. Store in an airtight container in the refrigerator for up to 5 days.

BROWN SAUCE

YIELD: ABOUT 2 CUPS (475 ML)
TIME: ABOUT 30 MINUTES

2 tablespoons extra-virgin olive oil

1 shallot, minced

2 garlic cloves, minced

2 tablespoons all-purpose flour

⅔ cup (160 ml) Marsala wine

2 cups beef stock

1 tablespoon unsalted butter

Pinch kosher salt

Pinch ground black pepper

In a medium sauté pan over medium heat, combine the oil, shallot, and garlic and cook, stirring frequently, for about 3 to 4 minutes, or until the shallot and garlic are translucent.

Sprinkle the flour into the pan, stir to combine, and cook, stirring, for 1 minute. Pour in the wine and stock while stirring constantly, then bring to a boil, stirring often.

Turn down the heat to a simmer and cook, stirring often, for about 12 to 15 minutes, or until the sauce coats the back of a spoon.

Add the butter and stir until melted, then season with the salt and pepper. Taste and adjust the seasoning if needed.

Remove from the heat, let cool completely, then transfer to an airtight container and store in the refrigerator for up to a week.

CREAMY ARTICHOKE SAUCE

YIELD: ABOUT ¾ CUP (180 ML)
TIME: ABOUT 10 MINUTES

½ cup (120 ml) Creamy White Sauce (page 81)

¼ cup (45 g) Marinated Artichoke Hearts (page 227), drained and chopped

1 tablespoon grated Parmesan cheese, preferably Parmigiano-Reggiano

In a medium bowl, whisk together the sauce, artichoke hearts, and cheese until well blended.

Store in an airtight container in the refrigerator for up to 5 days.

CREAMY VODKA SAUCE

YIELD: ABOUT 2 CUPS (475 ML)
TIME: ABOUT 20 MINUTES

1 teaspoon extra-virgin olive oil

1 garlic clove, chopped

1 cup (240 ml) Rustic Hand-Crushed Sauce (page 79)

¼ cup (60 ml) vodka

½ cup (120 ml) Creamy White Sauce (page 81)

In a medium sauté pan over medium-high heat, combine the oil and garlic. When the garlic begins to sizzle, start stirring with a wooden spoon and stir for about 1 to 2 minutes, or until translucent, being careful not to burn it.

Add the tomato sauce and stir constantly until it comes to a boil and the sauce is thickened and reduced, about 3 to 4 minutes. Add the vodka and stir to deglaze the pan, then lower the heat and cook for 3 to 4 minutes, or until reduced and slightly thickened.

Add the white sauce, stir to incorporate, and bring to a gentle simmer, stirring constantly. Remove from the heat and let the sauce cool completely in the pan. Store in an airtight container in the refrigerator for up to 7 days.

CREAMY
LEMON SAUCE

YIELD: ABOUT 1 CUP (240 ML)
TIME: ABOUT 10 MINUTES

1 cup (240 ml) Creamy White Sauce (page 81)

Grated zest and juice of 1 lemon

¼ teaspoon ground white pepper

In a medium bowl, whisk together the sauce, lemon zest and juice, and pepper until well blended.

Store in an airtight container in the refrigerator for up to 5 days.

CREAMY
WHITE CHEDDAR SAUCE

YIELD: ABOUT 1 CUP (240 ML)
TIME: ABOUT 15 MINUTES

1 cup Creamy White Sauce (page 81)

½ cup (120 ml) grated sharp white cheddar cheese

¼ cup (60 ml) white wine

Pinch ground white pepper

In a medium sauté pan over medium heat, warm the sauce. When it begins to bubble, whisk in the cheese until melted and smooth. Slowly add the wine while stirring constantly, then continue to stir for about 4 to 5 minutes, or until the mixture is smooth and slightly thickened.

Season with the pepper, then remove from the heat and let cool completely.

Store in an airtight container in the refrigerator for up to 5 days.

WHIPPED
RICOTTA

YIELD: ABOUT 1½ CUPS (350 G)
TIME: ABOUT 10 MINUTES

1 cup whole-milk ricotta cheese

1 tablespoon Creamy White Sauce (page 81)

2 tablespoons grated Parmesan cheese, preferably Parmigiano-Reggiano

1 teaspoon extra-virgin olive oil

Pinch ground white pepper

½ teaspoon kosher salt

In a stand mixer fitted with the paddle attachment, combine the ricotta, white sauce, cheese, oil, pepper, and salt. Start the mixer on speed 1 and slowly increase to speed 2. Then increase to speed 3 and whip for about 1 minute, or until the mixture is fully incorporated.

Stop the mixer and remove the bowl from the mixer stand. Using a rubber spatula, scrape down the sides of the bowl and along the bottom and gently fold the mixture until no streaks are visible.

Store in an airtight container in the refrigerator for up to 5 days.

ACKNOWLEDGMENTS

A lifetime of pizza behind the once-secretive walls of the professional kitchen would not be possible without the great men and women who have inspired me to keep moving forward, no matter how hard things became. Nor would the pizza renaissance of today have been possible without those who paved the way before me, and it's because of this that I am truly humbled and blessed to have been given the tools to carry the torch for the next generation.

To my pizza family around the world, the love and respect that you have shown me over the years has been what picked me up off the floor and allowed me to shake off whatever has been piled on top of me. This book is for you, and I hope that I can inspire you to continue spreading the pizza love to others as our family constantly grows.

To the thousands of students from around the world who I have trained in the art of pizza, thank you for inspiring me to do better each day and allowing me to be your maestro.

To my wife, Melisa. It takes a very special person to always put others before yourself, and I couldn't have accomplished all that I have done without your love and support. You are the foundation and lifeblood of our family and a role model for our daughters as well as me. None of this is possible without you!

To my daughters, Angelina, Isabella, and Giada. As you go through life you will encounter people and challenges that will make you question yourself. Don't ever lose focus of your dreams, stay kind, and continue to show the world what badass girls you have become. There's no such thing as failure if you are willing to work harder than the person next to you. If I can write a book, I can't begin to imagine what you will do in the future.

To my mom and dad. You taught me the meaning of family and home. You allowed me to dream and never said no, no matter how crazy the idea. As I grew up watching you both work your fingers to the bone, your lessons of where we came from and our incredible culture molded me into the person I am today.

To my brother and sister, Mario and Daniella. I know I haven't always been around as the big brother you needed, and our relationship often seemed long distance, but your late-night calls and messages have consistently given me strength and helped me remember where we came from. We grew up in a basement making soppressata, suffered scorching heat while simmering tomato sauce in the middle of August, and fought off swarms of bees while making wine in the backyard in October. But there has never been a time that I can remember when we weren't together. Our past is what inspires my future.

Thank you to my agent, Michael Psaltis, for taking a shot on a little pizza guy from Chicago who wanted to write a pizza book. I truly thank you from the bottom of my heart for never giving up and always listening to my ideas. Your determination made this happen, and I'm forever grateful for all your support.

To my family at Weldon Owen, especially Edward Ash-Milby and Kayla Belser. Thank you for loving pizza as much as I do and not wanting to write just another pizza book. What you have allowed me to write in these pages, in my own voice, has let the story and culture of pizza be told in a way that has never been done before, and I thank you for seeing through my rough exterior and bringing the real person inside of me out.

I want to personally thank some of my industry colleagues and mentors: Rich Labriola for teaching me the art of artisan baking. Scott Harris for showing me how to balance work and play. John Arena for your lessons of life and wisdom of pizza the old-school way. Peter Reinhart for teaching me what it means to truly be a teacher. Carlo Orlando and Fred Mortati and the whole Orlando Foods team for welcoming me to your family long ago and never looking back. Eddie Greco and the entire team at Greco and Sons for the years of support and for sourcing the best Italian products. Francesco and Enzo Marra for that first phone call that turned the page to the next chapter of my life and career as well as the entire Marra Forni and Pizza University team for allowing me speak on behalf of all of you "Piu Forte nel Mondo!" Everyone at Grande Cheese company for the many years of support and friendship. A huge shout-out to Antimo and Mauro Caputo for bringing Napoli to the entire world and supporting me for many years. Chefs Chris Bianco, Christian Petroni, Joe Sasto, Chris Cosentino, "The Franks" Frank Falcinelli and Frank Castronovo in Brooklyn, Marc Vetri, and Evan Funke for being like the big brothers I never had. Giulio Andriani for teaching me to respect the culture of Italian pizza and teaching Americans how to eat it. Scott Weiner for challenging me to understand pizza's origins and how to apply them to my teaching. The Chicago Pizza Guys—Gino and Lenny Rago, Bruno Brunetti, Tony Troiano, Tony Scardino, Robert Garvey, Gianni Gallucci, Derek Tung, and Jonathan Goldsmith—for making Chicago the greatest pizza city in the world. My family at the Associazione Verace Pizza Napoletana for maintaining true Neapolitan pizza throughout the world and ensuring that its roots are protected for many generations to come. Angelo Lollino for showing me that little guys become big guys if they focus on their own success and don't worry about what others are doing. And finally, the one person who single-handedly took a young, smartass kid making pizza in Chicago and taught him that there is an entire world of pizza out there to learn about. That was over fifteen years ago when Tony Gemignani invited me to my first pizza class in California. Thank you, Tony, for allowing me to study not only your pizza-making ways but also how to present oneself as a professional to the world and inspire others through teaching. For this I am forever indebted and hope that I have made you proud.

INDEX

ABOUT THE AUTHOR

Maestro Pizzaiolo Leo Spizzirri isn't just a chef with some good recipes in his repertoire. He's obsessed with all things pizza and shares his love and knowledge with all who encounter him. His passion toward pizza and Italian food have earned him the title, "America's ambassador of authentic Italian Pizza and Pasta products."

The significance of delicious, well-crafted food is part of Spizzirri's DNA. A first-generation Italian American, he credits his love for pizza with his earliest childhood memories. He spent hours watching, and assisting, his mom and nana in the kitchen while they created all kinds of traditional Italian dishes.

Since then, he's gone on to be trained by Head Master Graziano Bertuzzo and thirteen-time World Pizza Champion Tony Gemignani. In 2008, he was named a member of the World Pizza Champions himself. He went on to receive an undergraduate degree and several Master Certifications from Scuola Italiana Pizzaioli. In 2017, he was certified by the school as Master Instructor, a designation that fewer than 100 people in the world hold.

A Chicago native, he has had a hand in local pizza operations like Giordano's Famous Stuffed Pizza, Francesca's Restaurant Group, Labriola Baking Company, and the brands Gia Mia and Ella's Italian Pub by the BG Hospitality Group.

Spizzirri is the founder of Spizzirri Media LLC, which is known for such brands as "Ask Chef Leo," "The Pizza Garage with Leo Spizzirri," and a pizzeria consulting company where he helps build new pizza concepts around the United States for restaurant groups. He has traveled the world teaching and making pizzas, including for such celebrities as Johnny Depp, Justin Timberlake, Mr. T, Ludacris, Kevin James, and boxing legend Ray "Boom Boom" Mancini.

His tattoos and punk rock–loving persona is unmatched by his technical knowledge when it comes to the kitchen. The pizzas that he makes and the dishes that he prepares all share the one secret ingredient that has been passed down to him through the generations: the love that he puts into everything that he makes.

Spizzirri resides in the Northwest suburbs of Chicago with his wife, Melisa, and his daughters, Angelina, Isabella, and Giada.